To Mandy

Enjoy the books!

Love

Niamh &

Angel

First published in the UK by Gibson Publishing

CORRUPTED
Text copyright 2013 by Emmy Yoshida
Image copyright 2013 Emmy Yoshida

ISBN 9780957-508439

This story is dedicated to all the strong women in the world,
who never stop giving, loving, and living.
Your beauty is a beacon that fills the world with light.
Especially to the strong women in my life, who have always
taught me to believe in myself and hold my head up high.
My mum, my nan and my sisters, Yuri and Leah.
My heroines.

CORRUPTED

A Tale Of Sex, Scandal & Suspense

EMMY YOSHIDA

Gibson Publishing

CHAPTER ONE

"Don't worry love; the first times always awkward, like your first shag. And I've got plenty of money for you to practice."

The man who had just introduced himself as Terry sat before me; arms spread across the back of the red velvet and gold chair, his flabby torso spilling between the arm and the seat. His sweat patches were clearly exposed by his chosen stance and a tuft of grey chest hair brimmed from his white shirt; which he unbuttoned as if to signal his day of work was now done and it was time for him to kick back.

But unbeknownst to the people who associated with him in his day-to-day London rat-race existence, consisting of executive boardroom meetings and rub-shoulder, lick-arse lunches, Terry didn't choose to unwind in the stereotypical pint of lager, evening news kind of way one would expect he would favour at first glance. No, Terry preferred unwinding with a less conventional method, one which would shock and offend his colleagues and family in equal measure if ever brought to light; by watching a girl undressing and paying her for the pleasure. He shot me an impatient look, as if to say get the fuck on with it, and hesitantly I proceeded to dance.

Sandwiched between his ample thighs, my towering heels swayed beneath me worryingly. I was used to wearing heels but in these monstrosities it felt as if I were on a pair of stilts; my ankles were one awkward movement away from snapping. The copious amounts of champagne I had consumed had left me feeling flushed and only slightly bolstered my confidence, which had taken a remarkable nose dive since I had set foot in Centrefolds earlier that evening and seen the vast array of exotic beauty surrounding me. Big breasts the size of melons with egos to match, acrylic nails, fake tan, and hair extensions; I felt plain in comparison to the audacious glamour of the other girls, but whoever this man was he obviously wasn't looking for the archetypal playboy bunny type as I was the complete opposite.

He had approached while I had been sat on a bar stool watching dissolutely as every customer who walked through the door was quickly swept away by a throng of beautiful ladies. I was wondering whether I had made a mistake in coming to this alien world where I wasn't the centre of attention for a change, when he had disturbed me from my thoughts.

"Are you new love?" he asked, propping up the bar the way most alcoholic middle-aged men did, in a bid not to lose any precious drinking time walking from a table to being served.

"Yes, is it that obvious?" I laughed and took another deep gulp from the drink I had just bought myself, and couldn't afford on my student loan allowance.

"I can tell a newbie when I see one," he said. "So what's your name?"

I paused momentarily as I struggled to remember what the house mum had christened me earlier that evening. "Pearl," I answered, flicking my black hair off my face in an attempt to look seductive.

"So are you into pearl necklaces?" He laughed then; a dirty roar which displayed some silver crowns in the back of his teeth, and I resisted the urge to spring away from him and crawl under a rock to hide. It took a moment for me to register what he was implying. "I can definitely tell you're new," he said. "You've obviously not been corrupted yet. So will you give me the pleasure of having your first dance?" He spoke as if we were at a debutante ball not a strip club, and I nodded. I could hardly say no you're not my type could I?

I followed him through a sea of gorgeous, scantily clad women in various states of undress, dancing for a selection of delighted looking business men. Effortlessly they teased and seduced the customers before them, many of whom looked like they were about to combust with desire, mesmerised by the pure unadulterated sex appeal possessed by the women on display. They seemed so in control, every movement they made exhibiting the power they held over their customers. In comparison I felt like a car crash waiting to happen.

I took a deep breath, in the hope that the motion would alleviate my inferiority complex and absolute terror. Did I really want to go through with this? I knew now was the time to back out if I didn't.

We approached a secluded circular table at the back of the room; before I'd had the chance to make a decision either way we had reached our destination and my first customer had made himself comfortable for the show.

He tucked a twenty pound note into my garter and it suddenly seemed like a rather abysmal amount of money to take all my clothes off, for a man I would usually cross the street to avoid on a dark night. Still though, it was only for three minutes, and seeing the large wads of cash on many of the girl's garters was enough of an encouragement. Being a struggling student was losing its appeal; it was only to help me get through the final year of uni. Then I could move on to fulfil my real ambitions.

I had watched the other girls that night and began copying what I had seen, playing with the ties of my red lacy camisole, undoing each strap before finally easing it down my body, almost tripping over as the fabric got stuck on my stiletto. I struggled with the clasp of my bra, cursing inwardly as the hook got stuck, and noticed a smug look from a stunning blonde a few metres away as I did so. Meanwhile Terry seemed ignorant to my gracelessness, his eyes intently fixed on my body as I swayed near him, a serious expression on his face like he was studying a road map. He looked like he was afraid to blink, more than likely memorising every image for his own personal wank-bank, to store inside the deepest darkest corners of his brain for future use; probably for when he shagged his wife.

When the music finally came to an end I eagerly scrambled for my discarded garments on the floor, foolishly neglecting to realise that the whole point of the process was to get the customer to buy as many dances as possible. Still at least I had got the first dance out of the way now; it had been painful but quick, like ripping off a plaster.

"You forgot to take off your thong," Terry said, laughing as I adjusted my dress. "Don't worry though, we've all got to start somewhere love."

He ordered some champagne and I happily accepted a glass, drinking hungrily while he sat beside me, a grin on his face once more. I shifted uncomfortably in my seat, cringing at my amateur performance and he leaned in closer. "So, what made you want to become a stripper then, a lovely girl like you? You strike me as being a bit innocent for this kind of malarkey."

"The same reason most people do any kind of work," I said. "Money."

"Well I'm sure you'll be earning a fortune before you know it." He raised his glass as if my stumbling into the world of stripping was cause for celebration. "Here's to you making a packet then. Cheers."

"Cheers," I repeated, knocking my champagne flute against his.

"So how old are you anyway?"

"I'm twenty."

"Twenty!" he said in disbelief. "Bloody hell, you're the same age as my daughter! Usually I only get dances from the older girls. Still, there's something special about you Pearl."

"Thanks," I said, unsure as to whether his admission was supposed to be a compliment. The uncomfortable revelation made my thoughts veer to that of my late father, and I shuddered at the thought of him knowing what I was doing. With his strict Japanese values he would have been deeply shocked if he could see me now, but then he wasn't here anymore. The last time he saw me I was eighteen, innocent to the ways of the world. There was no one to protect me now, just a deep void that needed to be filled with distractions. Dancing was my main escape so I had figured working as a dancer would be an ideal job for me. Maybe I had been wrong?

"Well I feel honoured to have had your first dance. In a few months' time when you're one of the biggest earners here, I can say that I took your dancing virginity!"

Before I'd even had the opportunity to comment, a tall curvaceous brunette, with tumbling waves, and a long expensive-looking black dress, had perched herself on the arm of his chair. "Terry," she breathed, as if the man next to her were a George Clooney lookalike. She shot me a look of superiority and scepticism. "My favourite customer," she said, eyeing me with so much disdain that for a moment I felt like a piece of dirt caught under her perspex heel.

"Stacey, didn't realise you were here. Just had a dance with Pearl, it's her first night." Terry looked startled if he had just been caught committing adultery, but judging by the gold signet ring around his fourth finger Stacey wasn't the only woman he owed his misguided loyalties to.

"Hi Pearl," she said, a smile plastered across her face more false than her breasts. "Oh well, now you've had your fun with a beginner, I think it's about time a professional took over don't you?"

"Sorry sweetheart," Terry said to me, scarcely able to tear his eyes away from Stacey's ample cleavage which she had cleverly directed in his eye line. "I'm going to have to go back to my stripper wife now. Here though, take the champagne, think of it as a christening present."

"Ok then, thanks," I said, feeling pretty put-out. I took the bottle and backed away, seating myself so I had a good view of the exotic world of red velvet, poles, and mirrors surrounding me. Five hundred pounds. If I don't make at least five hundred pounds tonight then I won't ever be coming back.

I knocked back my drink in an attempt to calm my nerves. With each glass I drank the night went quicker and my inhibitions decreased, until finally it got to three am and I had managed to accumulate quite a respectable wad of cash on my garter; eight hundred pounds in total, which meant that I had managed to take my clothes on and off about forty times all in all. No wonder strippers had such great bodies, the dressing and undressing alone probably burnt about a thousand calories, not to mention all the dancing and charming. I was exhausted and stumbled into a cab after handing in my money to collect on my next shift. As the car shuddered off into the crisp London night air I wondered how much of a cut they would take, and looked forward to holding the cold hard cash in my hand.

CHAPTER TWO

I was used to being judged by men and my confidence had soared since working at Centrefolds, but still as the man sitting opposite evaluated me, I felt a wave of panic. It was one thing being judged on your looks but quite another to be judged on your mind. Ironic how I could dance around naked in front of men all night, but when it came to day-to-day occurrences, without the safety blanket of Pearl and the emotional crutches I used to become her, I was about as far removed from the girl who stalked the club seducing strangers as I was from the Queen. The man crossed his legs, made notes, and sucked on the end of his pen, scratching his bald head whilst carefully considering my answers. Then came the dreaded question, the one which I always wished wouldn't be asked but for some ridiculous reason always seemed to be.

"So Ria, what would you say your weaknesses are?" He adjusted his black framed glasses as if they could somehow zoom in on my deficiencies and waited for my reply. A million and one unsuitable responses raced through my mind, and I contemplated which would sound the least awful; time-keeping, a penchant for coming into work hung over, an inability to follow instructions or respond to authority figures; the list was endless. I swallowed back the urge to tell him I was an alcoholic party animal, and instead listened in bewilderment as the lie I had prepared for the occasion slipped out of my mouth.

"Well I sometimes find it hard to delegate tasks in a team situation, and as a result, I often find myself doing the lion's share of a project. I often have the attitude if you want something done properly then you need to do it yourself, but I realise that to be a truly efficient team player then I need to relinquish control over certain tasks occasionally." I smiled and he responded with a warm nod. The word bullshit was echoing through my head, but I had learnt from experience that bullshit was the food of love enthusiastically indulged in these situations, and it seemed my answer had done the trick.

"Wonderful reply," he said. "Well when you work here there are tight deadlines and it can be quite high pressured, but I'm sure you will find we have a great team and we are a very well-oiled machine. That's if you get the job of course." He winked and I could almost feel my chest bursting in reaction. A wink; surely that was a good thing? Do I really allow myself to believe that I could have just landed my dream job?

"We will be in touch very soon. Thank you for coming, it has been a pleasure to meet you."

I noticed his eyes sparkle as he spoke, glinting behind the glass of his specs. Was his liking for me based solely upon his assessment of my suitability for the job, or did he just fancy me? It was hard to tell. Either way, I couldn't give a shit. Perhaps after months of countless interviews and rejections I had finally got somewhere. I almost felt like I was floating as I stood up to meet the handshake of the impeccably dressed man before me.

"It has been wonderful meeting you too, thank you very much for your time," I said, a grin plastered across my face so wide, my cheeks felt like they were aching.

I left the office, a spring in my step, and made my way through the building, smiling to everyone I passed; my future colleagues with any luck. They bustled round the modern glass-fronted work spaces with purposeful steps, discussing designs around cutting tables, pinning mannequins, assessing beautiful garments hung from long rails around the rooms. Designers, pattern cutters, machinists; an eclectic mix of interesting people, some of whom looked like they had just stepped straight out of a fashion magazine. This is what I want; what I've worked for. I raced towards the tube entrance hoping that this weekend might be the last time I would ever work at Centrefolds, and that I was finally on my way towards having a legitimate career.

*

"Ria, your cab's here." I heard my mother calling up the stairs and quickly downed the glass of wine I had been drinking, before racing to the front door.

"Thanks Mum," I said, kissing her on the cheek and ignoring the look of disapproval on her face, which I wished I could have replaced with the look of pride she had worn on my graduation day a few months ago.

"Don't be drinking too much." She watched me warily from the front door as I made my way down the garden path, trying not to slip on the frozen patches. I hoped that she hadn't smelt the alcohol that was probably already on my breath; a lecture before I went to work was the last thing I needed right now. I could understand her concern though; I'm sure if I ever have a daughter then becoming a stripper wouldn't exactly be high on my list of career choices for her, but that's life and hopefully it would all change soon.

It had been almost a year since I had first started working at Centrefolds. Like everything else that was bad for you in life, it was addictive. Working a regular nine-to-five job had seemed a pointless waste of energy when I had been studying; I could easily earn in one night what I could in a month with an ordinary job. So I had continued to work as a dancer, hoping that I would eventually find a design job and be released from the cycle of drinking, sleeping it off the next day, only to get ready for it all again.

Despite my resistance, I had to admit that for all the times a customer was rude, a girl was bitchy, and I felt like walking out at the "I'm just shopping round love," comments, I just as often enjoyed myself; dancing could be a liberating experience. I did wonder at times though how men could spend such an obscene amount of money on what was essentially self-torture. They watched me getting naked with such pained expressions that I sometimes felt cruel; like I was eating a big mac and fries in front of someone on a fast. Still, I couldn't help it, it was my job; this is what these men wanted after all. They didn't call it a strip tease for nothing.

"Alright love," my driver greeted me as I lowered myself into the black cab. "Where you off to?"

"Centrefolds in Soho please," I instructed, and for a moment I could have sworn I could see his eyes bulging from his head in the rear view mirror.

"No problem."

I sighed and took a swig from the bottle of white wine in my bag as he pulled off. It was the first time I had been made to go in on a Saturday since my income had progressed from an average of six to seven hundred a night, up into the thousands. When you hit the high scores with regularity certain rules did not apply, and I had milked it, turning up if and when I felt like it. Truth be told I rarely did feel like it. Centrefolds was a hard place, behind the glitz and glamour of the girls were fragile egos and ruthless attitudes. That week though the house mum had insisted upon me working; obviously the new recruits were disappearing faster than usual.

Saturdays didn't tend to be worthwhile; the big players were usually at home with their disconcerted wives playing happy families, the hard-working façade they put on to dodge the myriad of questions fired at them when returning in the small hours during the week had to give sometimes I supposed. I would much rather have been with my girlfriends, downing jager bombs and dancing until the sweat poured off me in one of London's top night spots, but by the time we arrived outside the club, the wine and beautiful city views of London had got me into a money-making mood, and I was raring to go and begin my transformation into Pearl.

Boredom had led Brad Harrison to Centrefolds that night. Boredom and his insatiable appetite for beautiful women. If he didn't have a good looking girl hanging off his arm Brad felt bare; like a woman without a handbag. So after his mundane business dinner, instead of going back to his hotel suite and masturbating to pay on demand porn, he decided to venture into Soho and sample some of the delights that London had to offer.

He had heard good things about the club; it had a reputation for being the best in London, every taste catered for. For Brad, money was no object. In fact, much to the annoyance of his parents, he was as much of a spender as he was an earner.

After quickly making his way through his inheritance at the young age of twenty five, he had turned his own hand to business, to supplement his already impressive allowance. Property, entertainment, gambling; it didn't matter what Brad dabbled in. The rewards were usually returned quickly and at a high ratio. Whether he had inherited the Midas touch from his entrepreneurial father, or he owed his good fortune to having the safety net of one of the wealthiest families in Australia giving him the winning edge, it didn't matter. To Brad there were no risks: only the prize at the end of it. He had the determination and stubbornness of a fighter dog. Once he had sunk his teeth into something he didn't let go until he had his way. After ten years of business he was a renowned entrepreneur with celebrity status in his country, and his own wealth almost matched that of his father's which had taken him a lifetime to build.

Brad walked into the plush surroundings and made his way to one of the tables at the back. Although he could see heads turning already, it was a refreshing change not to be bombarded with women in the same way as he was in Sydney. Over here he was an unknown and he revelled in his anonymity. He could certainly relax more, knowing he wasn't going to have the usual clingers on hanging around his neck like a noose. Here he could be anyone he felt like. No holds barred. He selected the finest bottle of champagne on the list and noticed the attention it was drawing.

A girl strutted over confidently and placed herself into the seat next to him. "Hello, I'm Annabelle." She was petite, blonde, with ridiculously enormous looking breasts, and it was obvious she had fillers pumped into every orifice. Attractive looking enough, but Brad wasn't on the market for a Pammy lookalike tonight. She smiled broadly, sticking out her artificial tits as far as they could go, and grabbed the arm of a dark haired stripper who was walking past. "This is Naomi," she said, yanking her equally well-endowed friend over. They sat on either side of him like vultures, flicking their hair, and brushing Brad's legs not too subtly.

"Here have a drink ladies," he said, ushering over the waiter and getting two more champagne flutes. Sitting back he observed as the strippers laid all their best moves on him. Brad definitely liked an ego boost, but he also liked a challenge and was getting bored by the women on either side of him. He listened half-heartedly as they told him a story about some celebrity he had never heard of, and their evening of debauchery with him. God some women talked a load of crap, he thought, nodding along to their routine tiresomely.

That's when he finally saw a girl of the kind of calibre he was looking for. She had an unusual look; an exotic contrast of Oriental and Western influence, delicate features and kissable lips. She was sitting on a bar stool, laughing with a customer. Her laugh was wholehearted; she was as unaware of her surroundings as a child. Compared to everything else in the club, she stood out like a sore thumb. Every movement, flick of the hair and bat of the eyelids of the other girls, was false and pre-determined. But this girl, now, she had something different. Innocence.

Brad kept his focus on her, watching as the man she was talking to made his advances. Ordering her a glass of champagne, his plump body leaned in closer until his round gut was brushing against her legs. Brad felt himself growing agitated, observing as the man scanned over her body hungrily, licking his lips in a sickening fashion, and casually placing his hand on her knee. He felt the sudden urge to go and knock him out and was about to stand up and whisk her away, when she pulled his hand away from her leg, got up, and made her way over to the stage. Not one to waste any time, Brad stood up, thrust a few fifty pound notes at the women on either side of him, and got a seat by the stage for a closer look.

As she stepped up under the spotlight his pulse began to race, and he watched mesmerised as she swayed her body around the pole gracefully. Her long raven hair was like a veil of silk falling down her back, and when she finally eased off her red lingerie to reveal her delicate, perfectly formed breasts, he could feel his erection pressing against his trousers. He reached into his pocket and pulled out a fifty pound note, leaning forward to tuck it into her garter. She knelt down by him, a genuine smile on her face, and when their eyes met she looked flustered under the intensity of his gaze. He was pleased to see that he liked what he saw even better close up.

"God darlin, you're bloody beautiful," he said, and she blushed in response making him want her even more. He looked her up and down and imagined her lying naked in his enormous bed back in Sydney, swiftly making the decision there and then that she would make the perfect souvenir to take back home with him.

CHAPTER THREE

The eyes of the club were upon me as I climbed the steps of the stage; awaiting the display I was about to give them, like a crowd of spectators watching the black night sky in anticipation of fireworks about to erupt in the atmosphere. The place was buzzing as ever, champagne being knocked back like there would be no tomorrow, girls hustling, flashing their best smiles and just about everything else, their legs crossed towards the customers who were revelling in their attentions.

Scanning the room, I held the gazes of the men around me. The usual suspects were sitting at the front as they always did at the beginning of the night, their pockets filled deep with cash ready to be dished out accordingly as if they were giving out sweets in a playground full of children. Well I suppose in a way Centrefolds was a playground and us girls were battling it out to be the most popular girl at school. I certainly wasn't about to lose the battle.

I began to swing myself around the pole leisurely to warm up. "Dirty Cash" was playing and I found myself getting lost in the music, circling my hips and slowly playing with the straps of my dress, gradually easing it down to unveil each part of my body. The metal of the pole felt cool against my bare skin as I slid against it.

I winked at one of my regulars, remembering that I was up there for a reason; to get tips. Ignoring everyone while I just had a good time dancing probably wasn't the best way of doing that. My attention was lost though as I spotted someone new, someone I had never seen before, a man who was commanding more attention from the room than anyone including me. He was approaching the stage and everyone in his way was parting before him like the Red Sea of Egypt. Even the customers were giving him double takes as he sat down, directly in front of me.

He motioned at the lingerie waitress who had followed him like a shadow to his table, and within moments she and two others were serving him, pouring his drink and flapping around him with the excitement they would usually reserve for one of our celebrity guests. Looking at him it was no secret why. He resonated power, sex, and charm. It was displayed in every facet of his physicality; from his towering physique, to his confident swagger, to the perfectly tailored suit which hung immaculately from his muscular body as if it were a second skin. The girls were practically salivating at him, but despite their best efforts to compete for his attention he was brushing off their advances casually, as if they were specks of lint on his suit. There seemed to be only one girl who had caught his interest, and to my delight I realised it was me.

The discovery made me instantly aware of my every movement; I felt completely exposed as if Pearl had deserted me on stage; too intimidated to even look in his direction as I continued to slowly undress myself under the heat of the spotlights and his gaze.

Gradually I let each bra strap slip down, concentrating my attention on the other men seated at the front who were eagerly waiting for it to fall to the floor. I made them wait for as long as humanely possible before letting it ping off. One of them waved a note in the air and I crawled over to collect it, all the while very aware that the man with the dominating presence was still watching me; now with even more interest.

He stood up displaying his impressive stature once more, a note in his hand, and I could no longer avoid looking at him. I leant by him, my usual bravado melting away as he slowly tucked the cash into my garter. His hand grazed against my thigh and I felt a bolt of electric energy surge through me as his warm skin brushed against mine. His fingers felt smooth, he was obviously a man who groomed himself with precision, but in contrast to the rest of his pristine image was his unkempt hair which made him look like he had just gone for a swim, like a model from a designer aftershave campaign.

"God darlin, you're bloody beautiful," he said, and my heart leapt into my chest momentarily. I was caught off guard; it was surprising to hear the deep Australian twang and I felt myself blushing; a fire setting my cheeks aglow until I was radiating heat from within.

He was obviously as taken back by my reaction as I; I couldn't even remember the last time I had felt slightly shy over anything at work. I got up and tried my best to maintain my composure while I finished the stage show; while he sat opposite watching my every move as I danced, turning the girls who approached him away without even breaking his focus.

As soon as the three songs were up I went to the edge of the stage and began dressing, and he strolled over with a cocky air of arrogance about him usually only displayed by the rich and powerful.

"You're coming with me," he said, beckoning the hostess over and booking me for an hour.

I nodded, dumbstruck by how handsome he was. I certainly wasn't used to customers like this. His piercing blue eyes, sandy brown hair, and deep tan made a devastating combination; I daren't imagine what he would look like without the suit on, the mere thought of it was enough to make me want to break every rule in the book.

"I'm Brad," he said. "You're absolutely stunning. I was watching you on that stage; unbelievable darlin."

"Thanks," I said, searching for words. "You're not exactly bad looking yourself."

"So what's your name?"

"Pearl."

"Pretty but what's your real name?" he demanded. "Come on I'm planning on spending a lot of money tonight, so I want to at least get your real name."

"Okay then, I suppose it won't hurt. It's Ria."

"Now that is a beautiful name, a beautiful name for a beautiful girl." He raised my hand to his lips and kissed it tenderly. As his eyes met mine I was struck by how magnetic they were. Azure blue, filled with intelligence and a spark of something else I couldn't quite put my finger on.

"Would you like a dance Brad?"

"Not just yet, let's get to know each other a bit first," he said, pouring me some champagne. "So where are you from originally, you've got a really exotic look to you?"

"I'm half Japanese, half English," I replied.

"What an amazing mix," he said. "So what's a lovely girl like you doing working somewhere like this then?"

"I am just doing it temporarily until I find a job in fashion. I just finished uni."

"Well we all gotta do what we gotta do I suppose." He began playing with the string of pearls hanging round my neck, rolling them around in his fingertips slowly; I could almost feel the heat of his skin leaving an imprint against mine as he brushed against me. "You're an amazing dancer though."

"Well I've always loved dancing, I wanted to be a ballerina when I was younger."

"So does that mean you're quite flexible then, being into ballet?" he said, moving his thick eyebrows up and down comically.

"Depends on who's bending me," I giggled. "So what brings you to London?" I asked, uncomfortable with the level of sheer sexual tension in the air.

"Business. Would rather be back home any day. I live in Sydney, it's bloody beautiful. Got a place overlooking the harbour. Best view in the world. You would love it. It's summer there now; I can't cope with the weather here." He shivered dramatically at the mere mention of the English climate.

"I bet it's gorgeous. I can't stand the cold either, I'm a sun worshipper."

"I could take you if you like. I've got a beautiful yacht, we could go out on it, cruise through the harbour, lay in the sun and drink champagne all day long."

I laughed at his empty promise but despite myself I couldn't help but imagine for a moment being sprawled across a yacht, sipping a cocktail, and browning myself in the hot sun with him lying next to me. "That sounds nice but I bet you say that to all the girls."

"Actually I'm very particular, and I didn't get to where I am today by playing games," he said, a smirk on his face.

"Well I can think of worse ways to spend an afternoon," I said, unsure of how to take the man sitting beside me.

"There is no better way, trust me darlin," he said, a twinkle in his eyes, his attitude stirring feelings of annoyance and arousal inside me.

The hours flew by and Brad had whipped his card out more times than the girls had whipped out their tits. We had spent the night laughing and talking, and I was beginning to forget I was at work and was wondering why I was so desperate to leave, when I noticed someone watching from the opposite side of the room. He was seated by the stage, suited and booted next to a male counterpart, and the dancer accompanying them both was pointing at me, her finger stabbing the air in my direction in a threatening manner as she laughed. Stacey had always hated me, especially as I had taken away the attention of many of her regulars. I avoided her like the plague whilst she did the opposite, seeking out any excuse for a confrontation. I had got used to her behaviour but there was something a lot more unsettling in the air. As I glanced up I realised what it was; the man she was with looked vaguely familiar. I studied his face and he looked up at me; instantly I saw the recognition flash across his eyes. That's when it dawned on me who he was. It was the man from the interview!

"Are you alright?" Brad's voice was a muffled blur through the powerful sick sensation, spreading through my body like a shockwave.

"No," I replied, in a state of disbelief over my ill-fortune. "That man over there. I know him."

"How?" he asked, giving him the once over.

"I had an interview for a design job a couple of days ago and he was my main interviewer. I really thought I'd got the job but now there he is, and now he knows I'm a stripper."

"Fuck!" he exclaimed. "Are you sure it's him?"

Slowly I lowered my hand from my face for a moment long enough to steal a second look, only to be greeted by the view of the two men nudging each other and Stacey waving at me sarcastically, a look of smug satisfaction on her face. It was bad enough this was happening without her having to witness it as well.

"I need to go, I'm sorry," I said, standing up.

"Come on don't go. Let's just go to a more private area where the dickhead can't see us. Come on." Brad took my hand and led me towards a corner of the club, away from their prying eyes.

I looked down, deflated as we passed them, a sinking sensation of shame and disappointment lowering itself inside me; the high I had been feeling at meeting Brad evaporating alongside all hopes I had held for my new life.

"I can't believe it," I muttered, and sank into my chair.

"It's okay darlin, I'm sure you'll find something else." Brad squeezed my hand, I felt grateful he was here and I hadn't been left to face the bitter disappointment of the chance meeting alone. I looked up and saw the empathy on his face, his masculine features softened by his concerned expression. God how amazing would it be to have a man like him in my life; someone to take care of me, look after me, take me away from all the crap?

"I have been trying so hard though; perhaps it's time I faced up to it. Maybe this is what my life is going to be; maybe I belong here."

"Now that's the biggest pile of rubbish I've ever heard," Brad said. "Come on, do you want me to go and have a word for you?" He began to rise to his feet and I gripped his hand to prevent him.

"No, it's done now. I'm sure Stacey has fed him so much nastiness that there's nothing you could say."

"That the bitch who was pointing at you?"

"Yeah," I nodded, surprised at how annoyed Brad was getting on my behalf.

"Well I don't know why you'd want to work for that bald-headed loser anyway. A girl like you shouldn't have to work; you should be looked after, cared for."

"Is that an offer?" I said, laughing at the precariousness of my situation.

"It could be." He looked at me with his penetrating eyes and a promising look, which caused such a rush of euphoria, it almost cancelled out the loss I was feeling.

Just then the hostess Eve walked over. "Your show is finished guys, and I'm afraid the club will be closing soon. Here's the bill for the tab."

"Thanks," he said, passing her his card distractedly, not even looking at the amount on the card machine as we waited for it to be processed; eager to be alone again. Finally she ripped off a receipt, thanked him for his custom, and walked away.

"What's your number, I want to see you again Ria?" He took a gold pen out from his pocket and poised it over a napkin ready to scribble it down. I noticed one of the girls looking over; I would be in big trouble if she saw me giving my number to a customer.

"I can't give it to you, I'll end up losing my job; I've already lost one tonight I can't risk it. Sorry."

"Why don't you just tell me it then, I'll remember," he said; clocking the blonde by the bar staring at us icily.

"You're gonna memorise it? After all the champagne we've drunk; I can scarcely remember my own name!"

"Well I have a razor sharp memory; especially when it comes to important details, and you my darlin are a very important detail." He smiled then; a relaxed self-assured smile. The kind of smile that said I love myself and pretty soon so will you.

"Why don't you just come in again on Tuesday?" I suggested; partly out of fear of being caught giving my number out, partly because the idea of spending time with the handsome stranger in front of me, and earning a couple of thousands of pounds in the process was too great a temptation to resist. He seemed annoyed at my suggestion.

"Look Ria, I know how these places work and I'm not one of those guys. I want you and I want to get to know you outside of this place. And I know you want me too, so let's cut to the chase. Let me take you out and spoil you."

"Where are you going to take me then?" I asked.

"Well you're going to have to wait and see. I'm sure you won't be disappointed though." He threw me a look that said he knew exactly what game I was playing, and I felt the sudden urge to grab him by his collar and give him a lingering kiss on his sensuous mouth.

"Okay." I said. "I suppose some rules are meant to be broken."

It was hard to know how to behave with such a sexy customer. With the usual crowd comprising of old men and lonely workaholics I felt completely in control, but with Brad it was different. He was right, I did want him. More than anyone I had ever met, although I didn't want him to know that just yet. He probably had women throwing themselves at him all the time and I didn't want to be just another one of them.

"Whisper it to me." He pulled me in as close as he could without the risk of contravening any rules and I breathed my number slowly in his ear, feeling turned on by the delicious musky scent of aftershave on his neck. I could almost feel his heart beating through the crisp white cotton of his shirt. "God darlin, even you whispering in my ear is making me hard." He winked as I pulled away, a cheeky look on his face, and I smiled back as I stood up.

"I have to go now Brad my cab will be waiting for me, but I had a great night. Thanks." I turned to walk away and as I did so he took my hand and pushed a wedge of cash into it discreetly.

"No thank you Ria," he said, looking into my eyes intensely. "You're a diamond."

I stuffed the money into my bra quickly; I didn't feel like sharing it with the club. After making my way into the changing room, I unrolled the wad of money secretively. Amongst the thick wad of fifty pound notes, which amounted to a cool sum of a thousand pounds, was his business card. It was simple and to the point, black with his name and contact details emblazoned across it in silver print. Brad Harrison. I ran my fingertips across the lettering and wondered if I would ever see him again.

CHAPTER FOUR

My phone vibrated noisily against my bedside table, waking me from my slumber and making me conscious of the extremely bad hangover I had managed to acquire.

"Oh for fuck's sake," I muttered under my breath, as I glanced at the time and saw it was only nine in the morning. I had only managed three hours sleep so far. Fantastic! I turned my blurred focus towards my phone, pummelling the keypad in search of the perpetrator of my disturbance.

"One new message," it flashed at me tauntingly. If this is a message from Vodafone telling me my credit is running out, then this phone is going to be thrown at my wall.

"Thanks for a great night beautiful. You're an absolute diamond. Brad x."

My stomach flipped with excitement as I read and re-read the message. What was it he possessed that made me so giddy? I never usually got like this with men but there was just something about Brad that made me want him so badly. He had such a strong persona, was so cocky and full of himself, yet instead of finding him arrogant I just found him sexy and alluring. Brad was the kind of man who knew what he wanted and went after it until he got it, and I couldn't help but hope that he wanted me.

The delicious aroma of frying bacon wafted into my room, and I threw on my dressing gown to go and get a piece of the action. Padding down the stairs wearily, I was knocked out of my day dreams by my nan, immaculately made up as usual and no doubt on her way to wake me for breakfast. She caught an eyeful of my sorry state and almost jumped out of her skin in mock surprise.

"Bloody hell, look at the state of you," she tutted, shaking her head. "Another night on the tiles was it? Come on, get in that kitchen and get some breakfast down you girl, you still look half-cut!" She shooed me past; flapping at me wildly with her chequered tea towel as I gripped on to the bannister attempting to stay upright.

The sun was pouring through the windows of the kitchen; it was your typical Sunday morning scene. Newspapers were stacked upon the counter, the supplements pulled out and being flicked through, as only beauty and fashion could be digestible on such a beautiful morning. Some fresh flowers were stood in the middle of the pine breakfast table, amongst the place mats depicting different countryside settings. My nan had put radio two on and the sound of Terry Wogan's velvety voice filled the room, almost as delectable as the smells of the fry-up. Mum was placing a large pot of tea on the table and was looking as freshly turned out as the flowers on it; lipstick applied and white floral apron tied over her ample bosom. My sister Aia was in her silk dressing gown looking radiant, sipping at her tea delicately, my little brother Shinzo was downing his orange juice and playing with his cutlery; eagerly awaiting our Sunday morning ritual. Howard; Aia's husband, was sitting on the other side of the table reading the sports section.

"Morning," my mother greeted me, eyeing me suspiciously. Unsurprisingly I thought as I caught a glimpse of myself in the mirror. The seductress from the night before had now been replaced with a trampy looking fiend. Make-up was smeared over my face, making me look like I had just clawed my way back from the depths of hell. "Did you have a good night?" she asked, looking concerned at my appearance.

"Yeah thanks, it was quite a good night." I lowered myself onto the chair next to Shinzo slowly and rested my chin on my hand.

"Looks like you had the worst night of your life," laughed Howard. Shinzo joined in with the banter.

"Yeah, looking a bit rough Sis."

"Oh ha ha ha." I didn't have the energy to get into a full blown slanging match, not when my brain felt like it was about to explode over the neatly presented table. Let them have their laughs; I made over five thousand pounds last night entertaining one of the sexiest men I have ever met.

"Fancy a cup of tea love?" my mum asked.

"Oh yes please," I said. She filled my china cup for me and I stirred in my milk and sugar, and took a sip of the comforting warm brew.

"Did you make much money then?" Aia asked.

I hesitated, not sure how much I should share of the previous night with my family.

"Erm yeah it was really good. I met an Aussie guy and made about five grand."

"Five grand!" Howard repeated in disbelief. "Bloody hell, I'm in the wrong line of work."

My nan lowered a plate containing the most perfect English breakfast I've ever seen on the place setting below me. There were grilled Lincolnshire sausages, slices of black and white pudding and crispy bacon on one side of the plate. Beside the meat feast was a neatly poached egg, its yellow creamy yolk spilling out onto the triangular shaped fried bread underneath it. Beans, tomatoes, and mushrooms completed the feast.

"Mmm thanks Nanny," I said, tucking in.

"That should sort you out." She smiled and placed the rest of the plates on the table.

"Well Ria, I hope you're planning on putting that money aside and not wasting it on rubbish." My mum gave me a withering look and seated herself.

"Yeah well, I don't see how spending my money on enjoying myself while I'm young is a waste. I could get hit by a bus tomorrow."

She flinched in reaction to my statement. "God I hate that expression. You should be spending your energy looking for a real job. God gave you a brain and you should be using it, not sucking up to a load of perverts all night. Your dad would turn in his grave if he knew."

"Yeah Mum I know," I said taking a deep sigh, feeling instantly emotional at the mention of my dad. "I really am trying to look for a good job, there just isn't much out there."

"What happened to that job you went for the other day? You told me they had practically offered it to you." She stopped her chewing, lowered her fork, and waited for my reply.

"I don't bloody know do I? It was only a few days ago, they are hardly going to ring me over the weekend and make a big song and dance over it are they?" I carried on eating, hoping that we could move on to another topic of conversation; the weather, the latest celebrity scandal, the man with the biggest tumour in the world; anything would be better than this right now.

"Well I hope to God you do get it because I don't think I can bear you working at the club anymore. Look at you," she said, shaking her head at me. "You spend half your life hung over."

"Yes well I am hung over now too, so I would appreciate it if you stopped yapping in my ear for five minutes and let me eat." I stared down at my breakfast which was quickly becoming less appealing served with a side of guilt.

"Mum is just worried about you that's all, she wants you to make something of yourself," Aia said.

"Look," I said, rolling my eyes to the ceiling. "Fashion is a really hard industry to break into, it won't happen overnight."

"Well maybe if you hadn't studied fashion at uni and done something worthwhile, then you'd be able to find a decent job," Aia shot at me from across the table.

"God what is this, pick on Ria time? Just because I'm not bloody perfect like you." I looked at my sister, so composed, almost regal looking even in her bloody dressing-gown; no wonder my family were so critical of me, how could I possibly live up to her example? I wished that I could be more like her; stable relationship, good career, but being the black sheep of the family was like a curse; a dark cloud that followed me wherever I went and it seemed hopeless trying to change it. I could feel the tears welling inside me, I wished that I could share the truth of what had happened last night with them but I knew it would only give them more ammunition.

"Leave her," my nan defended me. "Why shouldn't she have some fun and make some money? All she does is dance. If I were her age with her figure I'd do it. Now all of you eat up before it goes cold," she said, not wanting her breakfast to be ruined. She gave me a knowing smile and I felt grateful for her turning down the pressure; at least she wasn't always judging me.

We sat in silence for a minute or two enjoying our Sunday morning treat, when the peace was abruptly interrupted by Shinzo. "Sis," he said pausing briefly, a cheeky grin on his face. "Now you're so rich could you give us twenty quid?"

CHAPTER FIVE

"Welcome to my world." Brad opened the door to the black Bentley parked at the end of my driveway and gestured for me to climb in.

I had almost forgotten how gorgeous he was, but standing against the backdrop of my home he looked like a cardboard cut out, too perfect a creature to exist in this mundane suburban street, the stark reality of my everyday life only serving to further enhance his features. He was wearing a silver-grey suit which contrasted against his tanned skin, while his tousled hair and designer stubble gave the classic look a sexy edge. He handed me the most exquisite bouquet of flowers I had ever seen consisting of striking orange and purple flowers that I didn't recognise, and gigantic fuchsia orchids.

"They're beautiful, thank you." I took the flowers and climbed into the smell of leather and aftershave, noticing the curtains of my mother's bedroom twitching as she and Shinzo spied at my date through the window.

"You are beautiful," Brad said and lowered himself next to me. "I was going to get roses but I thought you're far too exotic for them."

"I love them. Orchids are my favourite."

"Great minds think alike eh?" He winked and I felt my heart beat wildly in response. "Hey driver. Put my music on please mate," he instructed, before winding the privacy window up and pouring us a glass of rosé champagne. "Here's to a good night," he said, clinking his champagne flute against mine.

"To a good night," I repeated, feeling relieved I had bought myself a new dress for the occasion. I had trawled the streets of London frantically that day until I found it; it was a stunning emerald green colour with a plunging neckline and I had matched it with some sexy heels and diamante jewellery. Even with my new dress on though I felt out of place in Brad's chauffeur driven Bentley. "So where are we going then?" I asked, my curiosity taking over.

"It's a surprise darlin. You just sit back and enjoy."

As the car glided through London, I admired the handsome man next to me. Why was he so interested? He clearly could have had anyone he wanted in Centrefolds the other night. He called the evening after we met, all bravado and effortless Aussie charm, insisting upon taking me out at the first available opportunity. I had stammered on the other end of the line; failing miserably to play hard to get as planned, instead agreeing to meet with him on Tuesday night. I had expected him to cancel and prepared myself for disappointment, applying my make-up and styling my hair while glancing anxiously at my phone. Now that I was here with him I intended to enjoy every minute.

The car finally stopped outside a grand hotel in central London; an impressive architectural structure, softly lit and as majestic as a fairy tale castle. I had often wondered what it would be like inside and felt excited that I was about to find out.

The chauffeur opened the door for me and we were greeted by a doorman dressed in a top hat and red coat adorned with gold embellishments.

"Good evening Mr Harrison," he said. Brad led me up the steps and we reached the ornate double doors, which were opened by two more pristine young men, bowing as we walked past them.

"Good evening Mr Harrison," they said in unison. Bloody hell what was he the Sultan of Brunei or something? I tried to conceal my excitement from Brad and pretend such luxury was as commonplace for me as a trip to the local supermarket, but as we walked across the perfectly polished floors, visions of me tripping over and skidding across the floor flashed through my mind and I clung on to Brad's arm tightly.

He steered me towards the lifts and as the gold doors closed on us I gave him a nervous smile; surely he wasn't planning on taking me up to his room already? I wasn't that easy.

"I thought we were going to a restaurant or something?"

"We are darlin, the best in London, you're gonna love it." At that moment the lift doors opened to reveal our destination. Everything was black, from the black marble floors and bar, to the black varnished wood tables, all lit with red sculptural lighting which was casting an ethereal glow and ambience. The dark setting intensified the city lights of the London skyline. It was breathtaking.

The maître d' turned towards us; an impeccably turned out man, wearing a beautifully tailored three piece suit and a friendly expression. "Mr Harrison; how wonderful to see you."

"Nice to see you Charley," Brad said, shaking his hand warmly.

"And this must be the beautiful young lady you told me about." He turned his attention towards me now, his posh voice and mannerism making me feel terribly important; a talent that he had no doubt acquired through decades of service in similar establishments. "It's a pleasure to meet you."

"Pleased to meet you too," I said, smiling back at him.

"She is even more exquisite than you described," he said to Brad. "I have reserved your favourite table for you Mr Harrison, now if you would care to follow me."

He led us through the restaurant to a secluded table in a sunken booth. "Henry will look after you now Mr Harrison, enjoy your evening." A waiter appeared then and Brad swiftly ordered for us both, before I had even browsed the menu.

"Wow, I could get used to this," I said. "I like a man who can take charge."

"I could get used to you," Brad said, scanning me with his arresting eyes. "I'm so glad you came here tonight, you're even more stunning than I remember."

"Thanks. You're looking pretty dapper this evening too; Mr Harrison." The waiter re-appeared then, clutching a bottle of wine.

"Would you care to taste it?" he asked Brad.

"Let the lady taste it."

The waiter poured a small amount into my glass, I wasn't exactly a connoisseur but I did my best impression of one, awkwardly swilling the white wine around before taking a sip, pausing as if assessing its taste while they watched with expectant eyes.

"It's lovely," I said, giving him a nod of approval. He filled our glasses and left us alone.

"Cheers," Brad said and I lifted my glass to meet his. "So how have you been Ria, did you hear anything else about that job?"

"Yeah actually now you mention it, I had a phone call from his assistant this morning saying that they found someone better qualified for the position."

"God, the man must be out of his mind, if you ever turned up at my office for an interview I'd hire you without a second thought, I wouldn't even bother interviewing anyone else. I mean look at you, you're the best looking lady in this place by a mile."

"That's sweet of you to say but it wasn't a modelling job."

"Yeah but you've got brains as well, you're the whole package. The man's a hypocrite, I mean how can he turn you down for a job cause you're a stripper when he was in there himself?"

"Double standards I suppose, but hey that's life. I've just got to keep trying."

"Well I've got a great position in mind for you if you fancy it?" he said, staring into my eyes and trailing his finger-tips up my forearms.

"Oh; so that's that why you brought me here tonight to try and get me into bed?"

"That would be a bonus but that's not why," he said, his face becoming serious again. "I'd be happy just to spend time with you. There's something about you Ria, I can tell you're different, you stuck out in that club like a sore thumb the other night. I don't do this kind of thing for any girl you know, I don't usually need to bother, but I haven't been able to stop thinking about you since the other night."

"I've been thinking about you loads too," I admitted.

"Not just thinking though. I feel like you've put a spell on me; like you're inside of me."

"Ha!" I said loudly; the champagne and wine having successfully made its way into my system. "God you really are a professional player aren't you? And I thought I was good!"

"Look Ria, I am many things, but one thing I am not is a bull-shitter. I wouldn't bother saying it if I didn't think it was true. I really think you're special." He looked sincere but I still wondered how truthful he was being.

"Thanks, I think you're pretty special too," I said, looking back at him seductively.

"So what do you think of the place then?" He leant forward and laced his fingers through mine softly.

"Yeah it's lovely."

"This is always my home when I stay in London. I'm glad you like it, cause I'm sure you will be spending quite a bit of time here over the next couple of months."

"See there you go making your assumptions. What makes you even think there will be a second date?"

"I don't think. I know." He raised my hand to his lips and kissed me gently, and I shook my head at his audacity. "We were meant to meet Ria, and I am going to change your life in more ways than you can even imagine. You may as well surrender to it darlin."

He laughed again, and I couldn't help but smile at his bare-faced cheek. If he wasn't so astonishingly handsome there was no way he could have got away with it, but coming from him it was almost charming. Leaning back in my chair, I took in the plush surroundings and hoped for my own sake that he really was telling the truth; because I could already feel myself becoming addicted to him and his world, it was unlike anything I had ever experienced before.

CHAPTER SIX

Damp, hot, and tired, I lay next to Brad on the sweat soaked bed linen. My skin tingled with delight as he gently traced his fingertips up and down the curve of my waist and I basked in the afterglow of our latest steamy session. It had been four weeks since I had met him and he had been right; my life definitely had changed. I tried to forget that he would be leaving soon and it would all go back to normal again before long. My days of luxuriant sex with the most gorgeous man I had ever met, and of being treated like royalty wherever we went, were numbered. I felt sick at the thought of him leaving me and returning to Australia; to the other side of the world.

His embrace around me tightened as our breathing relaxed, and I enjoyed the sensation of his muscular body behind me; moulded next to mine so perfectly that he felt like an extension of my own body. He began to shower the back of my neck with soft kisses, and I felt an odd mix of happiness and pain ripping through my heart. Was this love I was feeling or just pure lust?

I heaved his heavy arm off of me in an attempt to halt my feelings from flowing and stumbled towards the fridge, dizzy from our exertions and my confused emotions. As I reached inside to grab a bottle of water, he called after me lazily.

"You alright?"

"Yeah, fine," I answered, my tone indicating that I was anything but. He heaved himself up and looked at me sleepily, his hair dishevelled, a white sheet scarcely covering his toned body. Why did he have to be so damn gorgeous all the time?

"What's wrong?"

"Nothing," I said flatly, trying to hold back the tears. I didn't want him to see me cry over him. No way. I wasn't ready to relinquish the power and admit the depth of my feelings.

"Come back to bed then," he said, flopping back onto the mattress and waiting for me to jump next to him.

"No. I'm gonna go home. I can't do this anymore Brad it's too much. You're going back to Australia soon. Let's just leave it now; I'm getting too involved for my liking." He sat back up and stared at me as if I were on crazy pills.

"Don't be stupid, come back to bed." He lifted the covers as a gesture for me to hop back in, but I resisted the urge and instead began pulling my clothes back on, seeking them from the floor of the dimly lit hotel suite that had become like a second home for me the last month. I had got as far as putting my underwear on when he lifted me up, and threw me back onto the soft mattress roughly.

"Ria! What the fuck do you think you're doing?" He stood above me, arms crossed. I was stunned by his reaction, but secretly relieved that he hadn't just let me walk out the door.

"I just really like you and you're gonna be leaving me soon so I thought I would get it over with and leave you, before I wind up getting hurt." I turned away from him, tears threatening to spill, my eyes beginning to blur as I looked in the opposite direction.

"Don't be stupid."

"I'm not being stupid though am I Brad? It's all been wonderful but let's not pretend it's anything more than it is. An extended one night stand." I pulled myself back up and began searching for my bra. He grabbed hold of my arms to stop me.

"Sit down and listen to me Ria, before I bloody lose it will you," he ordered. He had an expression on his face that I had never seen before and I instantly did as I was told; seating myself on an embroidered chair, curious to find out what he could possibly say that would change the situation.

"Now if you were a bit patient then I would have done this in my own time." He paced in front of me, before kneeling down. "I was never planning on leaving here without you. I want you to come with me darlin."

"What?"

"I want you to come with me," he repeated. "You didn't really think I was planning on going back without you did you?"

"Really?" I asked, not quite sure if I was willing to believe him.

"Of course. Why do you think I've been spending every moment with you? If I was just after sex I would have ordered a hooker and saved myself some time and money."

"But we've only known each other a few weeks Brad. How can I just move to Australia with you?"

"So what? How long have we got to know each other for, a decade? I know all I need to know, and I know enough to know that I'm never going to let you go. So what do you reckon then? Do you want to come with me?" He stared at me, and for a moment I thought I caught a flash of nervousness in his eyes as he waited for a reply.

"Yes definitely. Of course I want to come with you."

"Well that's settled then," he said pulling me onto the floor on top of him. "I'll get my PA to sort out your visa and flights."

He began kissing me passionately, holding my body against his so tightly I felt in danger of passing out. Before long we were rolling around on the floor of the hotel room, my legs tightly wrapped around him.

"I fucking love you," he groaned and I automatically replied.

"I love you too." The words rolled off my tongue naturally and fuelled his passion even further. He climbed on top of me, pinned my arms above my head and pumped his body against mine urgently, until we both came loudly. Whatever it was, love or lust, I knew I wasn't ready to give it up, and judging by the way he was clinging on to me, neither was he.

CHAPTER SEVEN

"You hardly even know him Ria, and now all of a sudden you're moving to the other side of the world with him."

I glared at my sister's reflection in the mirror. Why did she always have to be so negative about everything I did? We were supposed to be enjoying my last night and she was just using it as an opportunity to lecture me.

"Aia, please." I begged her to relent from her criticism of my decision. "I love him, he is a good guy. It's not just for him you know. I want an adventure and to get away. I'm getting nowhere here. I can't find a decent job and all I've done since I graduated is work in that crappy club. It's an opportunity to do something different Aia."

"If he's such a great guy, then what's he doing hanging round in strip clubs for fun?"

"I wouldn't expect you to understand. Everything's not black and white you know. I bet half the people you work with have been to a strip club before; it's not such a big deal. He was bored and lonely that's all. He's a good person."

"Oh you're so naïve; how can you not see it? He doesn't give a shit about you Ria, all you are to him is an object. A toy! Well he might have fooled the rest of the family with his bollocks, but he hasn't fooled me. Dad would have fucking hated him as well."

"God, why do you have to be such a bitch on my last night?" I said, on the verge of bursting into tears.

"I'm sorry Ria," she replied upon seeing my distress. "I just want you to be careful. I don't want to see you getting hurt."

"Look," I said solemnly. "I know it's a big step but if it doesn't work out I can just come home. It's not a big deal. I want to see Australia, it sounds so amazing. I just want to enjoy myself."

"That's all you ever want to do Ria, that's your problem," she said, her hand on her hip.

"Yeah well, if there's one thing I've learnt from Dad's death is that life is short," I snapped.

"Okay," she sighed, realising that my mind was well and truly made up. "It's just that there's something about Brad that I just can't put my finger on."

She looked at me with a worried expression. I understood her concern. I was a walking disaster at the best of times and I always had been. My older sister had always been the one who looked out for me. We were similar in many ways but in others the complete opposite. She favoured stability and lived for the future. I preferred excitement and living in the present. After years of picking me up after my falls, it was no wonder she was finding it so hard to believe that her hapless sister might have actually landed on her feet for once.

"I know Brad comes across as being a bit flash and arrogant, but there is a lot more to him than that. He is really kind and thoughtful and treats me with so much respect."

Aia looked down at the floor and when she raised her head back up, I could see the tears forming in her eyes as she fought to hold them back. "I'm just going to miss you so much," she cried, no longer able to contain her emotions.

"I'll miss you too," I said, tears filling my own eyes. We clung to one another for a few moments in the restaurant ladies room, comforting each other as only sisters could. "Come on, we had better go back out there now."

We dabbed at our eyes with toilet roll, trying to prevent trails of mascara from rolling down our faces.

"How's my make up?" Aia asked. I looked at my sister's beautiful face and smiled at her.

"Perfect."

We slowly began walking back into the restaurant, weaving through tables until we reached our own. My family were seated around a large circular table, enjoying one of the best Chinese meals I have ever tasted. Brad was deep in conversation with my younger brother, laughing and joking and I felt myself relax at the sight. How could Aia not like Brad? He was so perfect.

"Where have you two been?" my nan asked. "The food's going to be stone cold in a minute."

"We were just having a chat," I replied. I slid back into my chair, feeling happy to be surrounded by my loved ones. I would miss nights like these.

"Well, now we are all here I would like to make a toast," Brad said, standing up from his seat. "I want to thank you all for welcoming me into your family. It has been wonderful meeting you all, and now I know where Ria gets her good looks from!" He raised his glass in direction of my mum and nan who beamed in response; the expensive wine and festivities making their faces glow warmly. "I know it's going to be hard for Ria to leave you all and I just want to reassure you that I am going to look after her really well. Hopefully it won't be long before you can come out to visit us." Brad paused and raised his glass. "So here's to family."

"To family," we all said in unison. Brad grasped my hand underneath the white tablecloth as he sat down, squeezing it slightly, and I felt like the luckiest girl in the world to have met him. I couldn't wait to prove Aia wrong.

CHAPTER EIGHT

Thick snowflakes were cascading down from the heavens, leaving England and the town I had grown up in under a white blanket; a blanket that I suddenly felt compelled to bury myself under. It couldn't have been further removed from the destination I was travelling to; the complete antithesis. I was flying the nest and I couldn't be flying further away from it if I tried. It was a daunting prospect.

I had been looking forward to this day for weeks, so eager to get away from it all and to start a new adventure and life for myself. Yet now the day had finally arrived, I felt my heart wrenching with emotion as my family lined up by the front door waiting to say their goodbyes. Who knew when I would see their faces again, it could be months or years even, and I knew that when I did return, it would all have changed. Shinzo was only twelve, still a boy, but perhaps the next time we saw each other he would be a man.

I stood on the driveway and stared at the house, reliving the happy moments we had shared in it; moments that I had blocked out since my father's death. Our childhood memories were embedded in it, as tangible as the bricks and mortar from which it had been created. Memories of us playing together; our father and mother young and happy, Aia and I shrieking and running around after each other, the wind in our hair, the soft grass beneath our bare feet, our baby brother sitting on the lawn, gurgling with delight as he watched us play.

It had been sudden when he left us, a fatal heart attack which had left us all in pieces. Shinzo Kimura had been a good man, your archetypal Japanese father. Hard working, reliable; even though we didn't always understand his values and beliefs we always knew how much he loved us. My mother had fallen apart after his death; he was the only man she had ever loved. They had met when she was still only eighteen and soon after she had moved with him to Japan, where they had begun a happy marriage which had lasted more than twenty years before he died. She had taken a risk, leaving behind everything she knew to be with him, just as I was about to.

It had been two years and we had recovered as best we could from my father's absence but I still felt guilty to be leaving them; another missing piece to our fragile family unit. Tears were streaming down Aia's face, my own hot tears rolling down at such a pace, that collectively they could have melted the snow from here to the airport. I felt so selfish, like I was completely abandoning her.

I had been so focused on hanging on to Brad; our passionate relationship had been at the forefront of my mind. Act first think later, that was my motto, and that was precisely what I had done in this situation. Now I was finally thinking. I was thinking how Goddamn much I loved my family, and how much I would miss them. I would miss everything about them, even the things they did that drove me mad. With whom would I share my innermost thoughts without my Aia? Who would I argue with and borrow clothes from? Without Mum, who would be there to give me the encouragement and support I needed? Who would hold me when I was crying and make me feel safe? Who would cheer me up, make me laugh, and cause my heart to swell with pride and joy like my Shinzo? I knew Brad would compensate for their loss to a certain extent, but could he ever really be a substitute for their love?

I knew Aia would find it the hardest. We were so close, we were each other's best friends and confidantes and she had always been like a second mum to me. I couldn't imagine her not being there anymore. As Brad's driver struggled down the white pathway leading to his car with my over-sized suitcase, Aia cried more urgently.

"I am going to miss you so much," she said, her lip trembling as she wept. "I love you Sis".

"I love you too," I exclaimed, holding on to her tightly.

"I got you a gift, something to keep you safe. Open it on the journey."
She thrust a small bag into my hands.

"Thanks Aia." I took the gift and smiled at her.

"If you ever need me I'm always here," she said, wiping away her tears. "It doesn't matter how far apart we are, what time of the day or night it is, I am here for you. You got that?"

"Yes," I nodded. "I am always here for you too; always."

We gave each other our final hugs, and then Mum, Shinzo, Brad, and I crunched through the fresh snow to the car and began driving away. I looked out of the window for as long as I could at Aia's figure, blurred by my tears until she was just a dot in the distance against the white snow. Brad held my hand but looked surprised at the level of emotion I was displaying. It was okay for him; I was leaving my family, he was returning to his.

I reached into the gift bag Aia had given me and pulled out a navy blue jewellery box. Inside it was a silver chain, a small pendant with a picture of an angel hanging from it, and a beautiful card with an illustration of a ballerina on the front.

To my beautiful sister Ria, here is a guardian angel, to watch over you and keep you safe. Wear it all the time and remember I am always here for you. Love your sister Aia.

"Here, let me put it on for you," Brad said, seeing the gift. I turned while he fastened the clasp around my neck. Her gift meant more to me than anything. I knew I would never take it off.

The drive to the airport went all too quickly, the white scenic view and my salty tears clouding over my vision. I tried to join in with the small talk Brad was making with my family, but talking about check-in and flight schedules really seemed like an incredulous waste of the precious time I had left with them.

We stayed with them for as long as possible drinking coffee in the airport café before the time came for us to walk through security towards the boarding gate. Most people were descending upon the point of no return excitedly, eagerly striding towards it in anticipation of their holiday, yet as we approached the goodbye point I felt like I was being torn in half. The gates beckoned; a portal to an unfamiliar life, but it was also goodbye to my family, goodbye to the security I knew, and goodbye to being a girl.

"I love you Sis," Shinzo hugged me. "Ring us when you get there. I am going to miss you so much."

"I will miss you too Shinzo. Be good for Mummy. I love you so much Bruv." I wrapped my arms around him and felt his tears saturate my top as we cried.

Finally I said goodbye to my mum, who had so far managed to hold back her emotions but now the time had come for me to leave, she was sobbing.

"Work hard and believe in yourself," she said. "Your dad would be so proud of you right now." She held me tightly before pulling me back and looking me in the eyes. "No matter what happens you will always be my little girl. Be strong and make the most of every opportunity that comes your way. I love you so much."

With that we made our way through the crowds, Brad impatiently pulling me away from my family, while I looked back at them crying and waving. My mum and Shinzo stood huddled together, watching us until we were out of view. We turned the corner and I took a deep breath whilst contemplating how I could possibly live without them all and how I had neglected to realise just how much they meant to me sooner.

"It's gonna be alright darlin," Brad said, wrapping his arm around me. "You've got me now. I'm gonna look after you. From now on it's just me and you against the world."

CHAPTER NINE

It was an experience flying first class for the first time in my life. What might have been an agonisingly slow flight had been an adventure in itself; the first half spent drinking champagne and ordering from the extensive menu, the second half sleeping it off in my seat which was more like a luxurious cabin. The air hostesses were remarkably attentive, but respectfully absent when Brad made his way to my bed while I slept. His hand woke me from my sleep, creeping up between my thighs, the friction of his fingers rubbing against me, causing me to wake up feeling moist.

"Sshh," he said, putting a finger to his mouth, and as I opened my bleary eyes he began pulling my dress up and my knickers off. My modesty was concealed only by a thin blanket as he began kissing me and parting my legs.

"Brad," I said, still dazed. "What are you doing?"

"I'm bored; thought we could make our own in-flight entertainment."

He knelt down in between my legs and started kissing my neck, moving his hands down my bra and freeing my breasts, licking my nipples. I heard myself moan and he silenced me by pressing his hand against my mouth.

"Sshh," he whispered in my ear, making my skin prickle. I tried to contain myself as he worked his way down my body, until his tongue and fingers were in between my legs. He knew my body so well already, and my breathing quickened as my desire for him intensified.

Impatient for him I pulled him up towards me, unzipped his jeans and wrapped myself around him tightly. He slowly pushed himself inside me, covering my mouth to silence my groans so that the middle aged business man sitting in the next cabin couldn't hear my cries.

"Wow, that was amazing babe," I said as we quickly covered ourselves up and he laid himself next to me.

"Thought I should wake you up, we're landing in about an hour." He grinned whilst tucking his white top in awkwardly. I caught a glimpse of the tanned skin of his torso and instantly felt hungry for more. I took his hand to stop him as he began to do up his zipper. "There'll be plenty of time for that soon," he said pulling my hand away from the bulge in his jeans. "Besides if I were you I'd sort yourself out, you're looking a bit rough."

"Thanks," I exclaimed, feeling thoroughly offended.

"Ah, don't get upset with me darlin, just want you to be looking you're best. My parents are meeting us from the airport."

"What? I didn't think we'd be seeing them 'til tomorrow."

"Change of plan. Spoke to my dad while you were having your sleep. They want to pick us up, take us for breakfast, then we are gonna meet them for dinner tonight."

"Oh okay," I said, feeling nervous about meeting them for the first time. I felt hung over, tired, and completely unprepared. I had been dreading it; from what Brad had told me, his dad was a hard man to impress and his mum had been very judgemental of his previous girlfriends, apparently causing many a rift and tension between Brad and his exes. He was her only child so I suppose it was only natural she would be protective of him, I just hoped she would deem me as being good enough to be accepted into their privileged circle.

"Oh and one more thing," Brad said, giving me a kiss on the forehead.

"What?"

"Cover yourself up a bit. As much as I like your tits I don't really want them to be on display when you meet my folks."

"Oh," I said, pulling on the fabric of my dress to cover my modestly sized breasts.

Brad led us through the airport quickly and confidently; obviously it was a familiar path which had been walked many times by him before. I rushed behind him to keep up, feeling slightly more confident now I'd had the time to fix myself up. I was now wearing a nautically striped blazer with skinny jeans. Casual but smart; hopefully it would be approved.

The humid air hit me like a torpedo as we walked out of the glass doors of Sydney airport. I scarcely had a chance to take in my surroundings when I saw a tall man with silver hair striding towards us with the same confident air about him as Brad possessed, and I realised instantly it must be his father.

"Hello son," he said, slapping his back in a quick hug. "This must be Ria, lovely to meet you." He shook my hand vigorously.

"Nice to meet you too."

He smiled at me, displaying a perfect set of veneers. Even though he must have been about seventy years old he was handsome; his tanned, leathery, crinkled skin, off-setting the astonishing colour of his vivid blue eyes. He was impeccably well groomed; even Brad looked scruffy in comparison. I instantly liked him but was also intimidated. The man embodied power; it leaked from his pores and could have caused a fully grown man to stammer in his presence.

Arthur Harrison turned on his heels abruptly and Brad followed, leaving me behind with the chauffeur who was lugging the trolley containing our ample luggage awkwardly, struggling to prevent it from veering into the road.

"Mother's not feeling well today, she will be joining us tonight instead," I heard him explaining to Brad. I breathed a sigh of relief. At least I wouldn't have to meet them both at the same time.

The driver opened the door for me and I got into the blacked-out Mercedes next to Brad, once again engulfed in cool air conditioning. I felt like an intruder in a boardroom meeting as the men discussed their business dealings passionately in the back of the car, and so I used the opportunity to glance out at the new world which I had travelled to. We drove through the city streets of Sydney and although it was beautiful, I couldn't help but marvel at how small it seemed compared to London. As the journey progressed though we reached the monumental Harbour Bridge, and as we began to cross it my excitement grew. The sea was electric blue, stretched out as far as the eye could see, and interspersed in the vast ocean was a diverse city landscape, beaches dotted in between its abundant mass. Numerous ships were crossing across the distant horizon leaving behind them white tracks in the ocean, and as I turned to see the renowned architectural figure of the Sydney Opera house I felt giddy with joy. It looked like paradise.

We stopped at a scenic restaurant in the Harbour and had breakfast. I enjoyed the heat of the sun on my skin and felt sure I had made the right decision in coming.

"It's beautiful isn't it?" Brad's father said, noticing me scanning the view.

"It's gorgeous," I agreed.

"I will never forget the first time I saw it. I was seventeen, just emigrated over here with my parents. Back in those days of course it took weeks to get here; crammed on a boat. I just wanted to stay with my friends of course, but I felt it when we got here. Even though we had nothing to start with I felt a wave of excitement when we arrived that I could do anything here; so many possibilities. Are you feeling it too?"

"Yes," I replied. "I feel so excited."

"Well that's good, and you have Brad here to look after you so you've got even more opportunities. Well then, I will leave you two lovebirds to have a rest now, I have got to go into the office."

We waved him off and made our way back to the car. I was looking forward to catching up with my jet lag and waking up feeling fresh, with plenty of time to prepare for my first night on the town.

Although I had now been with Brad for almost two months and become used to extravagant surroundings, nothing could have prepared me for the opulence of his apartment. We pulled up in front of a modern skyscraper, the doormen at its steps anticipating our arrival.

"Mr Harrison, so nice to have you back," the concierge exclaimed and we walked into a gold mirrored lift. I felt my ears pop as we ascended to the top of the building.

"I've got the whole floor," Brad said proudly as we walked in and my jaw almost hit the ground at the view. It was a massive space, made to feel even huger by the ceiling to floor glass walls surrounding it. The view of Sydney was the canvas encircling it, so overwhelming that it felt like I was practically swimming in the ocean. The floors were marble, the space abundant, perfectly designed so that each unique element was assigned a task, and yet effortlessly formed part of the flawlessly designed whole. A sunken area adorned with carved wood and white leather furniture was in the middle, while across the other side was a futuristic looking kitchen and dining area.

"This is the best bit," Brad said, leading me out onto the terrace. I had to catch my breath, the altitude causing me to have a rush of vertigo as we stepped onto the balcony surrounding the apartment; dotted with exotic plants, modern sculptures, more sleek furniture and glass tables. We ascended some steps and arrived at a massive swimming pool which appeared to be flowing off the top of the building into the distance.

"It's fucking amazing!" I screamed, feeling like I had just won the lottery and the pools at the same time.

"Well it's your home now," Brad smiled, and I jumped up and kissed him all over his face. I couldn't wait to tell my family all about it.

"You should have a sleep before we go out tonight; catch up with your jet-lag. It's still only nine in the morning." He led me into a plush bedroom and I laid myself down on the soft mattress, stretching out my tired body against its luxurious silk fabric and yawned.

"Aren't you having a sleep too?" I asked.

"In a bit; just got to just make a few calls first. Sleep tight." He walked out of the room and I stripped off before falling into a deep sleep.

CHAPTER TEN

I woke up and glanced at the time. It was about midday so I had got a couple of hours sleep and was feeling refreshed. I sat up in the large bed and padded out in search of Brad. I was keen to spend some of the afternoon exploring my new neighbourhood. As I opened the bedroom door to the luxury apartment, I noticed a stillness in the air.

"Brad?" I called out, my voice echoing in the empty space. Walking into the kitchen I saw a note on the side.

Ria,
popped out will be back at one o clock to take you for lunch. Make
yourself at home
x

With just an hour to get ready I raced back towards the ensuite and propelled myself under a hot stream of water, washing away the staleness that was inevitable after a twenty four hour flight, first class or not. My family would be so excited if they could see Brad's place, I hoped that they would be able to visit me soon.

I stepped out of the shower and walked across the wet room. Taking in the amazing view at such a vantage point, while completely naked was liberating. I started to get ready hurriedly in time for Brad, eager to experience my new surroundings and have a chance to relax with him before dinner tonight. When I was finished I looked at myself in the mirror and felt a rush of joy. No more big winter coats and scarves for me. I looked elegant and summery in a white strapless sundress and heels, and revelled in the feeling of the hot summer air against my bare skin. I walked towards the seating area and waited for Brad to come back excitedly.

The minutes turned into hours and the hours rolled by so slowly it was painful. I tapped my foot impatiently staring at the door. Any minute now. I checked the phone in the apartment, lifting the receiver to hear the dialling tone. Surely he would just ring if he was held up? I tapped my foot, played with my hair, got a beer from the fridge and drank it. I looked at my watch again. It was now almost three and I was starving. Something important must have come up, otherwise he would be here making our first day here together special.

I lit a cigarette and watched the door. By the time I had stubbed it out I'd had enough; there was one thing which had never been my strong point; patience. I didn't have a clue where I was, I had no key to get back in but I wasn't intending on waiting around any longer for him. If he couldn't at least call me to tell me where he was then I would go out myself. I grabbed my bag and headed out defiantly. As I ambled through the modern lobby like a lost lamb, I saw the young man who had carried our bags up and walked over to him. He jumped when he saw me on the other side of the desk and began to turn red.

"G'day miss. Can I help you at all?"

"Erm yes, I want to go for a drink somewhere for an hour or so, can you recommend anywhere near here?"

"Yes of course, if you follow the path out of the building that will lead you on to Darling Harbour. There are loads of nice bars down that way." He pointed out the direction, his eyes shifting down me nervously as if he was trying to stop himself from looking, but his pupils were magnetically drawn to my chest.

"Oh and have you seen Brad?" I asked.

"Yes miss. He left the building about ten am, his driver took him somewhere," he stammered.

"Oh. Well if he comes back can you tell him I just popped out for an hour? Thanks."

I stalked off, in search of somewhere nice. I felt angry that he had just disappeared without so much as a phone call. It seemed out of character; usually he was so considerate.

I picked an open front bar playing melodic chill out music, lowered myself into a wooden chair, and took in the view. I hadn't expected to spend the first afternoon by myself, but I suppose a man as successful as Brad probably had to put business first sometimes to get to where he was today. I watched the eclectic mix of people drifting past while I sipped at my cocktail; tourists of all different nationalities, families talking animatedly, and couples holding hands. Before I knew it, it was five thirty. Time to go back.

I casually wandered back along the path I came earlier, admiring the yachts dotted across the harbour, as the heat of the sun beat down upon my back. I walked past countless bars and restaurants which were getting ready for their busy time, smart waiters smiling by their entrances, welcoming people into their establishments. As my path continued I searched for the side street which led me back to Brad's apartment, but to my distress it was nowhere to be seen. As the Harbour became busier I searched frantically up and down through the heaving bodies, my pace quickening until I was almost running. I looked at my watch. It was now half six. How could I have been so stupid? I didn't even know the name of the road I was looking for, or the building. It would almost be time to meet Brad's parents and they would all be wondering where I was. Great first impression I was going to make.

"Fuck!" I exclaimed loudly, overcome by frustration, my tears threatening to erupt from inside me. It was now almost seven; we were meant to meet them in an hour.

"Are you okay mate?"

I was surprised to see the thick Australian accent belonged to a young Chinese waiter wearing a bemused expression. I must have passed him several times in the last thirty minutes.

"No, I'm not," I replied in desperation. "I need some help. I just arrived here today and I am completely lost."

"No worries doll, I'm sure I can help you. Where are you trying to find?"

"I need to find my boyfriend's apartment."

"Oh right," he laughed. "Not sure I can help you with that one then mate."

"He lives in a really massive penthouse round here."

He paused and scratched his head as he tried to think. "The really tall building with the jetties coming off it?"

"Yes," I exclaimed, praying that he could help.

"I think I know where you mean but you're up the completely wrong end of the Harbour doll. You need to walk back that way and then you will come to some steps on the right. Go up them, turn right at that road, follow it down and that will lead you to it."

"Oh my God! Thank you so much!"

"No problem." He handed me a map he had drawn onto a napkin and I followed his directions, relieved when they led me to back to Brad's building.

I walked into the building exhausted and was escorted to the lift by the concierge. As the doors opened at the top floor, a frosty reception was awaiting me.

"Where the bloody hell have you been?" Brad was sitting in the same position I had been in earlier, suited for the occasion, a tumbler of whisky in his hand.

"I'm sorry," I said as I tried to take his hand. He pulled it away from me sharply.

"I've been going out of my bloody mind. We're supposed to be meeting my parents, now we're gonna be fucking late. That's one thing they really hate, lateness."

"I got lost, I've been trying to find my way back for hours, I'm exhausted!"

"Where did you go?" he snapped, slamming his glass down and studying my face suspiciously.

"I just walked to the Harbour and when I tried to come back I couldn't find my way. I've been walking up and down for almost two hours."

I could see by the way he was looking at me he didn't believe me. "Yeah well in future, tell me before you go anywhere." He stood up, coldly pushing past me to go and top his glass up.

"Well sorry, but I was waiting for you for hours, thought you were supposed to be taking me for lunch."

"Something came up with work." He took a sip from his drink; avoiding my eyes.

"And you couldn't ring me?"

"No darlin, I couldn't ring you, that's the way it is with work sometimes. I still expected you to be here when I got back." He was beginning to shout now, as if my suggesting him to ring was atrocious.

"Well I got bored, I'd been sitting there waiting for you all dressed up and starving for hours."

"Yeah, well you should have stayed waiting." His blue eyes flashed as he spoke and I felt myself growing angry, the frustration of the day rising inside me. If he thought I was going to be living by his rules from now on then he was mistaken.

"Whatever Brad. Now you know how I felt earlier, don't you?"

I pushed past him to go and get changed and as I did, he grabbed my wrist roughly. His eyebrows were furrowed with rage, and he wore an angry expression, biting on his lip hard as if trying to hold himself back from saying something. I watched him with trepidation; I had never seen this side to him before. He seemed to hesitate, and then the angry expression melted away as quickly as it had arrived, and was replaced with tenderness once more. He lifted my hand to his mouth and kissed it softly.

"Just don't do it again darlin. I'm supposed to be looking after you, so I need to know where you are. What would I say to your mum if something happened to you eh?"

"Sorry."

"Just hurry up, my parents are at the restaurant waiting for us." He slapped my bum as I rushed back in the room to get ready. "Oh and I got you something to wear, it's hanging up."

CHAPTER ELEVEN

The restaurant was heaving; we hurried in past the tables, the noise of chatter, and the clanging of china. The exotic aroma of Thai food filled the air. Arthur stood up when he saw us and pointed to his wrist sarcastically, indicating his annoyance at our lateness before we had even sat down at the table. Seated next to him was a frail looking lady with silver hair in an impeccable white suit, adorned in diamond encrusted jewellery; Brad's mother. Stephanie Harrison was elegant and remarkably striking for a lady of her age; every inch of her screamed powerful millionairess. With her remarkable bone structure and perfectly delicate features I could imagine she had once been an arresting beauty, but her light blue eyes seemed to be lacking any warmth and she was making no effort to conceal her disapproval of our delay. Her mannerisms were frosty and calculated, and as she held out her bony hand to shake mine there wasn't even a trace of a smile on her face.

"I am so sorry we're late, I got lost; went for a walk this afternoon and couldn't find my way back." I felt genuinely remorseful for the way in which our first meeting had transpired. She seemed not to hear me and instead turned to Brad.

"We ordered the tasting menu and a bottle of Krug."

"Beautiful," Brad said and smacked his hands together.

"How are you finding it so far?" she asked, turning her attention back over to me reluctantly.

"That's the problem, not really finding anything so far." I said nervously. She gave me a wry look and I had the sudden urge to kick myself under the table. "But Sydney is really beautiful; I am sure I will really like it. I love Brad's apartment, it's amazing."

"Yes I'm sure you do," she replied, raising a perfectly arched eyebrow in my direction. "Brad had it refurbished recently, spent about five million on the interior design alone."

"Wow." I tried to ignore the accusatory tone in her voice. "Well it's certainly out of this world."

"Yes it is." She lifted a glass of wine to her lips, taking a delicate sip before looking me over once more. There was a look of distaste on her down-turned mouth and I hoped it was the wine causing her sour expression and not me. "So Ria, what is it that you do in England?"

"I just finished a fashion degree."

"Fashion!" she exclaimed, as if I had just declared I had spent the last three years studying UFOs. "Fancy yourself as a bit of a designer then do we?"

"Well, yes. I love creating clothes."

"I personally favour classic styling. The fashion industry is based solely upon regurgitating past trends and making them appear new to make money. Quite a shallow business if you ask me."

"Well I disagree. I think fashion is one of the biggest cultural indicators we have and it reflects our society just as much as any other form of art does."

She laughed at my reply, a tinkling sound which sounded like it had been rehearsed at a finishing school. "Is that so? Well you told me she was a looker, but you didn't tell me she had brains too Brad," she said, the sarcasm apparent in her voice. "Unusual for you."

Many torrid questions then ensued over twelve courses of meticulously arranged morsels of food, and I cautiously constructed my responses so as to not offend her or disparage myself. By the time dinner was over I felt ready to jump off the Harbour Bridge, but I somehow felt like I had managed to overcome the false start of evening and had impressed Stephanie slightly.

We said our goodbyes and I breathed a silent sigh of relief as I sank into the back seat of Brad's car. "That was painful."

"I told you, they hate people who are late." I swallowed back the urge to argue as we drove to our next destination.

The car glided to a halt outside a glass fronted club, and we walked past the queue of revellers and up the stairs of the VIP entrance. Brad led the way and he was greeted warmly by everyone who worked at the club, particularly the women, who were treating me like I was invisible. We sat down at a reserved table and I took in the surroundings.

"What do you want to drink?" Brad asked, his voice competing with the loud music.

"A long island," I shouted back. I hoped the concoction of spirits might melt away some of the tension I was feeling after the trying day. Brad clicked his fingers at the waiter who appeared as if from nowhere.

"Well you look stunning in that dress darlin. I'm sure my mother liked you too. She has a funny way of showing it but trust me, I could tell."

"I hope so, just a shame we were so late."

"Oh they will get over it. Forget about that for now, got some more people I want you to meet." No sooner than he had finished his sentence a couple of men appeared wearing trendy clothes.

"Harrison!" they announced enthusiastically, back slapping him.

"This is my new girl Ria," said Brad. "She's just come back here with me from London."

"Exported her did ya mate, you old dog." They nodded towards me in a gesture of acknowledgement.

"Yeah well, you know me. Only the best for Brad Harrison."

I flinched at his remark, embarrassed at being objectified, and forced myself to smile politely.

"Hey come on mate, we got some catching up to do." One of them motioned towards the back of the club and Brad bent down quickly towards me.

"I'll be back in a minute darlin. Don't go anywhere."

It sounded like an instruction and I rolled my eyes, took a big gulp of my drink, and turned my focus on the music and the crowd of people surrounding me. I scanned the girls in the club. They were all very pretty, a sea of leggy blondes as far as the eye could see. I hoped I would make some friends soon.

I drank my drink and waited for Brad to return patiently, ordering another long island as soon as I caught sight of the waiter again and downing it. The combination of the wine at dinner and the cocktails was making me feel merry, and I felt the sudden impulse to dance as one of my favourite tracks erupted on the dance floor.

"Fuck it," I exclaimed, taking to my feet and allowing myself to get immersed in the music. I noticed a few glances in my direction as I got deeper into my dance trance and was actually beginning to enjoy myself when I felt someone tap me on my shoulder. I turned around to see a beautiful girl with platinum blond hair and red lipstick smiling at me.

"You're an amazing dancer," she said.

"Thanks."

I grinned back at her, took one of her hands, and we started to dance together, twirling each other round and laughing. After a few songs we sat down.

"Do you want a drink?" I asked, motioning the waiter over. "I'll put it on my boyfriend's tab."

"Yeah thanks, I'll have a vodka martini."

We raised our glasses and sank back some of our cocktails.

"It's my first night in Sydney tonight," I shouted over the music.

"Oh yeah? How's it going?"

"Yeah quite well I suppose. Just met my boyfriend's parents for the first time, was a bit awkward. I got lost before dinner and we turned up late. They weren't too happy."

"Oh you poor thing," she laughed.

"Yeah they are a bit scary actually."

"Oh well if you ever need someone to go out with let me know. I know all the best places in Sydney. I'm Sorycha by the way."

"Nice to meet you, I'm Ria."

"Where's your boyfriend then?" she asked, looking round the crowd.

"He went off with some friends a while ago," I said flatly, unable to conceal my annoyance.

"What's his name, maybe I know him?"

"Brad Harrison."

Her eyes widened in response. "You're kidding. You're going out with Brad Harrison! That's awesome."

"Yeah I suppose."

"Hey we should swap numbers. Need a girl to go out with."

We pulled out our mobile phones from our hand bags and then got up to dance again, and were joined by a tanned Mediterranean looking man, whose appearance caused Sorycha to squeal in delight. She hugged him drunkenly and he danced with us both, pouting his lips while he strutted to the beats. I had given up on waiting for Brad and ordered some more shots, which Sorycha and I knocked back with the speed of lightning. That's when I saw Brad.

"Who the fuck's this?" he asked, the look on his face alone causing the bloke to retreat into the crowd. "I leave you alone for one minute and you're dancing with some fucking wog."

"He's only been dancing with us for a minute."

From over Brad's shoulder I could see Sorycha pulling an awkward face and mouthing, "call me."

"You take the fuckin piss Ria. First I take you to meet my parents and you turn up late, and now I take you here and you make a fuckin mockery of me, dancing with some dickhead in front of everyone." His voice sounded menacing.

"I wasn't dancing with him, I was dancing with that girl. He's a friend of hers that's all."

"Whatever. Let's go home, I obviously can't trust you alone for five minutes."

He grabbed my wrist and led me out of the club roughly and into the car, slamming the door behind me. As he got in beside me I felt a surge of anger. I crossed my arms and looked out of the window, away from him. I couldn't believe how he had acted today.

"Sorry darlin. I just love you so much; it made me crazy to see some loser dancing round you. Come here."

"I was only dancing; it's not like I was grinding up against him for God's sake."

"I know, but I saw the way he was looking at you. Hey come on, don't be mad."

He took my hand and pulled me closer. I resisted for a moment before allowing myself to succumb to his arms, and as he held me in them, my temporary aggravation with him was replaced with lust. By the time we had reached his apartment my lipstick was smeared from our passionate kisses. He threw me over his shoulder and carried me into the lift and we had urgent sweaty sex by the front door, collapsing by it afterwards exhausted.

"I love you Ria," he said, kissing my forehead.

"Love you too," I replied.

CHAPTER TWELVE

"Who are you looking at?" Brad glared at me from across the table and I looked up at him, confused.

"No one, what are you talking about?"

"Don't give me that darlin, you were looking at that guy over there; I'm not blind."

I turned to see who he was accusing me of looking at. We were seated outside having lunch in a seafood restaurant in Woolloomooloo. There were people walking past along the jetty; it was a beautiful day and it was busy but I couldn't see anyone even remotely attractive.

"Brad how many times do I have to tell you this, I don't even look at other men, why would I, have you even seen yourself lately?"

"Just forget it," he said, getting his phone out of his pocket and typing out a message. "So what are your plans for the rest of the arvo?"

"Well I was planning on going back home after this, got an interview tonight."

That got his attention. He put his phone down and took a gulp from his glass of wine.

"You're not thinking of going back into dancing are you? Cause if you are you had better think again." The last thing I wanted was to work in a strip club again, he knew that, so why did he have to keep making a point of telling me that I wasn't allowed to? It was really winding me up.

"Didn't mind me working there when you met me though did you?

But no, if you must know it is for a bar job, thought I might make some friends."

"Are you kidding me?" Brad said, shaking his head. "My girlfriend working in a bar, that would be a total embarrassment, no way. Why would you even want to anyway, aren't I doing a good enough job of looking after you?" He looked offended and I knew I'd better tread carefully; he was so bloody touchy recently.

"Of course you are, but I just want to meet some people, I need to have my own life as well you know, I've been here for weeks and I hardly ever see you. What do you want me to do, stay at home missing you all day?"

"Yeah, now you come to mention it that's exactly what I want." He smiled and dragged my chair next to his, making a loud scraping noise that made everyone nearby turn and stare. I couldn't help but laugh at him, he changed as quick as a switch; one minute he was seething with jealousy, the next he was horny as hell.

"Well you can't always get what you want Mr Harrison," I said, determined not to succumb to his charms for a change.

"I think you'll find that I can and I will." He gave me a devilish look, ran his hand up my thigh and kissed me softly; tracing his tongue around my lips and pressing me closely against him. I could feel myself melting, but noticed a teenage boy on the next table gawping at us and pushed him away.

"There are people staring Brad."

"I can't help it darlin, that's the power you have over me. You're so fucking sexy." He picked his phone up again and made a call. "Hey Alicia, it's Brad. There's been a change of plan, won't be coming back to the office today after all, so can you reschedule the meeting for another day? Thanks." He hung up, swept my hair over to one side and began to bestow my neck with light kisses that made my skin tingle.

"So you're not working now then?" I asked, hesitant to believe we would finally have a whole day together, just the two of us for once.

"Well I can't exactly walk into work like this can I?" He grinned at me and I glanced down to see the fabric of his beige linen trousers straining under the pressure of a very large and very noticeable erection; I could see what he meant by not being able to walk in the office.

"Yeah, you could have someone's eye out with that thing." I giggled.

"Anyway," he said, taking my hand in his. "You're right; we need some more time together. So you've got me all to yourself for the day. What do you feel like doing? We could go out on my boat if you like, get some champagne and go for a bit of a cruise around, what do you reckon?"

"That would be amazing, but I need to be back by five Brad, my interview's at seven."

He shrugged his shoulders. "No worries darlin, I'll have you back in time."

We quickly finished up our drinks and walked back towards Brad's car. His driver was leaning against the Mercedes waiting for us, and he jumped up and opened the door for us to climb in. We drove back home, grabbed some champagne and our swimwear from upstairs and walked through the Lobby to the other side of the building where all the yachts were moored. I had been desperate to go out on his boat since we had arrived and was excited about finally being able to spend the day on it.

It was right at the end of the wharf, all white and gleaming in the sunlight, bobbing gently in the waves, and Brad hopped onto it and helped me down.

"How's the sound system on this thing?" I asked.

"It will blow your mind!" He flashed me a wicked grin and began unwinding the rope so we could get going.

"I'm gonna get into my costume," I said, eager to strip off and get my new Pucci bikini on.

"Just go down those steps, they will lead you to the bedrooms," he said.

I made my way down into the living room and kitchen. It was all white, and bright, and open, with a chrome kitchen and dining benches in the middle, and at the back of the room was a wooden corridor with several more doors. I pushed my way through the door opposite and found myself in a room which contained a king sized bed, surrounded by mirrored wardrobes. I felt the engine roar as I pulled up my bikini bottoms, and clung to the door to prevent myself from falling as we took off. When I was dressed I applied some more red lipstick, put on my massive sunglasses, and inspected myself in the mirror; not bad I suppose. Just then the walls began to vibrate with some funky house music; Brad must have fired up the sound system. Let the party begin.

I began to climb up to the top deck to join him, swaying up the stairs and gripping the railings as I made my way. When I reached the top I caught sight of him and my heart started to race; I felt just as I had the first night we'd met in Centrefolds. He was standing up steering the boat, wearing just a pair of white boxers, his rippling torso on view, a sun-kissed, bronzed picture of masculine perfection. He turned to look at me and grinned, his blue eyes twinkling in the sunlight.

"You look amazing Ria," he said, looking me up and down.

"So do you." I seated myself next to him as he navigated the Harbour. His apartment block was really far away already, the other boats we had been next to only ten minutes ago looked like little white dots bobbing in the distance. When there was a sufficient enough distance between us and the other boats, he turned the engine off and looked at me.

"Let's crack open some champagne then," he said and retreated to the lower floor returning soon after with an ice bucket, two glasses, and a bottle of Dom Perignon. He popped off the cork and I held the glasses up as he filled them.

"Cheers, here's to us," he said. "We're going to have a fucking amazing time today."

"To us," I said. "Just don't let me drink too much today Brad cause of this interview later."

"Fuck the interview," he said and took my glass away, lifting me on the flat surface behind the wheel of the boat. He kissed me passionately and pulled on the tie of my bikini top slowly until it fell to the ground, then leant me back and worked his way down my neck with his mouth. "You don't need to work darlin, you've got me now," he said in my ear as his hands explored my body.

"Brad," I said, trying to suppress myself from moaning so I could communicate my point. I pushed his hands away as they began to slide underneath my briefs, but all I could manage to say was, "I need a job."

"All you need is me, you don't need anything else. I promise I am going to make more of an effort from now on."

"Really?"

"Really," he said, silencing me by pressing his mouth on top of mine again and pulling my hands above my head. Lost in the moment I let myself surrender to my desire for him; now wasn't the time to fight, all I could focus on right now was what he was doing to me.

"How many times have I got to tell you this? It's you and me against the world. You don't need anyone else anymore."

Brad was stroking my hair, comforting me from the homesickness which was crippling me. It had been a couple of months since I had moved to Sydney and I'd never felt so lonely in all my life. I longed for my family, and now the novelty of living a life of luxury had worn off, I felt empty and lost. With no one to turn to but Brad, my days were filled with silence and solitude, eagerly waiting for him to return from work so I would have some company. All too often though I would be waiting to no avail, the massive size of his apartment engulfing me and causing me to feel even more alone.

Recently though, I often found myself wishing he hadn't come home at all, particularly when he was drunk. He would awaken me by ripping my covers off and questioning me on my day's activities, harassing me for details while he deciphered my every move.

"You're never here though Brad, I am by myself every day. I miss my family so much." My lip was trembling as I wept. He stopped stroking my hair, jumped up, and folded his muscular arms, the sympathy on his face rapidly evaporating.

"Of course I'm not here. Do you think I got all this from sitting on my arse all day? I need to work darlin."

"I know that, but you are out every night, you never even tell me where you are, and I'm just stuck here waiting for you all the time. I feel like maybe I made a mistake coming here. I might go home."

My suggestion made him jolt back over and he knelt down beside me. "Don't be stupid, you're not going home. Look I will make it up to you tonight, take you somewhere nice, just me and you. I'll finish work early and pick you up about seven. How's that sound?"

"You promise?" I asked, searching his face for any signs of insincerity. He looked back at me straight in the eyes.

"Yeah promise." He reached into his wallet and pulled out some cash; his answer to everything. "Go and treat yourself today, get yourself something new to wear for tonight. Got to go now, see you later." I took it resignedly and he kissed me on the forehead before hurrying off.

I looked at the cash in my hand and sighed. There was just over a thousand dollars in total. I had enjoyed having a rich boyfriend in the beginning but now I felt trapped, waiting for him to hand me over some guilt money; he seemed to think it was all I needed to lead a fulfilling life. It could never make up for his time, which was becoming less frequent as the weeks progressed. Maybe he was having an affair; he had women throwing themselves at him at every opportunity, and despite his excuses I couldn't see how he would have to work until three in the morning. We had spent all our time together in London, he hadn't been able to get enough of me then, but everything had changed since we came here. Now I felt like an expensive piece of furniture in his flat. He wanted to see me when he came home, to lay on top of me and enjoy having me there, but when he wasn't here I was forgotten. He never told me what he was doing or when he would return, but he expected to be informed of my every movement.

Despite the passionate feelings I had for him I could feel my love for him fading gradually; every day spent alone, every un-kept promise fuelling my disappointment. I'd thought it was too good to be true when we'd met and I was beginning to realise that perhaps I had been right? Maybe fairy-tale romances did only exist in novels and films? At that moment my phone started to ring and I ran over to the dining table to get it. It was my sister. I took a deep breath and answered her call.

"Hi Aia" I said, mustering up as much enthusiasm as I could in my voice so she couldn't hear I was upset.

"Hi Sis, just wanted to see how you were getting on?"

"Oh yes, everything's really good, still settling into it all really. How are things at home?" I asked, hoping to deflect the attention away from me. She didn't take the bait.

"Yeah, same as ever; just been a bit worried about you. We've hardly heard from you since you've been there."

"Oh I've just been really busy that's all, every time I want to ring you it's the wrong time of day."

"So everything's going alright with Brad then?" She sounded concerned, and I knew she could tell I was upset.

"Yes, really well," I lied.

"Alright Sis, well you know you can call me anytime if you need to talk. I miss you."

"I miss you too."

"So what have you been doing then?" she asked. I could hear the noise of the TV in the background; it was night time back home.

"Just relaxing really. To be honest Sis, I am getting a bit bored. Brad's always working. I still have to find my own feet."

"Why don't you get a job then? You'll meet friends and get out more, you should try to get a bar job and then maybe you can look for a job in fashion or something."

"Yeah maybe, it's just that Brad doesn't really want me to work. He gives me money, he keeps saying that he wants to look after me and it would be an embarrassment if I were to work in a bar or something." I felt embarrassed when I heard myself; I sounded so dependent, so weak. I could almost see my sister shaking her head at me disapprovingly.

"Oh right, so he'd rather have you cooped up in his flat all day waiting for hand-outs like a little kid?"

"No, not at all, but he is really high profile over here, quite famous. It's not like going out with anyone, he's got photographers and all sorts after him. I can't really just go and work in a bar. I have to be careful of what I do now."

"Oh bloody hell Ria, sounds like a load of old shit to me. He's just trying to control you. I knew this would happen."

"No he's not." I protested. "He's trying to look after me."

"Well he's obviously not doing a good job; you sound bloody miserable. Has he even taken you anywhere yet?"

"Not yet, he's been really busy with work because he was in London for so long, got a lot of things to catch up on. He will be soon though."

"Right, well as long as he does. I just hate to hear you down Sis. You went there because he promised to give you the time of your life and show you Australia. Sounds like all you've seen so far is his flash apartment."

"Yeah well hopefully he'll have more time soon."

"Fine, in the meantime though keep yourself busy, get yourself onto all the beaches, get to know the place, meet people. Enjoy it Sis, don't be hanging round waiting for him all the time."

I nodded and looked at the view below me; the city, the beaches and the boats gliding between it all. I had been watching it pass me by for the last couple of months; a spectator, not a participant. I felt so disconnected living so high up away from it all, I needed to go down and become a part of it.

"Yeah, you're right Aia. Thanks, I will do. It's just been hard getting used to it that's all, I feel really homesick. I miss you all so much."

"We miss you too, but we are always here if you need us, we're only a phone call away you know. Hey, I'd better go now cause me and Howard are about to have dinner, but I mean it Ria. Get out there today and make the most of it. I love you."

"I love you too Sis, take care." I hung up the phone. My sister was right; I did need to start making the most of it. No wonder Brad was losing interest when I was just hanging around waiting for him all day like some desperate housewife. I started to get my things together. Today I would go to Bondi, get an amazing dress for tonight, spend the day on the beach and enjoy myself, and tonight I would make Brad remember the independent, fun girl he had fallen for; hopefully resurrecting the charming man I had fallen in love with in the process.

CHAPTER THIRTEEN

It was eight pm and I had been clock watching for the past hour. It was a frustrating game and it was getting old very quickly. After spending the evening getting ready in anticipation of a night on the town, I was now sitting by the front door waiting for Brad to return, like a dog waiting for its owner.

"Look I will make it up to you tonight. Take you somewhere nice, just me and you. I'll finish work early and pick you up about seven."

Brad's words rang in my head as I went over them for the thousandth time. He had sounded so sincere when he had said them. So where was he? I had a sinking feeling as I realised that maybe he had been lying to me.

I was sick of being home alone and felt like I was going insane. He had promised me he would return and I had believed him, and now here I was alone, nursing a glass of wine by myself, again. If I was back home I would have just rung one of my friends and gone out but I had no one over here.

I glanced at my watch again. It was still too early to call my sister and I desperately needed someone to confide in. If I knew what Brad was doing then it wouldn't be so bad. What made it so much worse was that he would promise to come back, and then disappear off the face of the earth; unreachable and untraceable.

I looked around the stylish harbour side apartment, at its unabashed luxury. Its shine was wearing off after weeks of being inside it by myself. Yes it was beautiful, but it felt empty and vacuous; as did the space in my heart that was usually occupied by Brad.

I walked onto the balcony, clutching my glass of wine and admired the view. The Harbour lights shone in the distance. I was high up from here and could see most of the city. Leaning over the stone barricade, I looked down and an overwhelming rush of vertigo hit me making me feel dizzy. I felt a strange impulse to jump over and instantly backed away from the edge. Why was he doing this to me? Why couldn't he just answer the phone or better still call me if he couldn't make it? It was almost like he was deliberately torturing me.

I lit up another cigarette, watched it glow orange and sucked on the end of it greedily in the hope it would give me some sense of respite. Five more minutes and then I will call him again. I breathed out a long train of white smoke and watched as it filtered through the night sky.

There was a humming noise, and I turned to see my phone vibrating against the glass table. With a sense of relief I went over to answer it. Finally; about fucking time.

"Hello," I said in an irritated tone. There had better be a decent explanation for his disappearance this time.

"Hey is that Ria?"

I heard a girl's voice, causing my heart to leap into my throat. Maybe it was a girl he had been shagging, calling to rub my nose in it and twist the knife? Well if it was, then at least I would have some release from this wretched situation.

"Yes it's Ria. Who's this?"

"Oh hey, it's Sorycha. I met you a while ago remember?" I could hear some bassy music in the background, and she was shouting over it, in competition with the raucous to get heard.

"Oh hi!" I shouted back in surprise. "How are you?"

"Good," she replied. "Hey, what are you up to tonight? I am out in a bar in the Cross called Marco's. Come meet me, I'm with a bunch of people, thought you might want to come along!" She was talking enthusiastically, it was evident she'd had a few and I felt the urge to join her.

"Definitely, I will hop in a cab now." I jumped up from my seat and grabbed my bag.

"Brilliant. Call me when you get here. We're on the VIP list. Just tell the doorman you're with Sorycha. We're sitting by the main bar."

"Wicked, see you soon babe!" I felt so relieved to have escaped from my stagnant, helpless predicament. Striding into the lift I studied my reflection and put another layer of gloss onto my lips. Brad could get fucked. Let him wonder where I was for a change.

The cab pulled up opposite an open fronted bar, which was situated at the top of a flight of stairs, in the middle of the bustling Kings Cross.

"Here you go doll. That'll be twenty dollars."

"Cheers," I said, thrusting him some cash, eager to join the crowd outside. There was a huge cue to get in and I walked past it to the burly bouncer on the door. He gave me the once over, unhooked the red rope and ushered me inside, without so much as a raised eyebrow. I loved queue-jumping.

"Hey Ria!" Sorycha stood up as she saw me approaching. She looked as glamorous as I remembered; her platinum blond hair was swept into a style reminiscent of a fifties Hollywood movie star, and her petite frame was squeezed into an elegant black dress, which was doing an excellent job of showing off her hourglass figure. We air kissed each other and she introduced me to her friends; a group of remarkably good-looking and stylish men who were seated around the circular table.

"This is Hugo, Sylvain, and Angelo," she said gesturing towards them. "And this is Ria." She patted the stool next to hers and Angelo poured me a glass of champagne.

"Thanks," I said raising my glass. "So this must be where all the gorgeous people of Sydney hang out then!" I laughed.

"What these bunch of losers!" Sorycha teased. "These are nothing. You should check out the ones on Bondi beach with me some time." She nudged me playfully and I smiled. Finally some fun was on the agenda.

Five glasses of champagne and three shots later and Brad was the last thing on my mind. Angelo was being particularly attentive and I was revelling in it, pleased to have a confidence boost after the ego bashing I had been receiving from my once charming boyfriend. It was one o'clock and he still hadn't rung me.

"I love your accent Ria," he said, inching in closer to me, until we were sandwiched next to each other at the bar. His swarthy good looks were making my body ache with temptation.

"Thanks. Yours is nice too," I said, edging back.

"So what are you having?" He leaned over to order. "More champagne?"

"Oh yes please. And I'll have another Sambuca."

"What an animal!" he said and we knocked back our shots, slamming our glasses back down on the bar and grimacing at the harsh taste.

"Fancy a line?" he asked, gesturing towards the bathrooms.

"I don't know; I'm not into all that." I had seen the impact it had on some of the girls in Centrefolds who spent the large bulk of their earnings on the substance and had steered clear of it, but the invitation was tempting in my present state.

"Are you sure, you're looking pretty wasted? It will sort you out, keep you going."

I could feel myself swaying, the alcohol taking its toll and hitting me at once. I certainly could do with a pick me up and I wasn't ready to go home already. I had seen Brad do coke enough times and it didn't seem to affect him too much.

"Yeah, why not then," I said, and he led the way through the crowd to the toilets.

We squeezed into a cubicle together and he cut up two lines, rolling up a fifty and handing it to me. I bent over the toilet and snorted up the powder, feeling straighter instantaneously. There was a tingling sensation on my lips and I licked them, rubbing my tongue over my gums which were becoming numb. Angelo knelt down and snorted his line.

All of a sudden my phone began to ring. It was him. He had probably just got back home and seen I wasn't there. Finally, he could see how it felt and maybe he would understand what he was doing to me. I was in no rush to get back. I pressed cancel, cutting him off in the same way he had done to me on so many occasions before.

"Who's that?" Angelo asked.

"My boyfriend" I said, squeezing out of the cubicle.

"I should have known a beautiful girl like you would be spoken for."
He looked disappointed and I felt bad for flirting with him and leading

him on.

"Yeah well I don't know if I will be for much longer. He keeps disappearing on me all the time and I don't know anyone over here yet, so I've just been at home waiting for him, upset most nights since I got here."

"That sucks!" Angelo looked at me pityingly. "Well he must be mad. If I had a girl like you I would treat her like gold."

"Yeah, that's what they all say."

We walked back into the throng of the club, past people dancing to some pumping house music, enjoying the start to their weekend and I began dancing too; letting myself go and forgetting about all the problems.

The phone calls were getting more frequent and urgent. I could almost feel Brad's anger burning a hole in my handbag as my phone vibrated inside it. It was time to leave.

I searched for Sorycha to say goodbye. She was having a conversation with a man who was trying it on with her, and by the looks of it failing miserably.

"Hey Sorycha, I think I'm gonna head back now. Feeling knackered."

"Oh okay babe, it was lovely seeing you, we should definitely do it again soon. Angelo, walk Ria to the cabs will you, make sure she gets back okay?"

Angelo leapt up, happy to oblige and we made our way to the outside street which was lined with drunk revellers spilling out from the numerous clubs and bars. It was an unexpected crowd of people; transvestite prostitutes, smack heads looking for a score, local posers, and young foreign travellers as pure as the white driven snow in comparison to everyone else. We squeezed past them all and walked down the bustling street which was lined with strip clubs and bars, the flashing fluorescent lighting, doormen, and girls, tempting passers-by as they walked along. Finally, Angelo managed to hail a cab. As I got in it he handed me his card.

"Hey give me a call if you ever get rid of that man you're with. Or even if you just need a friend or someone to hang out with."

His beautiful brown eyes were filled with sincerity and warmth. He was nice. If I was single I would have jumped at the chance. Unfortunately for me though love was not a choice, it was a disease.

CHAPTER FOURTEEN

I took a deep breath and slowly turned the key in the lock, hoping against all hope that Brad would be asleep or still out; I really didn't want to deal with his shit right now. I pushed the door gently and it swung ajar to reveal the open-plan room. It was awash with darkness except for the lights of the harbour; casting menacing shadows against the marble floors. A still, silent and eerie sense of calm pervaded over the luxury apartment. I felt a wave of relief taking over from the sickening adrenaline pumping through my veins. If it wasn't for my deafening pulse hammering against my eardrums, you could have heard a pin drop. Brad wasn't there. Thank God.

I slipped off my jacket and quickly made my way towards the bathroom to cover up the evidence of the night's antics. As I walked past the kitchen I felt my heart leap into my throat as I caught sight of his silhouette. He was sitting at the table on the balcony, facing the front door, clutching a glass of whisky and staring right at me. My mouth fell open in shock. Why did he have to be home tonight of all nights? Why did I always have to be so unlucky?

I attempted to mask the feeling of dread at the pit of my stomach with some false bravado and an act of nonchalance. As I opened my mouth, ready to recite the explanation of my whereabouts, I was brusquely cut off.

"Had a good night did you darlin?"

His voice slashed through the tense silence like a machete, causing me to jump. He studied my face; searching for an incriminating slip up in my demeanour as if he were a human lie detector. Should I even look in the wrong direction while telling him my story I knew he would be ready to pounce. His paranoid personality meant that he was sensitive to every subtle detail in my body language, tone of voice and facial expression. Anything he could use to justify his psychotic and manipulative behaviour towards me he would, if only to make himself feel better for being such a bastard. I felt the sudden impulse to just run straight out the front door, but I knew that wouldn't be a wise move. It was too late now. I had to face the music.

"I just met up with that girl Sorycha. You know the one I met on our first night? Just went for a few drinks in town. Nothing major. I did try calling but your phone was off." My voice sounded strained and I leant against the balcony door, trying to act casual. I could see he was drunk. He was swilling amber liquid around his glass rhythmically. I watched as his big shoulders slowly started to drop as the tension that had hunched them together gradually released. Perhaps he believed me after all?

"Where did you go?" he fired, his glare softening slightly. For a split second, I thought I caught a glimpse of a wry smile, etching its way across his face.

"We just went to Marco's," I said, trying to hide the fear in my voice.

"So it was just you and Sorycha then, no one else?"

"No just us two," I replied coolly.

He seemed satisfied with my answer and took a big swig of whisky, gulping it down in one swift movement. Then all of a sudden, he crashed the glass back down so hard that it shattered to pieces all over the floor.

"You fucking lying bitch." He grabbed my hair and spat the poisonous words out in disgust, his flecks of spit spraying into my face like acid rain. I stared back at him in stunned silence. As he breathed in my face; I could almost smell his kidneys rotting away inside him. Brad had a good way of being able to conceal the amount of alcohol he had consumed, but I knew that smell straight away. Warning…danger! The pungent aroma filled my nostrils with terror. He threw me like a rag doll onto the floor, as I desperately tried to manoeuvre my landing away from the large shards of broken glass littered across it.

"I'm telling the truth," I cried tears streaming down my face. "What do you expect Brad, I am by myself all the time? I didn't come to Australia to live like a caged animal. I came to have fun."

"Fun! Fun!" Brad screamed in outrage. "Yeah well you had plenty of that tonight didn't you?" he said, squeezing my face in his hand. "Yeah that's right I know all about you're fun. One of my mates saw you tonight sitting with a group of wogs. I'll never be able to look them in the face again. You completely humiliated me, you fucking little whore."

"And how do you think I feel hey?" I shouted, my fear being over taken by rage. "I left behind everything I know to come here and you have treated me like shit since I arrived. Disappearing every night without any explanation. It's been almost two months. Two fucking months! All the promises of the places I would see and the life I would have. It was all bullshit! All I have seen are the four walls of your fucking pretentious flat." My body was quivering with anger as the realisation of what I had allowed myself to put up with suddenly registered.

"You ungrateful bitch," Brad snarled at me. There are girls out there who would kill to have all this. To be with someone like me. I have treated you like a princess since I met you." He looked me up and down in disgust.

"Oh yeah? Well they are welcome to you, cause this princess is leaving the fucking castle." I grabbed my bag and bolted towards the door. I had almost made my exit when I heard running footsteps behind me and I was knocked sideways onto the cold hard floor by Brad's large hand, smashing against the side of my head. My ears started ringing so loudly that I could hardly hear anything else. He leant over me, pushing his face into mine.

"You're not going fucking anywhere."

I yelped as he dragged me forcefully across the marble floor towards the bedroom by my hair. I desperately tried to grab on to anything I passed, chair legs, doors but it was happening too quickly.

"Let go of me," I screamed at the top of my voice, alarmed at his violent behaviour, hoping the neighbours would hear my cries. "Please Brad. I just want to go home. Let me go."

"This is your home now bitch," he said. His thick hands grabbed me by the throat as he straddled me. I tried to scream but his grip tightened and I could hardly breathe.

"You want to act like a whore. I'll treat you like a fucking whore." His other hand started to furiously tear at my knickers. I squirmed underneath him violently like a fish in a net, trying to get away, choking for air. Then I did the only thing I could think of. I stuck my long manicured nails right into his eyes. I gasped as my neck was released from his vice like grip and I got to my feet, but before I could do anything else, I felt a big fist crashing down against my face.

I raised my arms around me in defence as I felt another blow. His punch flew at me with such a force that the room became a blur as I flew across it; crashing into the dressing table and knocking its contents over with me as I went.

"Get off me you bastard!" I cried, attempting again to escape the catastrophic scene. I had just made it to the bedroom door, when I felt my hair being yanked back with such violence, that I landed flat on my back. An explosion of heat and pain spread across my face, as Brad's large fist cracked against my nose. I yelped with panic as I saw blood streaming out of it onto the white carpet below me.

The sight of my crimson blood across the floor, finally snapped Brad out of his rage and he instantly looked as terrified as I felt. "Oh my God. I'm so sorry darlin. I'm so sorry." His face crumbled and he started sobbing frantically in disbelief at what he had done. I felt myself being gently picked up and lowered onto the bed. The sound of the ringing in my ears and Brad's constant apologising made me feel dazed and I curled myself up into a ball while the room span around me. It felt like a horrific nightmare and I felt sick with the realisation of what had just happened.

"I want my mum," I sobbed as Brad held a cold flannel against my nose.

"It's okay Ria. I'm gonna look after you now. "

My whole body was throbbing in pain but it was nothing in comparison to the hurt I felt inside my heart. I cried silently with my eyes closed, too exhausted to move, too ashamed to escape and let anyone see me, and I was slowly released from my suffering as I surrendered myself to sleep.

CHAPTER FIFTEEN

When I came to, the sun from outside was streaming in through the ceiling to floor windows, the beautiful scene of Sydney Harbour cruelly mocking my predicament. It was an unfit backdrop for the anguish inside me. I lifted my face slowly which was stuck to the pillow with a combination of sweat, tears, and blood. I glanced down at the white sheets swathed around me, the spattering of my own blood across them, reminding me of the horror of the night before, and confirming that it had in fact happened and had not just been a nightmare.

The blue bruises across my tender forearms were pulsating in pain. Brad's hand prints were scorched across them, and it felt like they were burning away at my flesh. I grimaced in agony as I leant on them, trying gently to pull my battered body up. The back of my head was throbbing from where he had thrown me on the floor, and I felt alarmed as I realised my ear was still ringing loudly. What if he had damaged them forever? I had once known a woman who was half deaf from where her ex-boyfriend had screamed so loudly at her he had burst her ear drum. I didn't want to end up like that. I was so frightened at the thought of the harm he could have done to me.

My whole face was sore, my eyes were swollen and heavy, and I wondered if it was caused by my tears or by the beating. My nose was crusted up with blood and felt twice its normal size; I prodded it softly, pressing the tips of my fingers across its bridge, trying to assess the damage that had been done. How could he have done this to me? I stumbled across the room like a newborn colt towards the ensuite, to see my reflection.

When I got there I didn't recognise the girl who was staring back at me. My whole face was so swollen and enlarged that both my cheekbones were invisible; my eyes were black and so puffed up they looked like a couple of slits; my nose was so wide and bruised it had doubled in size. It wasn't just my outward appearance which shocked me though. When I looked into my eyes they seemed hollow and vacuous, like my soul had been beaten out of me. I felt like I didn't know who I was anymore. Gone was the confident, beautiful girl I had once known and in her place was someone weak, helpless. I had become a victim and I felt so ashamed. I looked at the poor girl in the mirror and I wept with disgust.

I collapsed back into bed flinching as my body hit the mattress. I couldn't believe what he had done to me. He had gone from the man who would have done anything to make me happy, to charm and entertain me; to a selfish creature who only cared about fulfilling his own needs. To him I was just a prize trophy that he could bring back to show off to his family and friends. I had been so foolish. I really thought he had loved me but how could that be possible? All the promises he had made me, of the destinations we would see before we came. "I can't wait to take you to the Whitsundays," he had whispered sweetly in my ear, charming me with fantasies of white sand, crystal clear waters and freedom.

In England I had held the cards. I had my family and friends around me, my independence and confidence, but I became stripped of that when I had entered his domain. He had basked in my dependence on him, my lack of control and my diminished support network, and he had tried to strip it away further from me, until I had become a confused little girl with no one else to run to, and no one else to care. The only place left to run had been back into the arms of the man who was causing my anguish. I felt so stupid.

Out of the corner of my eye, I saw my disposable camera poking out of my bag. I scrambled over to it, wound it up, and turned the lens towards me. I started clicking frantically, photographing the aftermath of destruction he had wreaked across my face and body. I aimed it at my ravaged eyes, and at my nose. At the blue bruises around my neck, my swollen face and my painful forearms. It snapped. Capturing the cuts on my legs from where he had pushed me onto the broken glass and the marks all over my body. I had just finished when I heard a knock at the door.

"Ria. Can I come in?" His voice pierced through my heart like an arrow, and for a moment I felt certain that I could feel it bleeding. Panicking I threw my camera back in my bag. I couldn't even bring myself to answer but before I had even had the chance, he swung the door open. I stared at the floor, noticing yet more of my blood sprayed across it. It had made an artistic looking pattern like a Damien Hurst polka dot painting. It looked kind of beautiful in a twisted way. I focused on it intently, my hair hanging over my face, imagining the white carpet was really a canvas hanging in the Tate Modern, art critics standing before it with a critical eye analysing the sprays of red, remarking on the artist's expressive and bold nature. Blood spray on white floor would be its title: simple, yet breathtakingly effective.

"I'm so sorry darlin."

He slowly moved closer to me, and I turned away holding my hands to my face. I didn't want anyone to see me, not even him. I felt a silent tear roll down my face, falling off the tip of my nose onto the piece of artwork below. I couldn't tear my eyes away from the sight of my own blood. I didn't want to see him, I didn't want to see myself. I didn't want to see anyone or to even exist.

He knelt down on the floor beside me. "Oh my God darlin. Look at what I bloody did to you. Look at what I did. Please forgive me Ria. Please forgive me."

He cried dramatically and tried to wrap his arms around me; every bit of pressure made me want to yelp in agony. I didn't want to see him. I didn't want to look at him. I didn't want him to exist. He buried his head in my lap like a child and wept, soaking my T-shirt. I didn't even have the energy to push him off. I just sat motionless, staring at my blood on the carpet and wishing that I was at home.

"Please Ria, let me hold you. Let me make it better." He forced me into his muscular arms and wept even more. "I love you so much," he said, kissing my forehead repetitively.

"You don't care Brad," I said pulling away. "You don't love me. Look at what you did to me." I pointed at my face and cried.

"Ria please, I love you so much. I never meant to hurt you. I was so scared you were going to leave me. I just want you to be happy. I was so upset when I came home and you were missing. I'm sorry I haven't been here for you, but I will be from now on. I'm all yours."

"Great!" I said sarcastically. "You're all mine and you're doing such a great job of looking after me aren't you Brad? First you get me to go to the other side of the world with you. Then you treat me like a prisoner, and now you have beaten the absolute shit out of me. Great. I am so glad I've got you. I am so lucky. So lucky!"

"I know Ria. I can't believe it; I have never raised my hand to a woman before." His statement left me wondering if it was my fault. If he had never hit anyone before then why had he felt the need to hit me? I never thought I would find myself in this situation.

"Look let me clean up in here and look after you," he pleaded. "I brought you some tea and a joint. Have a cup of tea it will make you feel better."

"Is a cup of tea going to heal my face Brad? Is a cup of tea going to mend my broken nose? Is a cup of tea going to take the constant ringing out of my ears? I can hardly fucking hear Brad, I can hardly fucking hear!" I gave way to the emotion which had been building up inside me like waves against a dam and I sobbed. I sobbed for my family who I missed so much, I sobbed for my horrifically battered body, but mostly I sobbed at the realisation that my Australian dream had become a living nightmare. Brad wrapped his arms around me again and this time I couldn't fight it. I relented, letting myself become enveloped by him for a brief moment. It felt so good to be held, so bitter sweet, even if it was by him.

I walked to the balcony and took a sip of my tea, lighting the massive joint and sucking in deeply, hoping it would eradicate my pain. Slumping on the sun lounger I allowed the sun's rays to warm my battered body. He followed and sat on the chair next to me, silently watching me while I inhaled the fumes greedily and tried to ignore his presence.

I looked down at the beautiful city I was in. It looked exactly like it did on the postcards. The Opera House surrounded by the crystal blue waters. The magnificent beaches and coastline dotted around the city like a paradise and the ferries and yachts gliding across the water majestically. I wanted to be a part of its beauty and away from the ugliness of my situation.

Once I had the energy and wasn't looking so horrific then I would get the fuck away from him. I couldn't fucking wait to be released from this fucking cage. In that moment I felt almost triumphant as I saw a glimmer of my fighting spirit returning, and I knew that I was going to be okay after all. I would enjoy my time in Australia if it was the last thing I did.

CHAPTER SIXTEEN

I looked down admiringly at my tanned skin, its rich mocha colour contrasting against the white silk sheets that I lay across. Always look on the bright side of life I thought, laughing at the irony of the situation. At least something good had come out of what happened. All this lying about in Brad's penthouse had given me a killer tan and I had lost almost half a stone.

It had been almost two weeks since the incident. Two weeks of hiding. Two weeks of engulfing myself in clouds of intoxicating skunk fumes. Two weeks of waiting for my face to go down so I could show it in public. I'd watched as Brad had transformed back into the person I had once known in London. The apartment was full of extravagant bouquets of flowers, their heady aroma masking the scent of the marijuana I was smoking. It looked like a scene out of a romance film but we both knew it was more false than a set from a Broadway show. You only had to walk round to the side of the stage to see it had been painted on.

I took a deep drag of my perfectly conical shaped joint, holding in the smoke for as long as possible, before blowing it out into a billowy stream above my head.

Brad had made it quite clear that he was worried about me being seen in public but still he was tip-toeing round me, checking up to make sure I didn't leave.

"Darlin you look a bit better but you're still can't go out just yet.

You're going to have to stay at home for a bit longer. The press will go crazy if they see you like this, the mags will go wild. Just let me look after you babe." He looked at me anxiously.

"You needn't worry Brad. I wouldn't be seen dead looking like this in public anyway." I threw my head back proudly, dark glasses hiding my feelings of hatred. The last thing I wanted was for anyone to find out, to admit the shameful truth to my family; the mere thought of it made me feel sick. I just wanted to recover as soon as possible and pretend it had never happened. In the back of my mind though, my thoughts were clouded with doubts. What if it was my fault? What if I had driven him to it?

"Can I have another please?" I sucked up the last remnants of the daiquiri remaining in my martini glass loudly with a little black straw, and thrust the empty glass in his direction.

"Of course you can darlin."

Only too happy to oblige, Brad walked briskly to the kitchen and poured more of the mixture into my glass through a silver cocktail mixer. Operation get Ria so inebriated that she loses her memory was high on his priority list. Higher even than his mysterious 'business' dealings usually were. My priorities were also on a similar wavelength. My main focus was on losing my focus. It was all I could do to mask my feelings of hatred and shame.

"So, I've gotta go to town a bit later babe, but when I get back I've got a surprise for you." He studied my face as if awaiting a reaction of excitement from me. I managed to muster a half smile.

"Great, see you later then." I said, raising my magazine up over my eyes to shield the sun. He kissed me tenderly on the forehead and walked out. "Thank fuck for that," I muttered, leaning over to my Ipod and turning up the volume, losing myself in the ambience of the music, alcohol, weed, and the stunning view. To the outside eye I must have looked like a young girl having the time of my life, but the massive sunnies and tendrils of hair were hiding a different story. The joint served its purpose of blocking out the thoughts swimming around in my head and caused me to feel tired. I rolled onto my front, and slowly faded away into a deep sleep.

I woke up fuzzy headed, my face sodden in spit, stuck to my beach towel. The heat and various other contributors made me feel dizzy, and I heaved my sweaty body up onto all fours, my Chanel sunglasses bouncing underneath my sun lounger as I got up. I immersed myself into the pool quickly to cool off, and then stumbled towards the kitchen for some water. I was taken aback when I realised I wasn't the only one there.

Sue Ting, the cleaner was busy scrubbing the kitchen, elbows deep in yellow marigolds. Her mouth dropped open with surprise at the sight of me. My arms instinctively crossed over my chest to cover my exposed breasts as I saw the embarrassment etched across her face. I searched my head for my sunglasses to cover my black eyes and realised they had dropped to the floor. Shit!

"I'm sorry Miss," she stammered. "I didn't mean to disturb. Brad said you were sick." Her eyes grazed the floor before stealing another fleeting glance at my bruised face. "Are you okay Miss?" Her eyebrows knotted together as she took in my altered appearance.

"Yes I'm fine, just getting some water." I hurried past her and poured myself a glass of water, avoiding eye contact; I knew I was on the verge of tears. Just one small act of kindness would cause the flood gates to open and that was the last thing I wanted to happen.

I walked past her quickly and was almost safely away from her, when all of a sudden she raised her head and looked at me again, studying the marks on my face.

"He hurt you didn't he?" Her eyes were filled with compassion and I looked down at the floor avoiding her gaze, trying to conceal my bruises by letting my hair hang over my face.

"I know it's not my business but that man is no good. I am sorry to tell you this Miss, but this is not first time I have seen him hurt lady." She paused and bit her lip. "Please don't tell him I told you this, but I am scared for you. You seem like nice girl."

Her kind expression touched my heart, and I felt compelled to run into her arms and sob into her chest like a baby. I held back my emotions with as much restraint as I could muster, feeling as if I were desperately clinging on to the reins of a wild horse.

"No I had a fight when we went out. Some girls started on me. It had nothing to do with Brad. I am fine Sue, don't worry." I pursed my lips together, straining a reassuring smile across my face to convince her of my story.

"Ok Miss. I hope u feel better, it's not my place. Please don't tell him what I said, I don't want to lose my job here." She returned her focus to the floor and continued scrubbing but as I walked away I could see her shaking her head out of the corner of my eye and I felt nauseous with guilt at lying to her.

I gulped down the water and immediately re-lit what was left of my joint. Sue had seemed frightened for me and it made me feel on edge. "This is not first time I see him hurt lady….I am scared for you." Her words washed over me alarmingly, waking me from the self-induced coma I had been living in. I knew the situation was bad but I hadn't realised the extent. I suppose I just hadn't had the strength to face it. It was easier to just hide away and pretend like it had never happened. I knew I wanted to leave Brad, but a sudden sense of urgency filled me as I realised the real danger I was in. Usually Sue was so shy, the biggest exchange we had ever had before was her muttering, 'hello Miss,' whilst mopping the floor. I knew it had taken real courage for her to warn me the way she had, and I wondered how many other women he had hurt. I needed to get away from him. The sooner the better.

I jolted in shock as I felt a hand on my shoulder.

"Are you okay darlin? Didn't mean to scare you."

I saw a perverse twinkle in Brad's blue eyes and realised that he had enjoyed seeing my reaction. His muscular tanned body was bulging from the crevices of his perfectly fitted suit, the sun reflecting off his golden hair, his tanned skin contrasting against the whiteness of his shirt. He looked amazing and I felt my heart leap despite myself. How could someone so handsome be so twisted inside?

"Erm I'm fine babe," I said, acting calm. I didn't want to give him the satisfaction of knowing that his presence made me feel tense with fear. The weed wasn't doing me any favours. Stay calm I told myself; paranoid that he might be able to read my thoughts and realise that I wanted to leave.

"Did you have a nice day?" He sat next to me, his own paranoid personality and sense of ownership over my life rearing its ugly head, despite his best efforts of covering his intentions. "What did you do?"

"Er what do you think I did? I snapped, the words falling out before I'd had a chance to consider them. Brad bit down on his lip and I saw his face begin to change before my eyes, as if holding back his anger. "Sorry babe," I interjected, cautious not to enrage him further. "I've just been so bored all by myself. I missed you."

"I missed you darlin." He grabbed my wrist and pulled me on top of his lap, positioning my body over his as if I were a puppet. "I missed you so much. It's been so long since I felt close to you."

He lowered his full soft lips onto mine, filling me with a strange sensation of hate and arousal. My heart pounded as I felt him stiffen in between my legs, my bikini bottoms still damp from swimming causing a wet patch to develop on his suit trousers. He pushed me down onto him and groaned with pleasure as I allowed myself to relent towards his advances.

"Oh God, I missed you so much. It feels so good to feel you next to me again. Oh Ria." He kissed me passionately grabbing my buttocks and lowering my pelvis down so I was rubbing against him even harder. "Tell me you missed me again darlin. Tell me you missed me," he said in between gasps of air.

"I missed you," I murmured reluctantly, whispering the words in his ear in a submissive fashion. He groaned louder in response.

"Oh God I love you Ria. Tell me you love me darlin. Tell me you love me."

"I love you." The words flowed out easily. I guess I did still love him. I also hated his guts and wanted to him to shut the fuck up.

He stood up lifting me with him, my legs wrapped around his muscular torso. Lowering me onto the sun lounger, he pushed my knickers to one side and I felt the heat from his tongue against my skin, probing me delicately. The contempt and shame I felt towards him and what was happening only excited me more, and I quickly felt a crescendo of pleasure ripple over me as I orgasmed loudly into his mouth, releasing some of the tension which had built up inside me over the last couple of weeks. He wasted no time and thrust inside me fiercely, causing the sunbed to collapse and me to climax again to his absolute delight.

"Oh I fucking love you," he said as he came too.

We lay on the sun lounger, our hearts beating rapidly. He wrapped his arms around me tightly and kissed me over and over. I felt tears sting my eyes and a nausea rising inside me; I couldn't believe I had just had sex with him. Nothing was ever black and white. I still did love him but I knew it would be the last time we would ever make love. I wish things were different. I wish he was the man I had thought he was. I wish that he hadn't let me down so badly. It had all felt like a dream come true when I met him but now it had to end. I sighed deeply and for a brief moment I allowed myself to forget it all, and to just feel the raw love which enveloped me when he held me in his arms.

CHAPTER SEVENTEEN

"Wow, it's amazing."

Brad looked at me proudly as he held up my 'surprise' present. It was a Versace dress, theatrical, a bright peacock blue, stunningly beautiful. One good thing about Brad I suppose; he always got me amazing gifts.

I heard the pop of a cork and watched as he slowly filled two champagne flutes up to the brim. "I have planned an amazing night for us darlin. Now you just get yourself ready and I will be back in a few hours to pick you up. Can't wait to see you in the dress."

I listened to his footsteps as he strode out of the apartment and closed the front door behind him. Hesitantly I waited for a disturbance of the peace; the keys turning in the lock and Brad announcing that he had forgotten something, but there was nothing. I glanced at the time. It was four thirty. I had about three hours to get the fuck out of there.

Sitting in front of the dressing table, I applied my make-up expertly, hiding the yellowy-brown bruises still visible around my eyes with concealer and smoky eye shadow. It had been a while since that night; most of the swelling on my face had gone down and my tan masked the majority of the damage he had done to me, but still I felt the need to cover up any evidence before I faced the outside world. It was ridiculous really; I was about to run away from a man who had beaten the absolute crap out of me, and yet here I was applying my make-up. It wasn't just make-up to me though; it was my war paint, and necessary for me to mask the feelings I was carrying inside.

It was the first time I had bothered with cosmetics for weeks, and by the time I had finished I felt like I had already regained some of my strength. I recognised the girl reflected back at me once again. She didn't look defeated, battered, and scared any more. She looked strong and beautiful.

I threw on some denim shorts, my Chanel blazer, and put on some platform espadrilles. Finally I felt like me again.

Hurriedly I emptied my draws, throwing their contents into the Louis Vuitton luggage that had been a present from Brad before we had left England; before I had known what a bastard he is. I checked the time on my watch. It had barely been thirty minutes since Brad had left, but in my panic I had lost all concept of time.

I checked the top drawer of the dresser for my passport. My hand searched for it frantically and I realised it was no longer there. "Fuck!" He had hidden it! I can't believe I didn't check sooner; I should have known. I cursed under my breath as I looked through all the drawers in the bedroom to no avail. That's when it came to me; Brad's stash. His paranoia caused him to conceal his drugs in strange places, but he had a particularly sacred box in which he stashed his coke supply. It was made of black onyx, and held within it was a solid gold snorter. It had to be in there.

I threw back the cushions of the sofa and found the box hidden in a compartment underneath. Placing the box on my lap, I slowly opened its black glossy lid, breathing a sigh of relief as I saw the dark red cover of my passport. Underneath it lay a wad of a hundred dollar bills so dense; it was comparable to the thickness of an encyclopaedia. Feeling tempted to take it all I stopped myself, and instead eased eight of the notes out of the elasticated wedge. No need to make him more mad then necessary. Eight hundred dollars would help pay for my flight back home; it was the least he could do. I threw the cushions back on the sofa, and tried to make it look like I hadn't just ran out of Brads apartment like a refugee escaping a brutal regime. I had learnt from experience that Brad seemed to like my fear of him; I didn't want to give him the satisfaction.

As I opened the door to exit the suite I had been living in, I glanced back quickly. It was so stunning, I had never even dreamt of such luxury before I'd arrived. And yet to me now the place was a cold, heartless trove of bad memories that I couldn't wait to forget and put behind me. I closed the door softly, pulling my suitcase behind me. The adrenalin was pumping through my veins. I watched the monitor as the lift ascended from the ground to the twenty-ninth floor. I felt a moment of panic as I imagined Brad standing in it as the doors opened, and I made a silent prayer to myself that he wouldn't be there. "Please God and angels. Please help me get away from here. Please don't let Brad catch me."

The doors opened to reveal the lift was empty, and as it reached the ground floor I heard a delightful ping as I was released from the cage I had been in for so long. It was still a beautiful day outside and the brightness of it blinded me as I quickly made my way through the reception, avoiding eye contact with the concierge. I stepped outside and inhaled the fresh air deeply into my lungs. I was finally a part of the big wide world again, and after staring at it from so far up for the last two weeks, it was an enormous relief. I was free to live my life again.

"Hello Miss," the concierge had followed me. "Can I arrange a car for you?"

"No thanks," I said, striding away from him purposefully. "I am getting a cab." I raised my arm confidently, and within a moment a white taxi pulled up next to me. As the driver loaded my luggage into the trunk of the car I looked back at the 'castle' I had been living in, controlling the desire I had to stick my middle finger up at it. "Bye bye you bastard," I said, my confidence returning as I could see the finish line on the horizon. "Good riddance."

With that I lowered myself into the passenger seat as the driver closed the door shut for me, and when I heard the engine start up, I slumped back into my seat and exhaled deeply.

"To the airport please driver," I said, happily watching as the luxurious building which had been my home for the last couple of months became just a mere insignificant speck in the distance. I felt exhilarated as I heard one of my favourite house tunes coming onto the stereo. "Oh and can you turn this up please driver, I bloody love this song!"

*

The white cab pulled up outside Sydney airport and I stepped out of it. Feeling slightly lost, I made my way through the crowds of people bustling past, and wondered where I was planning on running to? I had not given it much consideration before this point; my main priority had been escaping Brad unscathed, but now here I was. No plane tickets, no plan, and no clue.

I slowly rolled in through the revolving glass doors avoiding the glances from men as I walked past. It was still only six o' clock and hopefully Brad had yet to discover my departure from his life. I imagined the look on his face when he returned back to his empty apartment. He would probably be wearing one of his fancy designer suits, clutching an enormous bouquet of flowers; another one to add to the meaningless collection.

"Ria!" I could almost hear him frantically calling my name before stumbling into the bedroom and seeing the Versace dress still hanging in the wardrobe and all of my belongings gone. Rage and disbelief would contort his face and he would smash the flowers onto the floor stamping on them wildly, their velvety petals scattering across the room. My hand shook with nerves as I searched in my bag for my phone, checking for a sign that my absence had been discovered by him. I needed something to calm me down and headed towards the bar.

"Ah," I exhaled a sigh of relief and took a deep swig of the ice cold schooner of beer placed in front of me. I needed to think, and I needed to do it quickly. On the one hand I could go back to England. I missed my family terribly and wanted to get away from the drama of the last couple of months, into the safety and love of my own home. I imagined seeing the faces of my family waiting for me at the arrivals gate and the relief of being enveloped back into the familiarity of my old life. On the other hand I had been so excited about coming to Australia and I felt like a failure going home having not even seen any of it. Everyone would ask me, "how was Australia?" and I would have to hang my head in shame, and tell them that I hadn't seen past the four walls of Brads penthouse and had practically lived like a prisoner for the last two months. It was supposed to have been a time of freedom, liberation, and adventure; not oppression, captivity, and abuse. There was nothing else for it.

I downed the remainder of my beer, slammed it back down and belched loudly, much to the horror of the Asian business man opposite, who had been openly eyeing me up and practically salivating whilst doing so. I narrowed my eyes at him, gave him a wry smile and strode towards the domestic departures, my heels clicking against the floors defiantly. Why should I run because of him? If he ever so much as threatened me or came near me again then I would go to the press so quickly it would make his head spin. I remembered the photos I had taken after he had beaten me. I had my very own insurance policy in the form of a disposable wind up camera, deep in the depths of my Louis Vuitton hand luggage. If Brad thought his reputation would be threatened, he would back off for sure.

I approached the Jetstar booking desk, and folded my arms on top of it confidently. The lady behind the desk smiled at me in response. "How can I help you today?" she asked in her strong Aussie twang.

"I just want to know what the next available flights are and where they are going?"

"Well we have a ten-fifteen pm flight available to Darwin, there are still some seats left." She drummed her red talons against the keyboard rhythmically, searching for all my available escape routes.

"Is that the first flight I can get on?" I asked impatiently, biting on my lower lip. "You see I'm in a bit of a rush. Running from an abusive ex-boyfriend and I don't exactly want him to catch up with me anytime soon if you know what I mean."

She looked taken aback by my frankness and raised her eyebrow, arching it questioningly at me, before returning to her hypnotic typing. "There is a flight at eight-thirty to Byron Bay. I can book you on it but you are going to have to be very quick if you are going to make it. You will have to go straight to the boarding gate now."

"That sounds perfect," I said, thrusting her my passport.

"That will be three hundred and nineteen dollars. How will you be paying?"

"Cash," I replied, pulling some green notes out of my wallet hurriedly.

She printed the tickets and handed them to me and I hurried towards security, weaving through the human traffic with the focus of an Olympic athlete. By the time I got to the boarding gate I was panting and sweating like a dog but I had made it. A few final passengers were embarking and I joined them, catching my breath and feeling triumphant.

As I sat down in my seat my phone started vibrating, alerting me to the fact that Brad had returned home. I took great pleasure in pressing cancel. I felt in control again and powerful. I typed him a text.

"I am going home Brad and I never want to see you again. If you try to come after me then I will be going to the papers. Goodbye."

I pressed send and watched as the little envelope on my screen disappeared, sending him the news. I hoped that it would be enough to throw him off my scent.

The plane began its bumpy ascent and as I looked down at the city of Sydney, I couldn't help but be reminded of the scene from Jurassic Park when they finally manage to escape from the terrifying island in one piece. I felt a mixture of exhaustion, elation, and disbelief at the events which I had been through. I had done it. My Australian adventure was finally about to start!

CHAPTER EIGHTEEN

There was a balmy humidity in the air that night; even my shins were masked in perspiration, my cocoa butter weeping from the pores of my skin. I scratched myself agitatedly as I found yet another bite adding to the collection on my ankle. It was about nine pm, and it was my second night in Byron Bay.

I had spent the day on the beach by myself, looking in wonder at the endless array of white hot sand that stretched out further than the eye could see. The beach had been deserted; I had been the only person on it enjoying the serenity and peacefulness of the view. It was so tranquil, I felt like I had gone from a nightmare and dived head first into a watery paradise. As I walked into the crystal clear ocean, my footsteps had imprinted on the otherwise flawless landscape; the only sign of human life that could be seen for miles around. I felt myself healing as I immersed my body into the warm water, the waves lapping against my salty skin. I was happy for the first time in so long, connected to nature, and filled with joy.

As the sun started to show signs of setting, I had reluctantly pulled myself away from the paradise and headed back towards the hostel. So there I was sitting outside on a bench, swilling beer from a tin can, and scanning the horizon for possible travel buddies. It was a far cry from the luxury I had been used to in the past months, but I'd had enough of luxury, for a while at least. I knew I would be more likely to meet people somewhere like this, and I felt safer surrounded by fellow travellers than in a hotel room alone, with nothing but Sky TV to take my mind off of recent events. I was craving friendship; I needed a friend so badly. I hadn't seen my family for so long and hadn't had a proper conversation with anyone other than Brad for weeks. I was yearning for a confidante.

A crowd of people were gathered around an open barbecue with boxes of cheap wine stacked by their feet, and I decided to bite the bullet and try to mingle.

"Hey," I said walking over. "G'day, what's on the barbie?"

They looked at me questioningly and I cringed as I sensed the lack of warmth in their response. Working as a dancer had made me approach people in a direct, confident way, and I suppose it may have been a bit much at times. The three girls returned to their cooking and a German bloke smiled in response.

"G'day," he said in an awful attempt of an Australian accent.

"Hi I'm Ria," I smiled back. "I just got here last night. What are your names?"

"I'm Florian and these girls are Corinna, Aycha, and Ruth."

"Hi," they all said in unison, a barrage of different accents intermingling to form a confusing sound; what a mix of people.

"Do you want some goon?" Florian asked.

"What's goon?" Maybe it was some kind of new drug I had never heard of?

"It's Australian for cheap nasty wine," he said, and pointed towards a carton next to the barbecue.

"Mmm, that sounds delicious," I said and laughed. He emptied some of the cheap wine into a plastic disposable cup for me.

"Thanks." I took the glass, grateful for his friendliness and felt myself relax. Within a few minutes I had broken down the girls' initial defences and we were all having a good chat. The goon was flowing like water; my plastic cup was being topped up constantly by Florian.

Four plastic glasses of goon and an inedible hot dog later, and that's when I noticed him. He looked like I had felt a short while before. Ambling nearby trying to light a rollie, he was kicking at the dusty ground with his trainers, and scanning around hopefully for companionship. He looked innocent and cute with his blond hair which was flicked up at the front into a little peak, and he was wearing long khaki shorts. I ambled over casually.

"Do you need a lighter?" Before he could answer I had a flame posed before him and he smiled and leant forward, lighting his pathetic looking roll up awkwardly.

"Cheers," he said, and I felt a twinge of comforting nostalgia wash over me as I heard his voice.

"Oh you're English too. Where are you from?"

"I'm from Ealing." His London accent soothed me and I warmed to him immediately.

"Oh really? I'm from Wimbledon."

"Yeah I know Wimbledon," he said. His blue eyes were twinkling, the fire of the barbecue casting warm shadows across his face.

"Come and join us," I said, ushering him over to my newly acquired group of friends.

We traded our stories over the warm glow of the barbie. Two lost souls seeking adventure; finding common ground in our quest for freedom. My respect for him grew as I learnt that he had come over to Australia completely alone.

"None of my mates were up for it so I thought fuck it. Booked eight weeks off work and came alone," he told me. "I am going on a road trip along the east coast and then up to Darwin, it's something I've always wanted to do."

"Wow, that's impressive. Aren't you finding it scary driving around Australia by yourself?"

"Well I was hoping to find some company to be honest, not much fun completely alone. That's my beast over there." He pointed towards a campervan proudly, which was sprayed in garish graffiti. It was coated in blue and green paint with the words, 'the mystery machine,' emblazoned across its side boldly.

"Blimey no one's gonna miss you in that thing!" I teased. "You may as well hang a big camera round your neck, wear a hat with corks hanging off it and walk around with a map in your hand. Bloody pom!"

"Well I preferred it to the plain white version," he said and laughed. "Do you want to have a look?"

"Yeah, why the hell not!"

We walked over to the van and he slid open the heavy door. "This is where I sleep, eat, cook and do just about everything else," he said, pointing to a mattress which had a little fridge and shelves built around it.

"Wow, it's really spacious."

He laughed and opened the driver's door, "and this is where I sit, drive, and put on my tunes."

I climbed into the driver's seat. "Yeah this is pretty cool, quite a cosy little home you have. Sorry what did you say your name was again?"

"Call me Andy."

"I'm Ria, nice to meet you. Anyway loving 'the beast' but it's missing something vitally important," I said in a mock serious tone.

"What's that?"

"A Rastafarian style skunk joint," I replied, pulling a long joint out from inside my bra. "Ta da!" It had been a bit of a risk smuggling my supply on the plane but it had been worth it and necessary in such a time of crisis.

"In that case I'd better put on some Bob Marley." Andy climbed into the passenger seat and fiddled with his Ipod in the darkness until 'Could you be loved,' came on. We sat together smoking the joint while Bob Marley played in the background, relaxing in each other's company.

"So how long have you been in Oz?" he asked. "You've got an Ozzie accent already."

"About two months."

"You came alone too?" Andy took a deep drag, spluttering slightly as he inhaled it and promptly passing it back to me, his face showing intense concentration as he struggled to maintain his composure and not explode into a coughing fit.

"Well I came here with my ex-boyfriend. He is Australian, we met in London. I left him a couple of days ago."

"Oh I'm sorry," he said as he caught my eye, and got a glimpse of the emotion I was struggling to hold back.

"Don't be, I'm better off alone. I can enjoy myself now." I brushed off his kind words and put on a brave face, but I knew I couldn't hang on to my cool for much longer. I instinctively raised my hand up to my face, as violent images of Brad beating me flashed across my mind. It was still sore, and I felt the familiar feeling of fear hit the pit of my stomach as it had done on that awful night.

"Well thanks for showing me your campervan Andy. I am going to go to bed now." I smiled at him. It was nice to be with someone who reminded me of home.

"Let me walk you back to your room."

Slowly we made our way to the hostel room. The night was black but a million hopeful stars shone across the sky, their effervescent beauty illuminating my mood.

"Goodnight Andy," I whispered as we approached my cabin. The lights were all off in my room; as always I was the last one up.

"Hey do you want to come with me tomorrow?" Andy asked softly. "I was gonna drive up to Nimbin for the day, it's a good place to stock up on weed, supposed to be a really cool, hippy-type town."

"That would be amazing," I replied, glad to have found a friend and a rather cute one at that.

"See you tomorrow," I said and eased open the door to the room, the sound of sweet dreams emanating from the sheets as I slowly stepped inside it. I watched as Andy walked back to his van and I glanced back up at the stars, wishing on the brightest one I could see.

"Starlight star bright, first star I see tonight. I wish I may, I wish I might, have the wish I wish tonight." I closed my eyes. "I wish I have an amazing time here now, and that I am safe and happy."

When I was satisfied the wish had been sent out to the heavens, I opened my eyes and quietly navigated myself through the dark room to my own bed, folded back the sheets and climbed in. Surrounded by all these girls I finally felt safe again. The last thoughts on my mind before I drifted off were of my wonderful family on the other side of the world who were probably just waking up and starting their day.

CHAPTER NINETEEN

The veins in Brad's head protruded with rage when he realised that she had gone.

"That fucking bitch," he screamed, slamming the bouquet of roses he'd bought for her on the floor and stamping on them in frustration.

The drawers that had contained her belongings were empty; everything had been cleared out. It was hard to believe that she had even existed, there was practically no evidence that she had ever lived there with him at all. It was all gone.

"Fuck, fuck, fuck!" Brad had never been one for dealing with his emotions. The only way he knew how to, was to shout profanities and assault whatever was unfortunate enough to be in his path. He didn't ever discriminate. Whether it was a table, mirror, man, or woman, he would bash it with the ferocity of a tiger until he had unleashed some of his pent-up frustration. Then afterwards he would survey the aftermath of his destruction; shameless, guiltless. He had no conscience. There was only one person Brad really cared for and that was himself. He was the one who was supposed to decide when it was over. How dare she?

The Versace dress was all that was left of her, hanging on the door of the wardrobe, provoking yet more feelings of anger inside him. Yanking it from the hanger, he violently ripped at its delicate fabric and tore it to shreds.

"After all I did for that bitch; this is the way she fucking treats me!"

Grabbing the dressing table mirror he threw it against the wall, and enjoyed the sound of its shards of glass splintering, wishing it was her face he was smashing.

"I buy her a dress worth thousands of dollars, treat her like a queen, and she just fucking runs off!" Panting loudly and trembling, he attempted to control himself by taking long jagged puffs of air. When it didn't work he kicked a hole in the wardrobe door, slamming it with his foot before crumbling to the floor, his head in his hands, pulling his hair out in frustration.

For a few moments there was calm, just the sound of his heavy breathing in the room, until a malevolent glint of hope flashed across Brad's blue eyes, and he raced towards the sofa and pulled off its cushions. "Please still be there," he begged, hanging on to the last thread of promise like a desperate man being swept away by sea, clutching to a life buoy. He raised the heavy lid of his stash box. All that was left inside it was a wad of cash and some coke. It was gone. The passport was missing. Ria must have found it; she could be anywhere by now.

"Fuck! I should have tied that bitch up while I had the chance," he muttered, storming off to the phone and pressing the zero button. He paced the floor and took deep breaths while it rung. Finally, someone picked up.

"Hi Brian, it's Brad. Did you see my girlfriend leave earlier?" His fingers drummed against the table impatiently, and he tried to conceal the panic in his voice through gritted teeth.

"Yes sir, she left a couple of hours ago with some luggage. We offered her a lift, but she hailed a cab."

When he heard the concierge's reply, Brad clenched his fists so tightly that his knuckles turned white, and he pounded the table, causing everything on it to jump.

"Are you okay sir?" the concierge asked, sounding concerned. Brad was a very generous resident of the building, always supplying him with huge tips, and easing his boredom with friendly banter. Not to mention the endless array of eye candy that visited him, brightening up Brian's otherwise very dull job. Brad was the man. He didn't want to get on his bad side, it would cost him about four hundred dollars a week; cash which he needed. That extra bit of money was what was fuelling his late night drug-binges, without it he'd be fucked. He could see why he would be upset if that Ria girl had bailed on him though. She was a real glamour, maybe even one of the hottest girls he had seen Brad with since he had been working there; God what he'd give to be in his shoes for a day.

"Yeah, I'm fine mate just a bit pissed that's all." Brad spoke in a friendly tone, and wiped away the bead of sweat rolling down his face with the back of his shaking hand. "We had a bit of a spat and she's done a runner. Bit worried about her, she doesn't really know anyone round here. Did she say where she was going at all mate?"

"I think I heard her ask the taxi to take her to the airport," Brian said, scanning his memory for anything which might help his benefactor.

"Oh." Brad couldn't hide the disappointment in his voice when he heard his reply. It was what he was hoping he wouldn't say. The idiot should have called him on his cell or something. He could kiss his fifty dollar tips goodbye after this.

"I'm sorry sir, if I'd have thought that you didn't know about it, I would have called you. I just figured you knew she was leaving. I hadn't seen her much in the building the last couple of weeks, so I thought maybe you guys weren't together anymore and she was getting her stuff." Now Brian was worried. He could see his tips disappearing before his eyes. "Let me know if there is anything I can do."

"Just buzz me if there is any sign of her at all. I don't care if it's day or night."

"I will do sir."

Brad slammed down his phone with a thud. "Fuck!" He wondered whether she had gone back to England and remembered her excitement at coming over with him.

"I can't wait to see Australia," she had said breathlessly the night before they had left, as he had held her in his arms. Maybe there was a chance she was still there? If she was he would find her and bring her back, and if she brushed him off then he would make her pay.

"No one treats me like this and gets away with it." He picked up his mobile and dialled her number, half expecting it to go to voicemail when it connected. He heard it ring before being cut off. She pressed cancel. That little bitch!

He raised the phone in his hand and was about to throw it across the floor, when it beeped as a message came through. Could it be Ria explaining where she was? Perhaps she had had a change of heart? Rejection was unfamiliar territory for Brad, and his pumped-up body filled with insecurity and fear as he glanced down and read the text, wide-mouthed.

"I am going home Brad and I never want to see you again. If you try to come after me then I will be going to the papers. Goodbye."

The words were a shocking blow; they hit him full throttle with the force of an arctic lorry. "Aaargh!" he screamed, and hurled one of the vases containing the flowers he'd bought her across the room. The cleaner was going to have a lot of tidying up to do.

Then an idea flashed through his mind like a lit match in a dark cave. He grabbed his phone again and waited for an answer while biting his lip. It was picked up on the third ring.

"G'day mate, it's Brad Harrison here. Listen, I've got a little job I want you to do for me. If you get it done, there will be twenty G in it for you."

"I'm listening," said the voice on the other end.

"It's nothing major. Just need you to find someone for me. She got on a flight earlier today. Do you think you can trace where she went?"

"No problem mate, it's as good as done." Detective Inspector Griffwell smiled on the other end of the line. He loved being given easy work like this; kept his wife in Jimmy Choos and him in her good books. "What's the name?" he asked casually.

"Ria Kimura." Brad felt himself relax slightly. The bitch should have thought twice before fucking with him.

CHAPTER TWENTY

I straddled Andy, leant over him and kissed him passionately. We had rowed out to a secluded beach off of Noosa and after fornicating on the canoe, we had managed to make it to the white sandy paradise, where we had rolled around listlessly for hours by the shore.

Soft waves lapped at our feet delightfully while we made love on the wet sand. I eased myself down onto him, causing him to groan in intense pleasure.

"Oh my God Ria," he said, playing with my breast with one hand, and driving me down deeper onto him with the other.

I rocked my body over his with more urgency, causing his groaning to increase, until he yanked me closer and wrapped his arms around me tightly as we both climaxed. We collapsed in exhaustion, our skin coated with a combination of salt, sweat, and sun cream. I lay across his chest, breathing in the smell of coconut oil and sex, as he stroked my hair softly.

"That was amazing." I grinned up at him; my sexual appetite had definitely been satisfied. In fact we had been having so much sex the last couple of weeks; I could safely go without it for the next decade and still be happy.

"You're amazing." Andy kissed my forehead tenderly and we lay there on the sand while our breathing regulated, the sun beating down on us intensely. His blue eyes twinkled even more now than when I had first met him. It must be all the sex and sunshine. Neither one of us had tan lines as we got naked at almost every opportunity. I had never felt such a sense of freedom before in all my life.

The last two weeks had consisted of travelling along the beautiful east coast of Australia in Andy's psychedelic, beaten up old campervan, from one exotic destination to another. The days were spent lying on unspoilt beaches and driving down deserted dusty roads whilst singing along to music. The nights were spent either partying in whatever town we ended up in, or camping underneath the stars, in the middle of an overwhelming black space, smoking weed and trying to eat from our pathetically lit barbecues before it became too pitch-black to see.

When Andy had asked me to come with him I had been wary at first, but being the impulsive girl I was, I had eventually agreed. It was the best decision I had ever made. All the problems I'd had with Brad felt like they had happened almost a decade ago.

"Fancy some more goon?" I asked, pulling myself up from his grasp.

"I wouldn't say no babe." Andy crawled over to get his cup which was poking out of the sand and I topped it up.

"Oh my God Andy," I laughed. "Look over there." I pointed in the direction of a couple of blokes in a kayak going past in the distance. "They must have been there the whole time we were at it!" We looked at each other in amusement, and Andy creased up. The two figures started waving at us, confirming my fears.

"Oh shit! How bloody embarrassing is that!" I put my head into my hands and looked out from between the cracks of my fingers at the boys, who were obviously finding the whole thing hilarious.

"I'm not bothered" he retorted. "It's you they were probably looking at."

"Oh thanks, I feel much better now!" I said, brushing his hand away as he attempted to uncover my face.

"Well considering the amount of times we have shagged on a beach so far, we're lucky we've only been spotted once!" Andy smirked.

"You know what Andy. You're right. Who cares." I lifted my disposable plastic glass against his. "Let's make a toast. To sex on the beach."

"Sex on the beach!" he repeated, and we both took a gulp of the cheap plonk in unison.

Meeting Andy had been just what the doctor ordered. Just when

I'd felt on the verge of swearing myself off men for the rest of my life, packing up my bags and heading for a convent, he had arrived. I knew he wasn't going to be the love of my life, but right now I was enjoying him and he was enjoying me. He had an innocent charm about him, the kind of sweet face that you could read like a book. He was as endearing as a little puppy dog and I felt like I could trust him completely. I suppose in a way I was. If it had been any other man I had met after what I had just been through, I would have avoided them like the plague; I certainly wouldn't have trekked halfway across Australia with them in a campervan.

As if reciprocating my thoughts Andy gazed at me and smiled. "I'm so glad you came with me Ria. God only knows what I would have done out here without you."

"Masturbated a hell of a lot probably," I retorted, "and got lost."

"Er, I'll have you know that you are the one who has got us lost with your awful directions and your constant weed smoking," he said, nudging me playfully. "How's a man supposed to navigate through the outback, as stoned as a Rastafarian?"

"Well it's not that hard; it's pretty much one straight road." I laughed and he narrowed his eyes at me. "But hey it's not all about the destination Andy, it's about the journey." I winked at him, and rummaged around in our bag, pulling out a pre-rolled joint and my camera. "Speaking of weed," I said, lighting it up. Turning the lens in his direction, I wound up the camera and took a photo of him as he attempted to cover his modesty, a surprised expression on his face.

"That one's going straight on a gay porn site," I teased. I passed the joint to Andy and we lay in silence together, taking in the breathtaking view and the intoxicating feeling of liberation, allowing it to wash over us like the waves on the shore. After a few minutes Andy rolled on his side to look at me; his brows furrowed together.

"Ria. You never really told me about what happened with your ex." The seriousness of his voice startled me slightly. "Why did you leave him?" He studied my face intently and I looked away to avoid his eyes.

"It's not a big deal. I just don't want to think about it, I'd rather have fun and forget all about him." I was making a habit of brushing off any of Andy's questions. Any reminders of Brad were unwelcome. I reached for the joint and took a deep drag of it.

"Yeah well Ria. Sometimes it's better to face up to things. You can't always just run away from your problems and get pissed and stoned to forget about them."

I pulled my hand away from his in response. "Blimey Andy!" I said, flustered by his remark. "I don't appreciate the psycho-analysis thanks. Some things are better left unsaid. I am trying to have fun and I don't want him to ruin it any more than he already has." My annoyance grew when I saw the sceptical look on Andy's face. "Don't you see that's what he wants?" I pleaded. "He wants for me to be sitting here crying over him. I've cried enough now, I just want to move on and enjoy myself."

"I'm sorry Ria, I don't want to judge. It's just that when we first met I noticed quite a few bruises on you." He paused briefly, the concern apparent. "Did he hurt you?" He reached out to hold my hand again and I snapped it away angrily, and felt myself crashing back down to earth from paradise with a thud.

"Yeah, he fucking hurt me," I cried. "He hurt me real good if you want to know. He beat the absolute shit out of me, after almost two months of practically imprisoning me. Now are you satisfied?" As soon as I heard the words fly out of my mouth, I could feel the tears stinging my eyes. Andy flung his arms around me and this time I didn't stop him. My tears made tracks down my sandy face and collected onto his chest as I wept.

"It's okay. You're safe now." He gently rocked me like a baby and I sobbed in his arms. After a few moments I pulled away and began to search for a tissue in the bag. He anticipated my movements and held one out for me.

"I felt so ashamed Andy," I said, in between breaths. "I didn't even set foot outside for weeks after. I didn't want anyone to see me. I haven't even spoken to my family since. Everyone will think I'm so stupid if they find out."

"I don't think you're stupid Ria." He pulled me away from him and looked me in the eye. "I think you are beautiful and funny and intelligent. It's not your fault. How could you have known he would do that to you?"

"My sister warned me, she didn't trust him from the start and I never listened to her. It's my fault. I just thought he was so nice," I said, desperate to justify the situation. "I thought he would look after me."

"Well it's all over now Ria. He won't ever hurt you again." Andy pulled me back into his arms, and I looked through them at our serene surroundings, feeling so relieved to have finally confided in someone; I felt lighter somehow. I sighed as he kissed me; with his arms wrapped around me I felt safe for the first time in so long. Thank God I met him when I did; not only was he a much needed friend, he was my saviour.

CHAPTER TWENTY-ONE

Detective Inspector Tony Griffwell had gone into the force for all the right reasons. In his younger years he had once held a naïve sense of optimism and compassion for people. He was the kind of boy who stuck up for the fat kid being bullied at school, despite the fact that it also led to him getting a bashing as well every so often. He had clung on to his morals against the advice of his concerned mother, who had often pleaded to Tony to look out for himself and, "let the others fend for themselves."

It had always been his ambition to become a copper. There had once been a deep need inside him to protect others, which had perhaps been cultivated by being brought up by a single mother, who had fled from his abusive father after years of torment. Tony, at the tender age of four, would run downstairs when he heard the chilling sounds of his mother's cries, and bravely stand in front of her; his skinny arms spread apart, acting as a fortress between his parents.

"No Daddy," he would scream. "Leave Mummy alone!" When his mother had finally left his dad, Tony had felt responsible for her. He would comfort her when she came home from work; sobbing and dejected by her inability to provide Tony with the life she so desperately wanted to. Tony grew up with an aching desire to make his mum proud, and after years of struggling to bring him up alone, she had cried tears of joy when she saw him in his police uniform for the first time.

However years of working in the force had changed Tony's priorities greatly, wearing away against his optimism in the good of people on a daily basis, until his ideals were like a threadbare rug. They were still there if you scratched underneath the surface enough, but his good intentions and integrity were usually only reserved for his wife these days. Trying to help people who were unwilling to help themselves was a demoralising affair. He felt like he was swimming against a rip in the sea, and after years of trying so hard he had relented, and allowed himself to be swept away by the undercurrents of the society he served.

It had started relatively innocently; backhanders here and there to turn a blind eye to dealings which he could scarcely control anyhow. Gradually he had become allies with many of the seedier characters of the underworld and regularly took pay-outs from them, for tid-bits of information and the suchlike.

As far as he knew, Brad Harrison was one of the better characters of the bunch. He knew he was involved in drugs, but he was also a respected businessman, with plenty of other perfectly legitimate businesses on the go. Brad was similar to Tony in many ways, hungry for the finer things in life that money could buy, eager to make a crust. With a wife as demanding as Tony's, any ways of earning a bit of extra cash were welcomed, and as her appetite for spending increased, his questions and judgement diminished.

Tony's position in the force meant that he had easy access to information and could trace a person relatively quickly. He was now sitting at his desk, fingers poised above the keypad of his computer, ready to begin his search for this Ria girl.

He opened the manila envelope that Brad had sent him, containing photos of the girl in question. She was dark, looked very young and was extremely pretty. Tony felt his conscience tapping him on his shoulder, but with the promise of twenty thousand dollars for the completion of this menial task, he brushed his feelings aside and continued.

Her flight details came up easily. "Byron Bay, Jetstar flight number JQ912." So she was still in Australia. Well that was a start.

Tony's fingers clicked on the keypad as he pulled up her card details to try to discover where she had gone. What remained a mystery was where she was staying. Her card hadn't been used at all since landing in Byron. Perhaps this would be harder than he'd previously thought?

Picking up his cell he dialled Brad's number.

"Hey Brad, it's Tony," he said. "I've got some good news for you mate. Managed to trace Ria as far as Byron, she got a flight there from Sydney."

Brad felt excited as he heard the news. She was still here, still in Australia. His worst fears that she had gone back to England had subsided for now. Since discovering she had left, his anger had relented, and Brad was actually starting to miss her slightly. Maybe there was a chance she would take him back? "Yeah mate, so do you know where she's staying?" he asked, impatient for the information.

"Well, she hasn't used her card since she arrived so it's hard to be sure," Tony replied. "All I can do is wait for her to use it to find her location, and ring some hostels in the area to find out if she has been at any of them."

"Hostels!" Brad spat sarcastically. "Look she's not the type to be staying in a hostel with some smelly backpackers, trust me. If she is staying anywhere, it will be in a hotel with room service and a pool. She's not exactly one to slum it." Brad felt the corners of his mouth curling up at the absurdity of such a notion. Ria in a hostel. Yeah right!

Tony scratched his head. "Okay, well I'm on her trail. Only a matter of time till I track her down. In the meantime I will keep you informed of anything I find."

Tony lowered his phone onto his desk and slumped back into his seat. God he needed a vacation. He stared at his bleak office, its four bland walls closing in on him and he sighed. He was beginning to feel as impatient as Brad was to find this Ria girl, he could almost taste the cash reward waiting for him.

CHAPTER TWENTY-TWO

It was pitch black that night, even the stars had gone into hiding. Andy and I lay sweating in the campervan, with only the rectangular light on the van's ceiling, battling to illuminate the darkness. The mass of the outside terrain felt like a frightening wilderness, and with only the sliding doors of the van sheltering us from the unknown abyss of the outback, I felt a humbling sense of vulnerability. Judging by the way Andy was clinging to me despite the extreme humidity hanging in the air; he did also.

We had pulled over on the side of the endless, red dusty road after hours of driving. Exhausted and sticky with sweat we had finally relented from our quest to make it to Townsville; the comfort of a bed and shower still many miles away. It seemed like ages since we had seen any sign of human life. No passing cars had driven past, honking in appreciation at our vulgarly decorated home. No deserted gas stations had been dotted along the route like markers of our journey. There had just been an overwhelming nothingness. Nothingness and an inescapable heat. Even with all the windows down as we drove there was no relief from it; the breeze had not felt dissimilar to a blow dryer being held in our faces.

Turning off the engine, we had climbed into the back defeated, stripped off our saturated attire, and laid down across the back of the van, on the sandy mattress. For the first time in a long time, sex was the last thing on our minds. We were lost, again.

Andy reached for a litre bottle of water, which was now about the same temperature as the water I usually bathed in and passed it to me. I knocked it back, the glugging noise as its contents poured into my mouth, the only sound to be heard. I offered it back to Andy, struggling with the weight of it in my weary state. He tipped the water into his mouth, screwed the lid on tightly to ensure there would be no spillage, and slowly crawled back next to me.

We lay there in silence for a while, holding hands, feeling comforted by one another's presence. I now had a new understanding of agoraphobia; it felt like we were lost in space, a mere fleck of existence in the solar system.

I studied Andy's face in the dimly lit van and he smiled back at me softly. "Thank you," I murmured, squeezing his hand gently as I said the words. Reflecting on our adventures together, I suddenly felt enormously grateful for the experiences we had shared.

"Why are you thanking me?" he asked, sounding slightly bewildered, as he wiped the sweat from his dripping brow.

"Thank you for asking me to come with you. I've never had so much fun before in my life. I've never felt so free."

"Thanks for coming with me. It wouldn't have been so amazing without you here. I just wish I didn't have to go home so soon, I wish I could stay here forever. Maybe I should blow my family in Mount Isa off, pretend I got lost in the outback or something? Then we could have another week together."

His words reminded me of the sad fact that our journey was coming to an end. "I wish you didn't have to go either Andy, but you can't do that! Who knows when you'll get the chance to see them again," I said, as he ran his fingers through my damp hair.

"Well we can meet up in England soon when you come back," he reassured me. Then he added solemnly, "I'm gonna miss you though."

"I'll miss you too. I don't think you will ever realise how much you have done for me. I felt so bad after what happened with my ex. Meeting you turned it all around, so thank you."

He appeared to be genuinely touched by my admission and squeezed my hand. Trailing his fingertips softly across the perspiration on the surface of my skin he asked; "so what are you going to do now?"

"I don't really know. I want to do some more travelling but I haven't got much money left now. A few of the girls I met in England told me about a club in Sydney which is apparently really good to work in. I'll probably work there for a couple of months, get some money together, do a bit more travelling and go home."

"Sounds like a plan. Just be careful in case that Brad bloke is looking out for you."

"I will. Anyway I doubt he's still around, he is always all over the place with work. He's probably with some other poor girl by now and forgotten all about me."

I wondered who his new victim was and felt sympathy for her; I had escaped lightly. If I hadn't been the strong character I was then I would probably still be there right now. Perhaps money wasn't everything after all? I felt so much happier baking in this hot tin can then I had ever felt in the lavishness of his harbour side apartment.

"Well tomorrow when we get to Townsville we can go to an internet café and book your flight." Andy began his night time ritual of regurgitating our travel plan for the next day. "Then we can go find a nice hotel and have a bloody wash!"

"Thank God for that because you are really starting to stink," I teased, waving my hand across my face mockingly.

"And I suppose you think you smell like a bed of roses do you miss?"

"Compared to you I do; I'm not nearly as pungent!" I laughed and started to sit up for some more water.

"That's man smell babe. Caveman smell. Those pheromones are what have made you so horny these last few weeks."

"Oh really? I thought it was all the cheap beer and goon you've been plying me with."

"You love it," he said, grabbing the back of my head and burying my face into his sweaty armpit.

"Urgh, let go!" I shrieked, Laughing whilst struggling free from his grasp, I squirmed away and sat up breathless. "Urgh Andy, that was disgusting." I reached for the baby wipes so I could wipe his armpit sweat from my face.

"Well if you found that gross, don't suppose there's much chance of a blow job?"

"No chance!" I said, throwing him a pretend evil look. We quietened again, listening to the stillness of the night, and reflecting on our shared experiences.

"Are you sure you don't want to go home?" I knew Andy was secretly hoping I would return with him but I wasn't ready to go back to England yet. I knew there were still more adventures to come.

"I'm sure. I'm not ready just yet."

He sighed in response and threaded his fingers through mine. It was funny how meeting someone on holiday deepened the bond that would sometimes take years to create. I felt like I had known him for so long, despite the fact that it had only been about five weeks or so since we had met.

We curled up on the mattress, savouring what would be one of our last nights together; connected by our sense of vulnerability and affection for each other. It had definitely been fate that brought us together. As the night drew to a close I slowly drifted off, Andy's rhythmic breathing a comforting sound within our silent surroundings.

CHAPTER TWENTY-THREE

Tony breathed out a deep sigh of relief when he finally located Ria. It had been almost six weeks since Brad had asked him to find her, and he had been growing increasingly agitated as the weeks progressed. Tony had not asked why he was looking for her, but it was a question which was probing him a lot recently, as the calls from Brad had become more urgent and frequent.

"Any news mate?" Brad would ask. The friendliness in his voice had been replaced with an irritated tone of desperation, and in recent days he had sounded increasingly angry. He was questioning Tony whenever the urge took him now, all hours of the day and night, and often sounded highly strung, like he had done one too many lines of coke.

The last contact made between them had left Tony with a chill of fear down his spine. He had been woken in the middle of the night, by his phone vibrating next to him. His wife had stirred and groaned in annoyance at her disrupted beauty sleep.

"Hello?" Tony had said, failing to disguise his own annoyance.

"Any news mate?" came the fraught voice on the other end of the phone. Tony shuffled downstairs out of earshot of his wife before answering.

"No Brad, sorry, not yet. She must be using cash or something, or maybe she is with a guy who is paying for her." As soon as he had heard himself say the words he'd regretted it. It was apparent that this girl was obviously an ex, and Brad seemed like the jealous type to put it mildly.

"What the fuck Tone," Brad shouted. "You're supposed to be a fucking detective and you can't even track down a stupid fucking stripper. Jesus this isn't the case of the century." He laughed at him; a merciless sound that dripped with contempt. "You're fucking pathetic mate."

Tony felt his hand shaking; a mixture of anger and shock at the way he was being spoken to, causing him to tremble. This had become more hassle than he needed.

"Look Brad," he reasoned, trying to control the volume of his response. "Short of going there myself, there are very limited means of finding the girl. The number she was using before is not in service. Her cards haven't been used since she was in Ballina airport. I've checked out all the hotels in the area and there is nothing. I'm doing everything I can. Just give me a couple of days, and if there is still no sign I recommend you hire a private detective to go there and check it out. I'd do it myself but it will be too suspect."

"Hire a private detective; are you fucking kidding me? What the hell are you then? You listen you listen to me Tone and you listen good; I pay someone to do a job, I expect them to get it done. Simple. You had better find her soon mate or you and I are gonna fall out." The phone went dead then before Tony had been given the chance to argue, and he had reluctantly swallowed back the words that had been about to spill out. Brad might have money, but Tony was a man with power as well; he certainly wasn't used to being dis-respected like that.

He had climbed back up the stairs in his pyjamas afterwards and struggled to sleep, the sound of his wife's snoring and his thoughts keeping him awake until the early hours.

Detective Griffwell was now at his desk checking over the girl's details again. His conversation with Brad had left him wondering whether he was doing the right thing. He certainly didn't want to get on the wrong side of the man but he was beginning to fear for the girl he was looking for, and hoping against hope that Brad had nothing sinister planned for her. His opinions of him had completely changed now that he had seen a different side to the usually charming, friendly man.

He was actually hoping that nothing would come up so he could just wash his hands of the whole thing, when a clue as to her whereabouts unexpectedly flashed onto his screen. Her card had been used in a hotel in Cairns. She had checked in yesterday afternoon.

For a moment or two Tony sat hesitating, in deliberation over what he should do. Eventually though, his stronger instincts of self-preservation and greed quickly won the battle over his now shaky moral values, and he picked up his phone.

"Brad, it's Tony," he said pausing. "I've found her."

CHAPTER TWENTY-FOUR

I was woken up by Andy, shaking me from my sleep. "Ria. Wake up!" he said, jostling me into consciousness.

"What's the time?" I asked, peering at him through blurry eyes as I tried to evaluate my surroundings.

"It's ten o'clock," he answered, looking panic stricken as he leant over me. "We bloody overslept!" I bolted upright at the alarming news.

"Shit!" I shouted, and watched as Andy almost tripped over his boxers as he attempted to put them on. I joined in with the dance; the two of us hopping around the hotel room as we struggled to assemble together our belongings and dress simultaneously. There goes our relaxing breakfast together. I had been hoping we would have the chance to share our last meal in the downstairs restaurant overlooking the beach, and leisurely make our way to Cairns airport together, whilst reminiscing about the amazing times we'd shared. I'd visualised a romantic goodbye scene at the airport, boarding the plane looking impossibly fresh faced and beautiful, and instilling a lasting impression on Andy's memory of my radiance for him to dwell upon in my absence.

Instead it looked like I would have to make do with spraying my armpits with deodorant to mask my smell, pulling on a mis-matching outfit over my stale body, and rubbing the make up off from the night before with a baby wipe on the way, which was now smeared across my face causing me to look like an extra from 'Dawn Of The Dead.'

Well we certainly had enjoyed our last night together at least. It had been such a treat after weeks of sleeping in the campervan, to have spent the last couple of nights in a luxury hotel. It had been my treat to Andy to say thank you for such a wonderful time. It meant that I scarcely had a couple of hundred dollars to my name when I returned to Sydney, but it had been worth it. Memories lasted far longer than cash, particularly when the cash belonged to me; so spending it on making good memories was a wise investment as far as I was concerned.

We had spent our last night together in a beautiful restaurant, sampling the delights of the sea. Oysters Kilpatrick, Lobster Mornay and champagne - a winning concoction for a delightful meal. The night had ended with a skinny dipping session on the beach. We had peeled off our clothes and ran into the ocean, the moonlight reflecting off our bodies as we splashed and frolicked. When we had returned to our hotel, the novelty of having sex in an air conditioned room, on a bed with crisp white cotton sheets provided us with even more stamina than usual. The prospect of it being our last night together had been an even stronger aphrodisiac than the dozen oysters we had consumed.

"Quick, quick!" Andy ushered me into the van, hurriedly slamming the door behind me with such force that it caused the whole vehicle to shudder. Jumping into the driver's seat, he turned the key in the ignition, the trusty engine roaring to life as he slammed his foot on the accelerator and we sped off in the direction of the airport.

I took the opportunity to attempt to make myself presentable. I tried running a brush through my hair, which was now resembling a horse's mane after last night's shenanigans. Salt water, sand and sex definitely weren't a good combination for your tresses.

The van was rocking violently as I tried to apply some make-up; Andy was alternating between accelerating as fast as he could, to braking suddenly.

"Er I know we're in a rush, but I'd rather not die on the way to the airport thanks," I said.

He ignored me and jolted the van again, narrowly missing a car stopped in front of us at some traffic lights. I almost careered into the windscreen as a result of his reckless driving and now had eyeliner all over my face.

"Oh fucking hell, now look at the bloody state of me. Watch it will you."

"Sorry," he replied defensively. "I just don't want you to miss your flight, it's non-refundable."

I felt more anxious as he reminded me of the terms and conditions we had read briefly when booking the flight from the hotel the night before. "Well maybe if you had actually rung reception and arranged a wakeup call like I asked you to, then we wouldn't be in such a rush!" I snapped at him, irritated by the way our last morning together was eventuating. I began to clear up the mess on my face, every jerk of the van adding to my annoyance and not helping with my hangover.

"God I will be relieved to get out of this bloody stinky van," I said, trying desperately to hang on to the remains of last night's dinner and avoid bringing it up over the dashboard. As much as I had enjoyed it last night, I was sure it wouldn't taste quite so nice the second time around.

Andy looked at me with a wounded expression on his face. "Oh well it's nice to know what you really think of my van."

"Oh sorry, I didn't mean it like that. I just feel really sick."

"Here sip some of this," he said, passing me a bottle of coke.

"Thanks," I said, whilst hanging on to the side of the door, trying to keep myself from flying into him as we rapidly turned a corner.

We approached the airport and there was a cue of traffic lining up outside the departures terminal. "You're gonna have to jump out here and check in," Andy said, and pulled over by the taxi drop off point. "I'll park up and find you."

I hopped down and pulled my luggage off; the weight of it causing me to almost trip over as it fell onto the floor. Andy drove off, revving the engine of the van loudly, gusts of white smoke billowing after him. Finding the check in desk, I put my luggage onto the conveyor belt and collected my ticket. Slowly I made my way to the gate, my eyes searching for Andy as I went. Where the hell was he?

"Final call for Virgin Flight DJ812 to Sydney" the voice on the loudspeaker announced. Standing by the security gate I made one last frantic glance around my surroundings for him; I couldn't leave without saying goodbye. There was a cue of people waiting to go through and reluctantly I trailed behind them.

"Ria!" I heard a voice shout and I turned to see a breathless Andy. Red in the face and covered in sweat, he ran towards me and we locked in an embrace. We squeezed each other tightly, gradually managing to pull ourselves apart from each other's grasp and looked at each other, happy to have got the chance to share this last moment.

"You made it," I said and smiled.

"Did you really think I'd let you go without saying goodbye?" he said, taking me in his arms again. I breathed him in, savouring our last moment together; the warmth of his body enveloping me, the secure, content way he made me feel. When I opened my eyes again, from over the top of his scruffy khaki T-shirt I saw the departure board flashing and heard another flight announcement; I was going to miss it if I didn't move myself. Andy glanced up and grudgingly loosened his grip of me.

"Take care of yourself Ria."

"I will, don't worry I'll be fine. You take care of yourself, enjoy the rest of it with your family. And promise you won't forget me, I'm really gonna miss you."

"Forget you! I'll never forget you. How could I?" He gave me another quick hug and a kiss. "I'll miss you so much. The Mystery Machine won't be the same without you."

As I walked towards the gate I looked over at Andy as he stood on the spot, his hands in his pockets, a solemn expression. He gave me a strained smile when he saw me and we gave each other a final wave.

I ran as fast as I could once I got through the gate and was a breathless mess, but made it just in time. The flight attendant was taking down the flight number from the board and getting ready to embark on the plane himself. He raised one eyebrow at me as I thrust my boarding pass into his hand and I did my best to avoid eye contact with all the seated passengers who watched me with annoyance as I made my way to my seat.

As I squeezed past the strangers that were seated next to me I could feel some tears beginning to form in my eyes and I struggled to hold them in. I would miss Andy so much, I suddenly felt completely alone without him.

CHAPTER TWENTY-FIVE

"Oi watch it mate!" Brad shouted, as a scruffy looking blond boy ran into him. The collision caused the boy to fall backwards onto the ground and almost knocked Brad flying. He steadied himself, regaining his balance before looking down at the sorry specimen with a contemptuous glare.

Scrambling to his feet the boy picked himself up muttering, "sorry," under his breath before continuing to run.

"Scrawny little fucking scumbag," Brad cursed, dusting any trace of the boy off of his shirt as if he had just come into contact with an infectious disease. He had only just managed to control his feelings of rage, before the little shit had come along and fanned the flames of fury inside him again.

Brad strode through the airport purposefully with a look of conviction in his eyes. He was a man on a mission. The weeks of waiting for the information he needed had been tortuous, and had rubbed salt into his already raw wounds. His ego had been severely hurt; Brad wasn't the type of man to take kindly to being screwed around, particularly by a woman. He was the screwer; he was the one who kicked them out once he'd had enough of them, not the other way round.

What made it even worse was that he actually had feelings for the girl. He had hoped that she would have eventually been moulded into the kind of woman he wanted for a wife; the kind that would be there to pick up his dirty washing, to cook his meals and suck his cock after a long day at work. He had been doing a good job of transforming her too, not that there was that much to change, only that she was just a bit too damn sure of herself; needed to be taken down a peg or two. He knew that he had gone a bit too far that night, but she had deserved it. She had needed to be taught a lesson. A real lady should be at home waiting for her man to return, not going out all night, playing mind games and flaunting herself, trying to get one over on him. She had been taking the piss and he had dealt with it accordingly; end of.

It had been hard seeing her bruised swollen face afterwards though. Brad certainly hadn't intended on doing that to her but it had been an accident, he hadn't meant to. What with her threatening to leave him, he had just snapped. She would learn eventually what was expected of her though. Brad wasn't prepared to let her go that easily. She was a keeper and he certainly hadn't met anyone since who had even compared. Fucking a bunch of molls with inflatable tits was getting boring. He just wanted someone who would love him for who he really was, not just for his money and power. The other women he could have whenever he felt the urge, they were a dime a dozen, but Ria was different. She had made him feel like a God at times. The way she had stared up at him while they had sex, so adoringly through her dark lashed eyes; it almost made him hard just thinking about it.

He made his way through the exit of the airport and jumped into the first available cab. "The Ocean Plaza Hotel please mate," he commanded, slamming the door behind him. Ria was going to be in for a shock now, he thought to himself smugly. The plan he had concocted was flawless. He would find out what room she was in and knock on the door taking her by surprise. Then he would use all the charm he could muster to win her back with the little help of a diamond and sapphire ring, worth almost five hundred thousand dollars, which was now securely nestled in his breast jacket pocket. It was the most amount of money he had ever spent on a piece of jewellery before for a woman; how could she possibly resist?

One thing which was concerning Brad deeply however was a comment that Griffwell had made the other night on the phone. "She must be using cash or something, or maybe she is with a guy who is paying for her." His words had echoed inside him since, wreaking havoc with his mind and making his gut wrench with anger whenever he replayed them. Who the fuck did Tone think he was anyway? Well that pathetic son of a bitch would regret ever crossing him. Six weeks it had taken him to track her down. Six weeks! If Brad found out she had been with another guy this whole time, he would be holding him personally responsible for being the most pathetic excuse for a bent copper that he had ever met.

Anyway, Brad thought as he looked out of the window impatiently; Ria wouldn't do that. Whether she realised it or not she was still bloody crazy about him, how could she not be? She certainly wouldn't have got involved with someone else so soon. She was probably still upset about it all. Probably hoping for him to turn up and sweep her off her feet again.

The corners of Brad's mouth curled up as he imagined all the make-up sex they would soon be having. There was something about sex after a big fall out that felt so much more intense. All emotions and sensations were heightened. It felt all the more sweet fucking a girl after feeling that you had lost her. He remembered the day she had finally relented, the day she had run away. God it had felt good to be inside her again and she had enjoyed it too, he knew she had.

Yes pretty soon she would be back in his apartment, strutting round it in her expensive lingerie, joint in mouth and music on, waiting for him to come home longingly whilst draped across his sun loungers. But if he did find out that she hadn't been alone these past few weeks. Well then there would be hell to pay. Brad shuddered to think how he would react. He didn't want to hurt her again, but if she had done that to him he couldn't be to blame now could he?

The cab pulled up outside an elegant looking hotel, right on the seafront. Brad was familiar with the hotel having stayed there several times before on business. He was greeted by a tanned blonde on the reception desk, who was wearing a smile on her face so wide, he wondered whether there might be time for him to have a quickie before tracking down Ria.

"Hi I rang earlier, booked a room under the name of Harrison."

"Sure sir, you booked the clubhouse suite?" She glanced up coyly from the screen in front of her.

"Yeah that's right darlin."

"Sure sir, I just need some ID and a credit card please."

He handed it to her, taking delight in watching her bashfully shuffle around behind the desk. He enjoyed the effect he had on women sometimes. It made him feel powerful and in control.

"Here you go sir," she said, handing him back his driving licence and credit card. "You will be in room number two one two, I will get a porter to show you to your room. Is there anything else sir?" she asked, noticing him loitering slightly and hoping that he might ask for her number as well.

"Yes actually, I came here to meet a friend of mine, I was hoping to surprise her. Can you tell me what room Ria Kimura is in?"

"I will just check for you sir," the receptionist replied. Her wide smile faded slightly and she began to search the records for the handsome man standing before her. "Oh, her and her boyfriend checked out earlier this morning."

"What? She was here with someone else?" Brad desperately tried to disguise the temper which was rising through his body, threatening to erupt out of him like a volcano.

"Yeah they rushed out of here a couple of hours ago. Is something wrong sir?"

"No not at all, just a bit disappointed she's left already, an old friend of mine that's all. Where were they going?"

"They were travelling down the coast together in some psychedelic campervan with mystery machine written on the side of it. The valet was a bit surprised to be parking it the other day," she laughed. "Makes a change from the Porsches that's for sure. They seemed a really nice couple though, think they were on their way to Mount Isa, he was asking how long it would take to drive there the other morning. Anything else I can do for you sir?" she asked, ignoring the queue which was beginning to form behind him.

"Yes actually there is. Do you know any hire car companies?" Brad smiled at the girl warmly.

"Sure no problem, I will get the concierge to arrange something for you."

Brad paced across the lobby, clenching his fists as he went. His worst case scenario had been realised. He hadn't thought it was possible but there was no turning back now. Not only had Ria humiliated him, but now he finds out she's been screwing some other man, in a campervan of all places! He felt like such a fool; the diamond ring burning a hole in his pocket and reminding him of his rejection. That bitch will pay he promised himself. I will hunt her down and once I'm through with her no man will ever want to go near her again.

CHAPTER TWENTY-SIX

Andy was lying in the back of his campervan. He just had to get through this one night alone and tomorrow he would be with his relatives in Mount Isa for a couple of days of fun, before heading to Darwin for his last few days in Oz. Then it was back to old Blighty and back to reality.

The time had flown since he'd first arrived in Oz. Eight weeks of freedom and adventure had gone past far too quickly. Pretty soon it would be back to the rat race; the same old nine-to-five and the suffocating existence that he had escaped from.

Going travelling had given him a new perspective on the world. He had seen things in a new light. At the tender age of twenty six, in the eyes of most Andy had accomplished a lot. He had got a first class honours degree and had worked his way up the business in which he had landed his first job. He couldn't complain he supposed. There were others who had completed his degree who were still working thankless jobs. At least he had managed to achieve his career targets. He was exactly where he was supposed to be. Exactly at the point of his plan that he had visualised he would be at by now.

He was a trainee finance broker for a big firm in London, had his own office, and even a company credit card that he could use at his own disposal. Although he worked long hours, most of his afternoons were occupied with 'business' lunches, in some of London's trendiest hangouts. His colleagues were a nice bunch. His weekends were filled with friends and clubs and gigs, and yet the thought of returning to his old life was filling him with a sense of depression. Weeks of living the simple life of a traveller's existence had spoilt him. The days of driving on a long open road, marvelling at each destination he arrived in, and frolicking with a beautiful girl had made him feel really complete for the first time in his life.

He had spent years chasing a larger pay check, to surround himself with possessions and society's imposing vision of what qualified as a 'good' life, and now it seemed so very shallow. What was the point of it all? What was the point of life?

He stared up at the starry night sky, in awe of its simplistic beauty and he felt the sudden impulse to just pack it all in. Maybe he should just go and meet Ria in Sydney? Maybe he should just surrender to his overwhelming desire to be with her, forget his plans and enjoy the beauty of living a life with no plans, no ambitions? Maybe he should just leave it up to fate to blow him on the right course and drift like an autumn leaf, enjoying the moments of the present; drinking in what the world had to offer instead of doing what was expected of him all the time?

He thought of Ria and smiled. He hoped that he would see her again, that they would reunite one day soon, and she wouldn't end up being snapped up by another business mogul with a nasty temper. He worried about her deeply. She had such a trusting nature and there were plenty of people in the world who preyed on girls like her. Even he had sensed her vulnerability from the moment they'd met, despite her dazzling display of confidence and her extroverted personality.

Andy hadn't mentioned anything at first for fear of upsetting her, but the marks on her body had saddened him when he had seen them. They were barely visible, just a trace of the torment she had been through on her otherwise flawless skin, but it maddened him to think that someone could do that to her. God knows what they had actually looked like at first, for he had only seen the faded bruises, weeks after it had happened. He felt the need to protect her and wished she had come with him to Darwin and gone back to the UK, where she would be safe. She was too stubborn though, too hell bent on having fun. He just hoped it wouldn't lead to her downfall. The thought of her running into that Brad guy again scared him and made him sick to the pit of his stomach.

It was a cool night compared to many he had shared with Ria in the Mystery Machine. He took another swig of his beer in the hope it would help him drift off to sleep, and sat back on the edge of the van with his legs swinging over its side. It was so still, so quiet, not even the sound of wildlife in the background to appease him. Not having Ria there with him was strange; it would be the first night for over six weeks since he had slept alone. It might not have been so bad if he had been surrounded by other people in a hostel, but here there wasn't a soul in sight and he felt completely bare, just parked up on the side of the road.

He fiddled around with his Swiss army knife, flicked out its sharp blade and watched as the moonlight glinted off its sheath of steel. He swished it through the air; practice in case any nutters came along. If they did they would be sorry; he was prepared. The small knife was strangely comforting and managed to subdue his fears. Why was he so worried anyway? There was more chance of something happening to him on a night out, than in his van in the middle of nowhere. Clutching his weapon tightly, he flicked what was left of his roll-up outside and slid the van door shut; the sound of it closing echoing into the night. Curling up onto his side, knife still in hand, he gradually closed his eyes. Just one night to get through. Just one night.

BANG!

Andy was jolted out of his sleep by a thump in the darkness, against the side of his van. Feeling for the cold steel of his knife, he felt his pulse exploding in his ears, his senses heightened by the sinister sound of the crash against the door. Maybe it was just an animal that had run into the van?

Stay calm. Stay calm. It's probably nothing. His ears pricked up and he waited breathlessly for any more disturbing noises, trembling in anticipation. Perhaps he had just imagined it? Perhaps it had just been a bad dream?

BANG!

There it was again; a crash reverberating off the steel door, causing the whole van to sway. This time he didn't wait to assess what the perpetrator of the noise was. He scrambled up onto all fours and clambered in the direction of the driver's seat. The walls of the van began to spin around him and he struggled to see his surroundings, blinded by what could only have been some headlights shining towards him on the opposite side of the road. Whatever it was out there he couldn't see it, but they could see him; the knowledge made Andy feel even more vulnerable. His shaking hand reached desperately for the key which he had left in the ignition. Where was it? It had gone. Where the fuck was it? Bending down, his fingertips searched the floor beneath him manically, feeling under the foot pedals and grooves in his seat. Where was it?

Suddenly he felt a pair of eyes on him, studying him intently through the black of the night and his body froze instantly. Clutching on to his knife even tighter, the panic flowed through his veins like a bolt of lightning and he felt a bead of cold sweat rolling down his forehead. He lifted his head slowly in the direction of his spectator, not wanting to face his fears. This couldn't be happening? It must be a bad dream, surely? This can't be real.

But it was real. A face only inches away from his, the only thing separating them a thin sheet of glass. Andy's mouth gaped open in horror as their eyes met. He could only make out the outline of the shape of the face, but the eyes. The eyes he could see clearly. The eyes were menacing, piercing through him like daggers, glinting at him threateningly. They were devoid of compassion or humanity; cold, penetrating and cruel.

Perhaps it was another traveller who was lost? Maybe it was a policeman coming to tell him to move off the road? Andy desperately came up with explanations as to why this sinister creature would appear outside, without the intent of doing him harm.

Before Andy could convince himself that the whole thing was a big misunderstanding, the person standing before him dispelled all his hopes with one simple act. He pressed his forehead against the window and uttered one word, one word which chilled him to his very core, and caused his heart to spasm in his chest.

"Boo."

CHAPTER TWENTY-SEVEN

Diane Mackenzie sat opposite the girl and assessed her with a critical eye. She was well turned out in a wrap-over dress which revealed her pert cleavage. She was sexy but not slutty, fresh-faced and stylish. She also had a lovely English accent, a friendly manner and an exotic look which would stand out. So far she was ticking all the boxes.

Diane didn't audition her girls, but asked them to come in for an interview. From her experience it was personality as much as looks which attracted her discerning clientele and kept them spending. She liked her girls to have a touch of class, to be educated and charming, which was probably why Flirt was renowned as being the number one gentlemen's club in Sydney. There were plenty of trashy clubs in the city, the Cross was lined from one end to the other with them, but Diane's customers didn't just come to have a big pair of tits thrust in their faces. They wanted conversation, flirtation, and seduction.

"So have you worked in any clubs prior to this?"

"Yes, I worked at Centrefolds in London while I was studying at university, and I met a few girls who used to work here. They all told me it was the best club to work in, in Australia," the girl replied smiling.

"Oh really?" Diane felt flattered. She had worked hard to make her business a success and news that its reviews were crossing over to the other side of the Atlantic made her feel excited.

"Yes, Naomi was one of them, a really tall girl with dark hair?"

"Oh Naomi," Diane exclaimed. "Oh you worked with her? She was one of our best girls. Anyone else?"

"Yes an English girl called Bianca who worked here a couple of years ago. She is really funny, blonde, quite petite. Her stage name was Cassie."

"Oh yes I remember her, she was lovely. She had to go home because her visa ran out but she was a great girl. How is she?"

"Yes she was really well the last time I saw her, we did a few shifts together and went out a few times. I told her I was coming to Australia and she insisted on me trying it here. She told me about you actually and how nice you are."

The girl was certainly good at charming; she had heard enough. Another gorgeous girl to add to her bevvy of beauties; the customers always loved a newbie.

"Well Ria, I really think you will do well here. The customers will adore you with your Asian look and your accent. You'll make an absolute fortune!"

"I hope so," the girl replied.

"Welcome to Flirt!" Diane smiled. "We treat our girls really well here. There are no house fees, and you get to keep all your cash tips to yourself, and we pay you at the end of your shift, so there's no waiting round for days to get the money you earn. We only take thirty percent as well."

"Well it all sounds great," the girl said warmly.

"Fabulous," Diane said rising to her feet. "Well, Natalia is the manager, so I will get her to have a sit down with you now and explain everything. Good luck with your first shift and let me know if you need anything."

"Thanks a lot; I will see you soon then." The girl stood and shook her hand confidently.

Diane walked back upstairs to her office, to check on a few details before going home. It was funny how life worked out sometimes. Never in a million years would she ever have anticipated that she would end up becoming the owner of a strip club, but she had always been a vivacious and adventurous character, and when the opportunity had arisen to buy Flirt she had snapped it up, instantly recognising it for the gold mine that it was. She had natural business acumen, charm, and was an excellent hostess; the business was perfectly suited to her.

Diane was a beautiful woman who exuded glamour and style with a timeless grace and elegance that never seemed to fade. In her heyday, her looks could have rivalled the best of the girls who now worked for her, and with her blond locks and curvaceous figure, she still had the ability to make the heads spin of those she passed.

She treated her dancers like people not commodities, which helped to create a more positive atmosphere in her club. She cared for them all and often became like a mother figure to many of the girls. She loved hearing about their adventures and experiences, it made her feel young again. Her own social life revolved around the club too, and her friends and comrades often gathered there sharing some champagne and conversation over one of the candlelit tables.

Recently however, she had tried to distance herself a bit. The partying was taking its toll on her and she often became too involved with her girls', feeling responsible for them and despairing whenever they got themselves into scrapes, which seemed to happen on a daily basis. Still, however much she tried to get away, Flirt was her home and her girls were her family, there was just no escaping it.

She walked out of the club and was hit by the daylight in the bustling street outside and quickly pulled on her shades. People rushed past her in their tailored clothes on their way home, finished with work for the day. Diane was going home to get ready for her work, it seemed ironic, but she had always been a creature of the night. Daytime was a time for reality, a time when people kept themselves hidden and conformed. Masked by the cloak of night, people became their true selves, their hidden agendas and fantasies were unleashed and the responsibilities of their lives were forgotten for a short while. She understood this and so she provided the perfect establishment for facilitating it. Flirt was a haven for escapism, a light which called out to the lost souls of the city who fluttered towards it like moths in the night, and Diane was proud to be its owner.

CHAPTER TWENTY-EIGHT

Panting with exhaustion, Brad struggled with the weight of his load as he dragged it across the dusty terrain. His shoulder seared with pain and his arms ached, but he knew he only had a few hours to dispose of it; so he continued further into the outback, fear and adrenalin taking over to complete the task for him.

Finally, when he was satisfied he had ventured deep enough into the wilderness, he threw the body down beside a dried-up creek, and begun the grim business of making it disappear as effectively as possible. It wasn't long now until sunrise and the risk of being spotted meant the task was a rush job. Brad almost felt afraid, an emotion which was alien to him and he quickly covered the body with some loose soil; just enough so it would go un-noticed.

He reached into his pocket for his phone and felt a square velvety object in his hand; confused as to what it was, he pulled it out to identify it. The ring. The mere sight of it was like a red hot poker, stabbing him, mocking him, taunting him. He opened the box, pulled it out and hurled it with ferocity into the bush. "Fucking bitch!" he screamed. It was all her fault. He hadn't meant to do it. It hadn't been planned.

Brad had searched for the van for hours in the black night down the long stretch of the Flinders Highway. He had been about to give up when he had seen it there on the side of the road. It wasn't exactly inconspicuous.

He parked opposite and watched for a while. Listened for any signs that its inhabitants were awake but it had been deadly peaceful; the silence before the storm. They must have both been asleep; the perfect time to strike.

He circled his prey, walking around the beaten-up old campervan, silently assessing it before acting. What an insult, it made his blood boil to see it; Ria had gone from being with him to living in this shitty van! Unbelievable. Well she would regret it now; no one took Brad Harrison for a mug and got away with it.

He peered in through the windscreen to try to catch sight of her and was distracted by a key in the ignition, its metal surface glinting in the darkness. Slowly, he squeezed his arm in through the gap and removed it. He wasn't going to give her the chance to do a runner this time.

Brad circled the van a few more times and attempted to decipher a plan of action, but as usual his anger got the better of him and hungry for revenge he kicked the side of the van, slamming it with all his force like a thug on the way home from a bender. He felt a rush of adrenalin as he heard some startled movements from within.

The rush caused him to breathe heavily, and his heart to race with intensity. I am going to enjoy this, he thought. That bitch is going to pay now. He backed up and ran towards it, his foot flying into the side of the van again, causing the whole thing to shake.

A terrified looking young blond boy climbed into the front. Brad listened for Ria's startled screams but there was nothing. He watched with amusement as he saw the boy looking for the key, trying to escape. Slowly Brad approached, until he was just a few inches away.

"Boo."

The boy jumped with terror and he laughed in response. So this was what he was up against, this measly little kid? This was going to be a whole lot easier than he'd previously thought.

He opened the van door and pulled him out of the driver's seat by the scruff of his neck, and the boy rolled across the dusty ground before scrambling to his feet.

"Where the fuck is she?" Brad shouted.

"Who?" he replied, his wide eyes shining with terror.

"You know who; Ria. Where is she?" Brad shoved him, slamming him against the side of the van.

"I don't know who Ria is," said the boy.

He refused to tell him anything, denied all knowledge of ever knowing her, yet his solidarity told him that he was lying to protect her. "We'll soon find out if you're being honest mate," Brad said, and slid open the door of the van. Reaching in he pulled out a rucksack and noticed the stale, pungent smell of skunk, which was hanging around in the back. She had been there.

"Have a good time smoking weed and fucking my girlfriend in your shitty van did you mate?" Reaching into the boy's ruck sack he pulled out a camera. There were photos of Ria smiling, submerging her naked body in the ocean. Photos of her sitting in the van, legs akimbo, stretched out over the seats, cigarette in hand. Smiling; again. Why did she look so goddamn fucking happy in all of them? It was a joke. This little shit was what made her happy? He had seen enough.

"Do you think I'm fucking stupid mate?" He grabbed the boy by his hair and dragged him across the floor towards his car. "Where is the little bitch? I've come a long way to find her and I'm not giving up now. Show me where she is, this isn't a fucking game."

"I don't know and I wouldn't tell you if I did," he shouted, instantly pulling his arms around to cover his head in anticipation of the blow that he knew was coming. Brad swung his foot back and kicked him in the stomach as hard as he could and he whimpered in pain like a dog.

He asked him again, but the boy had just kept his mouth clammed shut, adding fuel to the fire. It was his fault, Brad thought. If he would have just told me straight then I wouldn't have done it.

He kicked him again, hard in his side and the boy started to splutter and knelt down on the floor, clutching at his knees. He wasn't even trying to defend himself; it wasn't as much fun without a bit of a fight.

"Get up you fuckwit." Clutching him by the throat Brad dragged him further towards his car, as the boy bucked his legs and gasped for air. His hand fitted easily around his neck; the weedy little fucker. Finally they reached the side of the hire car and Brad released his grasp and threw him down by the wheel. The boy got on all fours like an animal, wheezing.

"You're fucking pathetic mate," Brad spat at him. "Well it doesn't matter whether you tell me or not. I'm going to track down that little bitch and she is going to pay."

The boy charged towards him, leaping at him through the air. Brad swung out of the way and felt a sharp pain in his shoulder as a knife penetrated into it forcefully.

"You stupid little shit," he shouted. "Now look at what you've gone and done."

Brad cracked his fist into his face, smashing it so hard against his nose that blood splattered across the windows of the hire car, and the boy fell backwards onto the dirt, the little knife he had used to stab him falling to the ground. He stretched his arm out to reach for it as Brad stood over him, but he was too slow. Within moments Brad had his weapon, his only means of defence in his hand. He thrust the blade into his stomach. The boy spluttered and Brad watched with fascination as he squirmed, the life draining from his body, until there was no movement left, only stillness.

"Fuck," Brad shouted when it was over. "Look what you made me do! Look what you made me fucking do!"

CHAPTER TWENTY-NINE

I lay motionless across the long crimson tablecloth surrounded by sensuous, appetising delights. The chef at Flirt had exceeded my expectations and created a Japanese feast fit for a king. Japanese cuisine is all about presentation and I'm sure the customers who were due to walk into the club were to be pleasantly surprised, as the majority of the delights had been presented across my naked flesh.

My breasts were adorned in an assortment of nigirizushi, and rolls of maki were artistically arranged across my torso down towards my own eastern delight. It was taking all my self-restraint not to lean down and eat some myself, but I knew the slightest movement could cause it all to tumble off onto the floor. It was almost torturous being covered in my favourite food and not being able to take a bite, and I giggled at my predicament. To make matters worse I hadn't even eaten that morning as I was in such a rush to get to work and begin my transformation into a modern day geisha girl.

My black hair was swept up into a dramatic up do, my lips painted red and my almond shaped eyes were emphasised by my white eyelids and expertly applied kohl eye liner. The Japanese theme was certainly playing up to my assets, especially as I was the only Asian looking girl in the whole club. Today was definitely going to be a fun, welcome distraction from the feeling of dread that had hung over me like a shadow since returning to Sydney.

It had been almost a month since I had begun working at Flirt and I had been made a part of the delightfully dysfunctional, well groomed family from day one. However as I lay awaiting the festivities that were about to take place, my mind wandered and I began to think about Andy. There had still been no message from him.

I tried to ring him the day I first arrived back in Sydney, seated at the bottom bunk of a hostel bed in the Cross. The isolation I had felt when I had first arrived in Australia was beginning to creep over me again, as the comedown of our road trip adventure started to hit home. I just wanted to hear his voice, to see if he was okay, to tell him I was fine. There had been no answer. Just the disappointing sound of his phone's endless ringing, as I made excuses for his disregard for me in my head. I had tried again the next day; the phone was dead. Perhaps he was with his family? Maybe he had lost his phone? After weeks of further attempts, the realisation that maybe he was no different from the rest had finally sunk in. Perhaps I had meant nothing more to him then a fling in the sunshine and now he was back home in England, boasting about how he had bedded a stripper, laughing about our most intimate moments with his cronies over a pint in the pub. I felt wounded at the thought of it. I thought Andy was different. Maybe all men were the same?

I had thrown myself into my work at Flirt to take my mind off the rejection I felt. At least here I was surrounded by people and not alone with my thoughts, with only a can of Victoria Bitter to keep me company.

I feared seeing Brad again, the paranoia from living in such close proximity to him made my stomach lurch with dread at every corner I turned, every street I walked down. I felt vulnerable when I was alone and imagined seeing him, behind every turn, his scowling face and his dangerously pumped physique waiting. Was he pining over me, in fury over my departure from his life? My intuition told me that it was not over yet, but I reasoned with myself that his sights were most probably fixed on his new prized possession by now and that I would be forgotten, another notch on the bedpost, a disposable commodity which could easily be replaced.

Between my fears and loneliness it would have been easier to go home, but my time in Australia was just beginning now I had my freedom back. Aia had begged me to come back when I had finally plucked up the courage to call home. I had given her a watered down version of the events that had happened but I knew she had it sussed out. Still there was no way I was going to let someone like Brad get the better of me; I still had a lot of adventures yet to come. I was determined to have the time of my life and no one, not even Brad would stop me.

I heard footsteps descending the stairs of the club and Bobbi and I looked at each other and tried not to laugh. She was decked out in sushi as well and from the look on her face she was finding it difficult to contain herself. The customers grinned from ear to ear when they saw the feast before their eyes. It was party time.

"Konichiwa," I greeted them. Vinnie who was quickly becoming my most valuable customer, made a beeline in my direction, clapping his hands together in glee when he saw my predicament.

"Konichiwa," he enthused loudly. "You look delightful!" He smiled broadly and leant over, chopsticks poised, ready to select one of the tasty treats on offer. "Now which one shall I have first, the one resting on your right nipple, or the one by your navel?"

"Save best one for last," I said in my Japanese accent animatedly. The crowd of gentlemen descended over me like a group of ravenous vulchers, chopsticks in hand, hastily consuming the array of sushi displayed on me, some attempting to feed me as part of the fun, until there was nothing left but a few grains of rice stuck to my skin. It reminded me of a scene from a wildlife documentary; I was the bait thrown into the water, and they were the sharks devouring me.

"I hope you enjoyed the food gentlemen," I said, kneeling on the table and blowing kisses in their direction, to which they responded by taking to their feet and applauding me enthusiastically.

Heading for the dressing rooms, Bobbi and I began to change into our costumes ready for the day ahead. The Flirt shut door lunches were notoriously famed for being the most extravagant and exclusive days of fun amongst the men in the city, and for being outrageously lucrative for the handful of girls working at them. It was still only one o clock and already the day had transcended my imaginings.

"That was weird," I said to Bobbi as we exchanged bemused expressions. "I was scared they were going to start eating me for a minute then!"

"They probably would have done if Terry wasn't standing there," Bobbi laughed. Terry was one of the burly doormen who worked at the club, and if he hadn't been employed by Flirt, he could have quite easily been trusted with protecting the crown jewels singlehandedly; such was the level of his covert operation in the club. His watchful eyes never missed a trick, if a customer so much as tried to have a feel of himself through his pockets during a show Terry would be behind him in an instant, his glare fixed on him, bulging arms crossed like a guard dog ready to pounce.

"So have you found a place yet Ria?" Bobbi asked. Her eyes were focused upon her lithe figure in the mirror, while she brushed herself down liberally with body glitter until she shimmered all over.

"Yes, I finally found a flat. It's great, right in the centre of the Cross, so I can walk to all the bars and cafes. It's really nice; you should come over for a drink after work sometime."

"Oh my God," Bobbi exclaimed clutching at my arm. "We should have a house warming party for you. Invite over all the girls and maybe a few boys."

"Mmm yeah, that would be good. Let's invite some people tonight, but keep it a bit select, quite small. I think twenty people would be enough."

"Perfect," Bobbi said smacking together her glossed lips in the mirror and pouting at her reflection. Our preening session was interrupted by Natalia the manager, poking her head round the door.

"Girls, sorry to break up the party but you are due on stage in five minutes." She ushered us impatiently through the door onto the club floor, tweaked our costumes and handed us some decorative fans. "Do your stuff, all the customers are waiting." We looked at each other excitedly, it was my first 'show' at the club and our burlesque style performance had been rehearsed only briefly the night before.

Exotic eastern music filtered through the club; our cue to make an entrance. The lights dimmed, the chatter subsided to a din, and Bobbi and I strode in holding hands, fanning ourselves in time to its rhythm. Wearing cropped kimono tops, black silk knickers and Perspex five inch heels, we made our way through the crowd of spectators, leaning over selected targets on our way, seductively gyrating and flicking our hair over them as they gawped wide-eyed and wide-mouthed, the

Japanese shamisen's alluring sound playing in the background.

Ascending the stairs onto the stage, the music quickened, as we began our strip tease, slowly removing each other's robes, until our breasts were exposed. Pressing ourselves against the metal pole, we swung ourselves around it, synchronised with each other's movements as we teased the audience, treating them to glimpses of our flesh in between the sweeping movements of our ornate fans. Then tiptoeing out of our heels we stood at the back of our stage and took it in turns to bend over, whilst slowly removing each other's silky knickers.

A shell shaped pool lay in wait for us and we stepped into it. Bobbi picked up a jug of warm water and trickled the liquid down my chest. The sensation of the water over my bare skin gave me a rush of delight, and I reciprocated the gesture, sponging down her naked flesh until there were white suds of soap clinging to her curves. Water glistened off of our slippery forms under the stage lights as we continued with our erotic, Japanese inspired sponge bath, slowly and deliberately, as we allowed the water to wash over us enticingly. Then as the music came to an end and the stage lights slowly dimmed, we grabbed our fans, pressing our wet bodies together and sharing a pretend kiss behind our fans.

Our audience rose to their feet in a standing ovation, banging their hands together wildly. Bowing in a demure Japanese geisha fashion, delighted by their reaction, we carefully stepped out of the pool into the robes which the cocktail waitresses were now holding open for us. A circle of men stood by the edge of the stage, each holding out notes of money and we smiled while we collected our tips gratefully, noting their colour. Clutching a wad of green and yellow bills we made our way backstage to count up our earnings and divide them between us, like a couple of kids with a bag full of sweets on Halloween.

"Fifty, one, fifty, two, fifty, three, four, five, fifty, six, fifty, seven, fifty, eight, fifty, nine, fifty, ten," Bobbi said, slamming the notes down with the skill of a bank teller. "A grand!" Bobbi exclaimed. "That's five hundred each."

"Wow," I said, holding out my hand while she gave me my share.

"Plus Diane gave us three hundred to do the show, that means we just earned eight hundred dollars in the last fifteen minutes," Bobbi informed me.

"Bloody brilliant," I said grinning. Working at Flirt really was another world altogether. I had thought Centrefolds had been a lucrative place to work but it wasn't even comparable to the amount that could be earned here. Customers practically threw their money at you and it was so much fun. None of this hounding people for lap dances as it had been in London; the effort of getting a twenty pound dance an exhausting charade. Here the men booked you by the hour, and after ten minutes of dancing they would usually ask you to sit next to them and join them in a glass of champagne. Often the private rooms would be filled with bodies, a group of men and two or three dancers creating a party like atmosphere. The time flew past quickly and by the end of the night I would usually go home with at least a thousand dollars, sometimes even three or four. If it kept up like this I would have enough money to go around the world a few times over!

"Girls that was great," Diane enthused, walking into the dressing room, a picture of elegance with her perfectly coiffured blond hair and stylish black dress. "The customers loved it, you two look great together! We will have to get you to do some more stage shows! How did you find it Pearl?" she asked me, smiling.

"I loved it!" I exclaimed, still buzzing from the adrenalin.

"Well once you're ready girls then come and sit with us; Vinnie and his friends want to have a drink and some shows with you. In fact I believe there's a bit of a queue for you both!" She sauntered back to join her friends and we followed shortly after, gasping for a drink and eager to join in with the merriment.

"My favourite ladies!" Diane announced as we approached their table. "This is our new girl Pearl, she has been making waves since she started. The customers adore her." Flattered by her introduction, I shook hands with her circle of comrades. "She is so exotic isn't she?" she enthused, to a rather wealthy looking gentleman to the left of her.

"And my little Bobbi," she added, being careful not to miss out my new friend. "Best ass in Sydney!" she laughed, putting her arm around her.

"I'll toast to that," said Vinnie raising his glass. "To the best ass in Sydney!" We clinked our glasses and sunk back our champagne. Swept up in the delirium of the moment I laughed and chattered with the extraordinarily fun group of people surrounding me.

Looking up I noticed the DJ, Eddie peering at me shyly with his deep brown eyes and I smiled at him. He was another character unlike any I had ever met. The eclectic mix of music he played at Flirt made my stage shows enjoyable and we were becoming friends quickly. He had the largest collection of records of anyone I had ever met, almost every request I made he managed to dig out for me, even the most obscure of the old school acid house tracks. We shared a love of music and marijuana and at the end of the night, that is where I found myself; sprawled across the floor in his cave of wonder, lined from floor to ceiling with records spanning every genre of music imaginable, smoking a joint and laughing, while he mixed some classic house tunes on his decks. Heaven.

CHAPTER THIRTY

Eddie Steele had wanted to be a DJ for as long as he could remember. Music was like a drug for him, he needed it like most people needed air to breathe. It was an essential part of his existence. Gradually though as the years had progressed, the reality of surviving on a DJ's salary, playing the odd Saturday night in one of Sydney's clubs had hit home. His mother's insistent nagging to get a real job was starting to get to him and he had begun reconsidering his dreams and looking for a nine-to-five. That's when he had landed the job at Flirt.

It had saved him from a fate worse than death, the monotony of normal life had never appealed, and now he was able to work almost every night of the week, playing music and as an added bonus he was surrounded by some of the most beautiful women he had ever clapped eyes on.

He had never been to strip clubs before, had never understood the appeal of watching something and not being able to touch. He had seen dancers as being money grabbing, shallow girls, selling their bodies for cash but his mind had been quickly changed. They were mostly intelligent fun-loving girls, wanting to escape from mundane life just as he had and they were using their best assets to do it. Seeing the amount of money they sometimes earned it was not surprising. It was obscene sometimes. If he was a woman he would have given it a go himself.

One thing that never ceased to amaze him though were the countless girls he saw in destructive relationships with men who offered them nothing in return for their generosity but tons of grief and a black eye. No doubt about it, they seemed to attract the wrong sorts and Eddie found it frustrating hearing their stories. He had become a trusted confidante for many of the girls who saw him as the 'good guy' they could trust. That's as far as it ever went though, he needed some normalcy in his life. Getting involved with a dancer usually ended in drama, they seemed to attract it like a magnet and any decent guys were usually chewed up and spat out by them. Perhaps that was why they always seemed to end up with the wrong men?

Despite his resolve not to fall for a stripper, recently that was exactly what was happening to him. He was falling hard and no matter how hard he tried to prevent it, he couldn't seem to stop himself from thinking about her. She was on his mind constantly, every time he picked a record and put it on it somehow reminded him of her. She was different somehow he told himself, a diamond in the rough.

He went round the back to have a quick cigarette break and there she was sitting on the steps, her presence took his breath way. Her dark hair was swept off her face, her scarlet lips parted, blowing out a stream of white smoke. God she was beautiful.

"Hey Eddie," she greeted him, shifting over on the step to make room for him to sit. "How are you?"

"Yeah good Pearl, how are you?" he asked back casually, trying to conceal the grin on his face that always appeared when she was near.

"Yeah not bad, just want this night to be over with, got a customer who also happens to be the most arrogant arse in the world." She took another long pull of her cigarette and rolled her eyes.

"Oh, Gary? Yeah he is a dick. If he's being rude you can end the show you know. You don't have to stay in there with him."

"Yeah thanks Eddie, feel like I have to get on with it though. He's booked me for a couple of hours now, still got loads of time left."

"Yeah well if he is making you feel uneasy let me know."

"Thanks Eddie." She smiled sweetly at him and he felt the urge to take her in his arms and run out of there with her.

"I'd better go back," she said standing up. "See you later?"

"Yes see you later," he nodded, hoping that they would be having a drink again after work together. They had been spending a lot of time together recently but he wondered if she was doing it out of boredom or because she genuinely liked him. He knew she was wary about getting involved with anyone and needed a friend, and he didn't want to make a move and risk losing her. He loved spending time with her, the hours floated by as they talked, and what had begun as a bit of flirtation and friendship was deepening every day. He was beginning to feel like he wanted to protect her from the world, feelings which always surfaced when he fell for a girl; feelings which could be dangerous when working with the girl in question in a strip club.

As he returned to the DJ booth, he watched the camera screen of private room number five intently for any signs of Gary mistreating Pearl. He looked rowdy and drunk as usual, the only reason they allowed him entry to the club was because he was good friends with one of Flirt's highest spenders; if it hadn't been for that Diane would have probably barred him ages ago. He had upset the girls on quite a few occasions, making nasty comments about their bodies, anything he could to cause a reaction. The more experienced girls of the club now avoided him like the plague and so he always went for the new girls knowing their inexperience made them more vulnerable.

Pearl entered the private room and he motioned for her to sit next to him. He handed her a drink and whispered in her ear. Judging by the expression on Pearl's face she wasn't too eager to listen and was trying to back away from him subtly. Eddie felt a stirring of anger rise inside him as he saw him putting his hand on her knee, and Pearl pulling it away. He was just about to call the bouncer over when Pearl got up on the table; obviously in an attempt to distance herself from him, and started to dance. He watched mesmerised as she took her clothes off and as she turned away from Gary, he looked on in horror as the grotesque man unzipped his pants, pulled out his penis and grabbed hold of Pearl's arm, yanking her on top of him.

"Fuck," Eddie exclaimed, ushering over the bouncer Terry and making a beeline for the private room.

"Get off her you fucking moron," Eddie snarled, pulling a shell-shocked Pearl away from him. Terry came to his aid, grabbing the man by the scruff of his neck roughly and dragging him out of the club, his pants round his ankles as he fumbled to pull them back up.

"You're barred mate, don't ever show your face round here again or you're dead," he said, kicking him up the stairs.

"Get your hands off me! This is fucking assault," the man screamed.

"No what you did is assault mate and we got it on camera. If you don't piss off now we'll be taking it to the police."

"Whatever, I'm sick of this place, it's full of a bunch of dirty molls anyway."

Terry responded by grabbing him by the throat and pulling him off the premises, as onlookers watched, stunned in silence as the scene unfolded.

"Are you alright?" Eddie asked. Pearl was noticeably shaking. He jumped up and helped her step back into her dress. "Come on, the man's a dickhead, don't let him upset you."

"I think I cut myself Eddie," she held up her forearm, which was gushing with blood.

"Oh my God," he exclaimed. "Come on, I'm taking you to the hospital. Natalia," he said, motioning to the unusually quiet hostess standing behind him. "Put one of the CDs on and tell Diane what happened." She nodded and disappeared, doing what she was told quickly to restore some semblance of normality to the club again.

"I'm fine, it's nothing, I just need a plaster," Pearl insisted. Eddie inspected the wound closely.

"Are you mental? It's pretty deep - you're gonna need stitches."

She nodded reluctantly, her expression dazed as he picked her up, hailing a cab to the hospital, pressing a towel against her arm as they sat in the back of it. When they were finally seen by a doctor, he helplessly watched Pearl wincing in pain as the doctor stitched up her delicate looking forearm and she squeezed his hand tightly.

When it was all over she turned to him, her beautiful face tense with emotion. "Can I come back to yours tonight Eddie? I don't want to be alone." He felt his stomach flutter at her request.

"Of course you can. I'm always here for you. You know that Pearl."

"It's Ria by the way, not Pearl. I want you to call me by my real name from now on."

Ria. So that's what her name was. He had been wondering for a while and now he knew. He smiled and led her towards the cabs outside the hospital, glad to be able to spend some more time with her. When they were finally back at his, he made up a bed for her and handed her a cup of tea. His T shirt was swamping her frame, making her look vulnerable and innocent.

"Thanks," she said, taking a sip.

"No problem. Now rest up." Eddie walked out of the bedroom and stole a glance at her before shutting the door. Her black hair was fanned out across the pillow like an exotic silk, even without a trace of make-up on she was stunning. Closing the door gently he let out an exasperated sigh and he knew in that moment that he was well and truly in love. There was no escaping it.

CHAPTER THIRTY-ONE

The cool breeze whipped back my hair as I stood at the front of the yacht admiring the view of Sydney Harbour. Girls were strewn across the front of the boat in designer swimwear, tanning themselves as we made our way across the silken ocean, house music pumping out loudly setting the party atmosphere.

Bobbi came over to me, her cut away swimsuit showing off her petite frame. She lifted up her sunglasses, looked me in the eyes and laughed. "Not a bad life is it?"

"Yeah can't complain. Thanks for asking me to come today it's been really fun."

"No problem, Vinnie asked me to get you here anyway. I think you're his new favourite. He's a good guy, make the most of it while you can, he's very generous when he likes someone." She looked downwards and I could tell she was a bit envious of my new elevated position as Vinnie's "favourite girl."

"Yeah well I have decided to save up as much cash as I can and go travelling again soon. Then I'm going to go home. I miss my family so much," I said, in an attempt to reassure her that she would soon be reinstated to the number one spot on his list.

"God, you're crazy. You'd leave all this behind to go back to freezing cold England?"

"Well I'm sure I will miss it when I leave but it's not the same when you don't have your family around. Still I am going to enjoy every minute of it now while I can."

"So what's going on with you and Eddie?" she asked, pulling down her shades and staring at me inquisitively.

"Nothing, we're just friends."

"Just friends? You have been going back to his almost every night after work. Everyone's noticed it."

"Well I do really like him but I don't want to get too attached."

"Well he likes you too, won't stop going on about you. You should marry him and then you can stay. I don't want you to leave."

"Ha, marry him! Yeah right." I laughed at her suggestion.

"Seriously he is smitten with you," she said, adding another layer of gloss to her plumped lips.

"Hey ladies, you enjoying yourselves?" Vinnie had sauntered over and was leaning casually against the rail of the yacht, smiling at us.

"Vinnie!" she breathed, wrapping her arms around his neck. "Yeah it's been an awesome day so far."

"Your boat is amazing." I added.

"Well you let me know if you ever want to come out with me on it. I'm always going out for the day. Would love the company of such a beautiful lady." Vinnie smiled at me.

"Thanks, I will," I said, knowing full well it would never happen.

"Great, well all the guys are having a great time; you've managed to get together an amazing bunch of girls as always Bobbi." She leant her body back against the rail, and fluttered her eyelashes at him, glad to have his attention back on her.

"Only the best for you Vinnie. Christiana and Lana are getting ready for the show so you might want to get all the guys together."

"Great I'll go round them up." Vinnie turned back and we made our way on to the upstairs deck, Bobbi clutching a CD picked by the girls for their performance, the men sitting round in a circle, eagerly awaiting the show. As the music came on Christiana and Lana climbed the stairs, dressed in PVC bodices, yielding long whips, and cracking them against the floor as they strutted. They began to peel off each other's clothes in a dirty performance, the men were practically salivating as they kissed and started to lick each other's erect nipples. When they were both naked they pulled out a can of whipped cream;

spraying mounds of it onto each other's bodies. Groaning as they licked it off each other and rubbing it around their chests, they each picked a victim and straddled them. Their faces' were a bemusing combination of embarrassment and pleasure as the girls bounced around on their laps, their cream covered tits jostling in their faces. The rest of the men burst into laughter at the sight of their cronies, and a passing boat stopped as they saw the festivities, the young lads on it honking and shouting at the two curvaceous blondes dancing next to each other, and caressing each other's sticky bodies.

"That was raunchy!" I laughed as the music ended and the boat erupted in rapturous applause, the girls bowing and smacking each other's bums before going downstairs to get dressed again.

"Yeah well they said they wanted a bit of girl on girl action for the show and Christina and Lana are pretty good at that kind of thing. Don't mention it to them but they aren't getting paid any more than we are."

"Oh yeah, course not," I said, feeling slightly awkward. As the crowd dispersed and the drinking continued I went over to Vinnie who was at the wheel of the yacht, navigating the party through the picturesque harbour.

"Can I have a go?" I asked.

"Sure darl you look like a sailor in that hat. Just don't turn it too sharply or we'll end up like the titanic."

I took the wheel and holding out one arm I shouted, "I'm the king of the world." Vinnie laughed at me, and I caught a glimpse of Christina and Lana exchanging sneering glances at me. "God what's their problem?"

"They're just jealous. It took them about five surgical procedures, fake hair extensions and veneers to look that good, whereas you my dear, have it naturally."

"Why thank you Vinnie."

"No need to thank me, it's the truth."

"Here can you take my photo?" I asked, handing him my disposable camera which I had seldom used since I had arrived. It would be a shame not to get one shot of me to look back on when I'm old and wrinkly.

"What's this old piece of junk?"

"My camera, wind it up like this and press the button," I instructed him.

"Didn't know they even made these things anymore, I will have to get you a new one Pearl; this is ridiculous." He was holding it in front of him as if he couldn't quite believe it wasn't a hologram. Anybody would have thought I had just pulled a live lobster out of my bag the way he was looking at it.

"I'd rather spend my money on shoes and booze. Anyway, I quite like disposables, bit of a surprise when you go to pick up your photos. Digital cameras are boring." I leant my body against the wheel and posed while he snapped the camera.

"Hey Pearl, glad I've caught you alone, I've been meaning to talk to you, wanted to ask you something." He had a serious expression on his face and I hoped he wasn't about to proposition me for sex.

"Oh really, what did you want to ask me?"

"Well, as you know, you have become my favourite girl since you started at Flirt, and well every year I go on holiday for a week and take a girl with me. Last year it was Bobbi and I was hoping this year you might like to come."

"Oh I don't know Vinnie, I'm really flattered you asked but I don't want to cross over that line."

"You can ask Bobbi, it's not a sex thing, just nice to have a gorgeous woman like yourself to keep me company. We'd have loads of fun. This year I am going to Fiji. Obviously I wouldn't expect you to do it for free I will give you ten thousand dollars to come with me." He lit a cigar and took a few puffs, surveying my reaction, while I tried to work out what would be the best way of putting him down. Having sex for money had never appealed to me; I was earning enough as it was without having to overstep that boundary. I had made myself a promise a very long time ago that I would never consider it, no matter how much I was offered.

"Ten thousand dollars. Wow that's a lot of money but I don't think I can."

"Is it because of Eddie, are you two together now?"

"No we're just friends," I said, unsure of what he was becoming to me.

"Right, well think about it and let me know if you change your mind because I'd really like you to come. We can negotiate the money if you want more."

"Okay Vinnie I'll think about it," I said, eager not to piss him off and lose my best customer.

"Alright. Well enjoy the party, I will see you in a minute. And here," he said taking my hand and filling it with a wedge of cash. "Don't tell any of the other girls but here's a little tip for you. You look amazing today."

The day progressed and the music began to soften and fade as the sun set on Sydney harbour. The girls and I were now wearing long maxi dresses and as the yacht pulled up to be moored, we all went our separate ways, despite the desperate attempts of the men to get us to party on with them. Most of them were so drunk now they were slurring their words. We all made our excuses of being expected at work in a few hours.

"Don't forget what I asked Pearl," Vinnie said as he helped me off the rocking boat.

"No, I won't," I said, catching a glimpse of a scowl from Bobbi as she overheard.

Diane greeted me as I walked into Flirt later on that evening, still feeling slightly tipsy from all the alcohol I had consumed.

"How was the boat party darl?" she asked, eager to hear all the gossip. She was dressed in a plum coloured dress, the deep V neckline displaying her ample assets. She poured me a glass of champagne and I sat next to her, eager for a chat.

"Yeah it was really fun."

"Good. Are you feeling okay after the other night?" Her face was etched with concern. She had been so kind to me since I had started at Flirt; it had been such a comfort with my family so far away. I smiled at her appreciatively.

"Yeah I'm alright; glad Eddie was there to help me."

"Let's have a look at that arm of yours." She winced as I showed her the wound. "Ouch, still looks pretty sore."

"Yeah it's not too bad," I said covering up the gash in my arm with my dressing and a studded sleeve I had fashioned.

"Well I've told Natalia you don't have to do any stage shows tonight if you're not up for it. Don't want you tearing your stitches."

"Thanks Diane."

"So what's going on with you and Eddie?" She raised her eyebrow and smirked.

"Oh nothing really. I really like him but I don't want to get involved just yet, not after my last relationship."

"Why darl what happened?"

"Oh I was with this Aussie guy and he turned a bit nasty on me towards the end. Put me off men for a while."

"Oh how awful, sorry to hear that sweetie. Is he from Sydney?"

"Yeah you've probably heard of him, his name's Brad Harrison."

"Brad Harrison, you were with him! He's a bit notorious round here; I used to know his dad. Wouldn't trust that Brad character as far as I could throw him I never liked him." She leaned in closer and lowered her voice as if worried someone would overhear. "He's very arrogant, no respect for women whatsoever. He used to be with one of our dancers and he mistreated her. He hasn't been back in the club since, that was years ago now."

"Yeah well I can believe that," I said, relieved to find out that he wasn't going to be walking into the club any time soon.

"What did he do to you?" she asked.

"Well we met in England and I moved over here with him and he just started being really controlling and possessive. Then one night I went out and didn't tell him where I was. He didn't take it too well, let's put it that way."

Diane gasped in response. "Oh you poor thing. Did he hurt you?"

"Yes," I nodded solemnly, my heart sinking as I remembered what he had done to me.

"You should have gone to the police. That man needs to be dealt with." Diane's voice was peppered with anger and she shook her head at my revelation.

"I was too scared, I just wanted to get away from him."

"Well I can't blame you, it's best to stay away from men like him. His family are very powerful he probably would have bribed his way out of it somehow anyway. You shouldn't let him put you off men though. You're too young; you've got to kiss many frogs before you find your prince."

"Yeah you're right."

"And Eddie is one of the good ones darl. He adores you too; maybe you should go with it if you like him."

"Yeah Diane, maybe I will."

"Go on then girl, go and have a good shift and remember I'm always here if you ever need a chat. I know you don't have your family around to talk to."

"Thanks," I said, grateful for her kind words.

She waved me away with a flick of her heavily jewelled hand and as I walked away, I relayed her words in my head and noticed Eddie looking at me from behind the DJ booth. I smiled at him and he reciprocated; a broad grin across his face as I approached him.

"Ria. Where have you been, not seen you since the drama the other night? Are you okay?"

"Yes I'm fine, I missed you though." I said, holding my breath as I waited for his reply.

"I missed you, here come up." He pulled me up the stairs that led to the DJ booth and we sat on the top step together concealed from the club; stealing sideways glances at each other.

"Thanks for helping me out the other night," I said eventually when the words came.

"Don't be stupid that's what I'm here for. Been trying to call you since; what happened?" I paused trying to think of an excuse before settling for the truth.

"Just been thinking loads."

"What about?" he asked gently.

"About us." I said shifting closer to him.

"What about us?"

"Just how much I adore you." He looked at me and I felt a spark of excitement in his eyes.

"Well you know how much you mean to me, I'd do anything for you. Come here." Pulling me closer to him he kissed me softly, a kiss which quickly progressed from soft and lingering, to deep and passionate.

"Come back to mine after work," he said, holding me tightly.

"Maybe," I replied, feeling overwhelmed by the emotions stirring inside me.

"What Ria? You're always giving me such mixed signals; I feel like I don't know what to think."

"I'm sorry Eddie I'm just scared, I don't want us to get too involved because I've decided that I want to go home soon. I am just saving up some money to go travelling for a few months and then I'll be going back to England."

"Well that doesn't mean we can't be together. A lot can happen in a few months you know. Maybe I could come with you." He looked hopeful but I couldn't help but wonder if getting involved with someone else now would be such a good idea, considering the track record of my past relationships.

"Well maybe, but I want to take things slow I don't want to rush into anything now, it will make things too hard."

"Okay," he agreed. "So do you still want to come over for some drinks after work as usual?"

"Definitely." I pulled him closer and felt a rush of excitement as our lips interlocked again. "I'd better go back out there," I said, releasing myself from his embrace. The track was about to end and he leapt up to put another one on before the club descended into silence.

"Oh and by the way, you've got a bit of lipstick." I pointed to his red mouth and he grinned and wiped it away quickly.

"Better?" he asked.

"Better," I said, pushing the door open to the DJ booth slowly so not to attract too much attention. Diane observant as always was smiling from the other side of the room and held up her glass towards me. I smiled back at her and laughed to myself. Nothing was ever a secret for long at Flirt!

CHAPTER THIRTY-TWO

I was being chased through the outback, my bare feet scrambling across its dead soil, screaming screams which no one else could hear, searching for a hiding place in a vast open space where there was nowhere to hide. The footsteps grew quicker and louder behind me, and I froze in terror as I sensed my assailant just inches away. An icy cold chill shot through my body like a bolt of lightning as my pursuer tapped me on the shoulder. Too scared to look round and face my attacker, I tensed up in anticipation of their next move. Their hot breath lingered by my ear making all the hairs on my body stand on end, as they whispered; "this is all your fault bitch."

I woke up panting; it was just a dream. I looked around my bedroom; my strewn clothes spilling from my suitcase, the pictures of my family sellotaped to the walls, and the half-smoked joint still in the ashtray next to me alongside many cigarette butts. It had taken me a very long time to go to sleep last night. For a few moments I felt bewildered and half-asleep, and a sense of calm took over from the panic. Everything was okay. But then reality began to creep in and I remembered that the horror of my nightmare was not too far detached from the facts. I shook my head and felt nauseous as it dawned on me. Last night really had happened; I definitely hadn't dreamt that.

It had been a top night in which I had been in high demand but it was interrupted abruptly, when in the middle of a private show with a very generous customer, the shadows of two police officers had formed on the other side of the translucent curtain.

I had not thought much of it at first; there usually were uniformed officers appearing at some point in the night on their patrol, their presence an unwelcome entity causing many a girl and customer to stop dead in their tracks, even when they weren't doing anything wrong. Diane despaired of the visits which were unnecessary and imposed on the ambience of the club. Half the time the cops just came in out of boredom, to liven up their shift and leer at some nude girls for free.

However this night, nothing could have prepared me for the news they would bring.

"Cops," Eddie had warned whilst walking past, and sure enough less than a minute later they were standing outside, looking in at me while I sat naked on the table. This time though they didn't move on to the next room. The moments passed by slowly, their overbearing shadows on the other side of the curtain making me feel anxious; had I done something wrong? My discomfort quickly turned to shock when they parted the sheer fabric and came in.

They stood over me threateningly, disapproving looks crossing their faces as their eyes scanned over my exposed body. One officer was tall with a Mediterranean look, probably in his late thirties; the other a short stocky woman with cropped hair, a hard face, and a piercing gaze.

"So this must be Ria," the male officer said, startling the customer sitting opposite me. Eddie stood behind them, eyeing them cautiously.

"Actually it's Pearl when I'm at work," I said bluntly, annoyed by the way they had just revealed my identity to my customer, who had been pressing me for it since the beginning of the show. "What's going on?"

"Sorry mate, show's over," said the lady, shooing the friendly middle-aged man from his seat and taking it herself, her colleague following suit.

"I'm sorry Clive," I said to the man, who couldn't get away from the situation fast enough. "We can finish our show later." Then turning to them I asked, "Have I done something wrong?"

"I am Constable Harlow," said the woman, "and this is Constable

Mikos," she said gesturing towards her male counterpart.

"We've got a few questions for you Miss," said the male officer, who seemed to be enjoying my vulnerability and was doing his best to conceal a smirk which was appearing on his face.

"Yeah, well I think you can let her get dressed first," Eddie piped up, bending down on the floor to get my dress for me.

"Yeah sure take your time," said the policeman, looking slightly disappointed that he had lost his opportunity to question me naked. I scrambled up, hastily pulling my dress back over my head, my hand probing the floor for my g-string. Eddie spotted the flimsy garment and quickly handed it to me.

"Here you go," he said, with a comforting expression on his face. I stepped back into it awkwardly, my heart pounding with fear as they watched with cold expressions. After successfully managing to pull my clothes back on I sat opposite them and Eddie seated himself by my side. "What is this about anyway?" he asked them, angry at the way they had just burst in on me. Ignoring Eddie completely, Constable Harlow reached inside her leather Filofax and pulled out a photograph from it.

"Do you recognise this boy?" she said, passing me a picture. I studied the face on the photo in front of me and my heart sank as I instantly recognised its subject.

Blond hair, baby face, blue eyes; Andy was smiling back at me. He looked just like he did when I first met him; relaxed, happy, and slightly paler than he had been when we had said our goodbyes, before weeks of sun-worshipping and a lack of washing facilities had hit him.

"Yes," I said, brows furrowing as I tried to figure out why they were asking me about him. The notion that Andy was in trouble with the police seemed ridiculous, he wasn't exactly the kind of bloke that would go around looking for trouble. I couldn't imagine him breaking the law, certainly not to a level where it would warrant two coppers coming into question me like this. Well whatever he had done I certainly wasn't going to drop him in it, I would keep my mouth shut.

But then it hit me; what if it wasn't something he had done? A wave of dread washed over me and I felt sick with fear. Here I had been cursing him and feeling hurt, thinking that he had been ignoring me. I should have known better. Maybe something had happened to him?

The officer studied my reaction, curling her upper lip disdainfully and I felt myself panic. "Why are you asking me? Is he okay? Did something happen to him?" I asked, my voice wobbling with shock.

"Well that's what we are trying to figure out," the man said, his harsh demeanour softening slightly at the sight of my distress.

"He has been missing for six weeks," the police woman said bluntly. "And you were the last person seen with him."

"Oh my God!" I exclaimed. My hand began to shake uncontrollably as I held the picture of him and stared at it. Something was seriously wrong here. Eddie reached for my other hand and held it in his.

"He was going to go to Mount Isa," I said, shaking my head in disbelief over what was happening. "He had family there, was going to meet them. I haven't heard from him since."

"No, no one's heard from him since the twelfth of March," Constable Mikos replied. "He was last seen at a hotel in Cairns with you. His family rang him the next day but he never answered the phone. Then the day after that his phone was dead. It hasn't been used since." He pulled out his note pad and poised his pen above it, ready to write down my responses, whilst the woman sat on the edge of her leather seat eyeing me suspiciously.

"We found his campervan in the middle of the outback. There has been no sign of him at all. Now we have a distraught family that we are trying to deal with," Harlow said.

"Oh my God," I said again, my hand covering my mouth in shock. Not Andy, please let him be ok. I felt hot tears threatening to spill in my eyes. "I can't believe it."

"Can you think of anyone that you met who may have wanted to hurt him?" Detective Harlow's face hardened further and her thin lips pursed as she awaited my response.

"No way, Andy is a lovely bloke. We travelled together for a few weeks, he was friendly and nice to everyone we met. I can't think of anyone who would want to hurt him." This couldn't be happening, it felt like a nightmare. My head swam as my thoughts whirled around it and made me feel disorientated. I felt Eddie's hand squeezing mine tighter.

"Look we are hoping that we will find him," Detective Mikos reassured me. "A lot of kids go missing travelling over here, and then a few weeks later they turn up out of the blue. It's not unheard of."

"The circumstances of his disappearance are very suspicious though," Harlow added, noticeably irritated by her colleague's soft approach. "His van was abandoned in the middle of nowhere, his phone is out of use and he left all his possessions, even his passport."

I gasped and desperately searched my memory for any clues which could help, or alleviate the horror of the situation. "He did say he wished he could stay in Australia," I offered optimistically, the recollection of the conversation we had had on one of our last night's together, offering a small glimmer of hope. "Maybe he met some people after I left and he went on with them?"

"Perhaps," Detective Mikos shrugged.

"We also found a stash of marijuana in the glove compartment. Do many drugs when you were together did you?" Detective Harlow snapped at me, causing me to stammer in response.

"Well, er we smoked a bit of weed together but that's about it." The disapproving look on her face grew.

"You do know we could have you deported for that," she warned.

"Look, Ria hasn't done anything wrong," Eddie jumped in. "She is in shock over what you've just told her, so don't take advantage."

"It's relevant to the investigation," she said, acknowledging Eddie's presence for the first time with a scowl. "If Andy was mixed up in drugs in some way then we need to know."

"Andy isn't a drug addict. He isn't even that much of a drinker," I said.

"Perhaps he was corrupted by a stripper then?" She glared at me, looking me up and down as if my mere existence was an offence to her.

"No," I cried, the tears beginning to well in my eyes. "That's not fair. You don't know even know the first thing about me!" A combination of anger and shock proceeded to make me tremble.

"A stripper with a drug problem and a temper?" she retorted.

"How dare you!" I snapped back, outraged by her insensitivity.

Eddie, sensing the danger of the situation jumped in. "Look I don't think this is the time or the place officers. Why don't you just let it sink in a bit; Ria is obviously in shock. Can we come into the station tomorrow instead?"

"New boyfriend?" Harlow asked, arching her eyebrow. "Get through them quick don't you?"

"Actually we're just friends," I said, offended by her attitude. Just because I was working as a stripper didn't give her the right to treat me like dirt. "Anyway my friend is right, this is all a lot to take in. I'll come into the station tomorrow, anything I can think of to help I will."

"Fine," Detective Mikos said, thrusting his card into my hand. "How's midday?"

"Yeah fine."

"Okay, well have a long hard think about this tonight," he said. "Anything you can think of that will help us to locate him, however minor, could prove to be invaluable."

"I will do."

The officers rose to their feet and I fell back into my chair shell shocked, as I watched them disappear through the club, leaving a trail of open-mouthed dancers in their wake.

"Are you okay?" Eddie asked when they were out of sight.

"I just can't believe it. I hope Andy is alright."

"Don't worry Ria. I bet he is okay. You'd only known him for a few weeks he could have had other plans or met other people and gone off with them."

"Well he was talking about packing it all in the last few days I was with him. He said a few times he wished he could stay in Australia and give up his job, maybe he decided to do it? I don't know though, why wouldn't he have gotten in touch by now? Oh God Eddie, what if something has happened to him?"

"I'm sure there's an explanation for it all Ria. Come on." He stood up and pulled me to my feet. "I'll get you a cab home and I'll pick you up tomorrow and take you to the police station."

"I need a drink after all that," I said, turning in direction of the bar.

"No you don't." He took my hand and steered me towards the changing rooms. "You need to go home and get some rest. You need a clear head Ria, you're supposed to be remembering everything you can tonight, not forgetting it all."

"Yeah you're right; I just don't want to be alone Eddie, I feel so scared."

"It's alright, there's nothing to be scared of." He pulled me into his arms and held me tightly. "Just give me a call me if you need me. I'm sorry, I would come home with you now if I could but I don't have anyone to cover for me. I'll see you in the morning though, okay?"

"Okay," I muttered, and he walked me up the stairs to collect my things.

I threw on my jeans, grabbed my bag and Eddie led me out to the pavement to hail a cab.

"I'll tell Diane what happened," Eddie promised as a cab veered towards us. "Just go home and chill out, I'm sure your friend is fine."

"Thanks," I said and collapsed onto the back seat of the taxi.

I returned to my flat in the Cross, dazed by what had happened. I lay in my bed, too afraid to switch off my bedside lamp, the image of Andy alone in the dark campervan, haunting me.

Questions raced through my mind for hours while I tossed and turned. Where was he? Why would anyone want to hurt him? Could it be possible that he decided to stay, his new found sense of freedom too alluring to return home? Maybe he just dumped the van and went off with a group of randoms? Or perhaps I was just searching for less horrific alternatives to the possibility that he could have been attacked by a nutcase and dragged off into the outback. Andy would have been a helpless target for a psychotic madman all alone in the van. The thought of it terrified me.

Eventually I had drifted off into a fitful sleep and was awoken by the bad dream which had left me breathless. I barely had time to gather my thoughts and wipe the cold sweat from my forehead, when I heard a knock at the door.

Cautiously I peered through the keyhole and was relieved to see it was Eddie. I swung the door open to him.

"How are you feeling?" he asked.

"I'm alright," I said, not quite sure how I was feeling.

"You look awful! Here, I got you some breakfast." He placed a McDonald's bag and a coffee on the table triumphantly.

"Er thanks," I said giving him a weak smile, grateful for some support.

"Look Ria," he said, holding my hand and looking me in the eye. "You just tell them everything you can remember today and maybe it will help. That's all you can do." He paused for a moment before adding, "Oh and promise me you won't drop yourself in it again. I really don't want you leaving me just yet."

"I'll try not to," I responded, unconvinced of what would happen. I then proceeded to get myself ready, my stomach swilling with a disastrous combination of fast food and dread as we walked out of the flat. I just hoped that it had all been a big misunderstanding and that Andy was alright.

When we finally got to the building, the imposing stature of the police station towered above me and made me feel very small. I felt sick as the harsh reality of the situation hit home. It hadn't just been a bad dream. Andy really had disappeared and God only knew where he could be. Poor, sweet Andy.

CHAPTER THIRTY-THREE

Detective Tony Griffwell paced through the corridors of the police station, feeling invigorated from his recent holiday. He and the wife had just vacationed in Bali, and after a week of luxury living and escapism he had returned to work; refreshed, rejuvenated, and ready to take on the lowlifes of the Cross.

Casually glancing into the interview rooms as he passed them, he stopped in his tracks when he saw a girl who looked vaguely familiar. Exotic looking and attractive, she possessed a distinctive face, and he hovered by the glass of the office looking puzzled as he tried to remember where he had seen her before.

The girl was sitting opposite Detective Harlow and Mikos. Her fresh face looked anguished as they questioned her; she was obviously not accustomed to the kind of situation that she was in. She definitely didn't look like the type that would usually grace the interrogation rooms of Kings Cross station; typically a nice wholesome mix of ice addicts, crack whores, and seedy drug traffickers.

He searched his memory, until dumbfounded, his mind finally registered where he had encountered the girl before. Hurrying back to his office, he dug through one of his drawers looking for the evidence to confirm his beliefs, stopping when he finally reached a big manila envelope he had been given months earlier. Tentatively he reached his hand in and pulled out a photograph.

Her pretty face was devoid of the tortured expression he had just seen her wearing and she was wearing less make-up then in the photo, but it was her all the same. It was the same girl that Brad had paid him to track down! The girl he had finally managed to find after weeks of searching, and then against his own better judgement, had blown the whistle on. The question was; what the hell was she doing in the station?

Tony felt a sense of uneasiness wash over him as he began to worry that his dodgy dealings might have finally caught up with him. What was she doing in the interrogation room? Perhaps she had come to report Brad, maybe he had been hassling her? Tony tried to calm himself by deducing the many other possibilities which could have led her to the station. It could be for an entirely unrelated reason, she obviously would be more susceptible to getting involved with the wrong sorts than the average Joe on the street; she was a stripper after all. It could be drug related. Who knows, she could even be a prostitute or have been involved in a nasty altercation at work?

Tony looked at his watch nervously, a present he had treated himself to; another luxury item now a stark giveaway as to his dishonesty for anyone who cared to look. All it would take was one rousing suspicion voiced amongst his peers and he could lose it all. His job, his lifestyle, and his wife would certainly follow suit. Gravely shuffling away the paperwork now strewn across his desk, he slowly slid the photo carefully back amongst his files, closed his desk drawer, and locked it behind him. Warily, he made his way back down to the interrogation rooms hoping to get some information that would put his mind at ease.

He knew his dealings were risky and could possibly lead to trouble, but there had never been any sign of danger before. Something about this situation felt different though. Usually he handed over information about other crooks, or set up drug busts to help disengage the competition of dealers. The rewards had been fruitful and he had still managed to remain detached from their real outcomes, in blissful ignorance.

He should have refused when he had first seen the girl's photo, but his greed had taken over. Brad had seemed like a gent compared to the sorts he was used to dealing with, but he had been wrong. The man had scared him and Tony had been relieved to get him off his back and wash his hands of the whole situation. He had worried about it a few times afterwards, but it had since become a distant memory, no longer threatening his conscience. Still at least he knew now she hadn't been harmed. She was still alive and that was a bonus.

He caught Harlow and Mikos leaving the office, and walked towards them casually. "Hi guys, who was that girl you were just interviewing?"

"Just some stripper." Detective Mikos volunteered the information, eager to share the gossip with his senior colleague. "You know the case of the English boy Andrew Wilson who went missing recently in Queensland?"

"Yeah, I have heard about it," Tony replied.

"Well she was the last person seen with him. They stayed together in a hotel in Cairns and the next day he went missing. Cops found his campervan on the side of the Flinders Highway, just outside Hughenden. No trace of him but there was blood in the van."

"Really?" Tony said, trying his best to cover the panic in his voice. "So do you think he might have been murdered?"

"Well it sure seems that way," Detective Mikos said ruefully. "Course she didn't have much information which could be of any use to us, but probably knows more than she is letting on I'd say."

"They always do," Tony agreed. "I will see you guys later. Keep up the good work."

Walking away from his colleagues, Tony made his way out of the station as quickly as he could, eager to break free from the institution which he had sworn to serve all those years earlier. He could feel himself suffocating and loosened his tie from his neck with anxious yanks as he approached the station's entrance. Swinging open one of its glass doors, he caught a glimpse of his reflection and felt a sense of shame so overwhelming that it made him feel physically sick. That poor boy had been killed, and it was all because of him. What kind of a person had he let himself become?

CHAPTER THIRTY-FOUR

Brian was sitting in his beaten up old yute, bleary eyed and dishevelled. It had been almost an hour now. His eyes scanned his surroundings, desperately searching for any sign of Damo. He hated waiting. What was it about dealers? They took the absolute bloody piss.

It had taken long enough for him to find the meeting place, and now he finally had he was wasting yet more of his time in a side street in Sydney, when he could have been in a club sinking back some piss by now.

His mates were all counting on him to deliver the goods and he sighed as his phone flashed again, illuminating his dark, smoke filled car. Brian read the fifth text from his friend that night.

"Where are ya mate? Still no luck?"

He played with his phone and fought back the urge to ring Damo again. He didn't want to get in his bad books. There weren't many dealers who would supply him on tick these days, and since he had got on the wrong side of that Brad dude from work he rarely had the cash to pay upfront.

A smile suddenly broke across his face as he thought of the perfect distraction to pass the time. Maybe he could see if he could hook up with that glamour he met the other night? Now that would be an awesome way to end the evening. He would have to play his cards right though, she had seemed a bit frigid last time. Still though, nothing an eccie wouldn't fix if he ever managed to get hold of them.

Lighting up another ciggie, he leant across to put his pack away and almost jumped out of his skin as he heard a tap on the window.

"Jeez Damo. You scared the bloody life out of me!" he exclaimed, when he realised who it was. His dealer hopped into the passenger seat, a grey hoodie pulled down over his head.

"Drive down the road mate. It looks too suspect me just sitting in here and jumping straight back out again. There are cops all over the place."

"No worries mate. I'm heading towards the Cross if you want a lift?" Brian pulled out onto the road, cautiously eyeing the street for any sign of police.

"Nah, just drop me at Pitt Street mate. I got another drop off to go to round there."

They crawled along past the night time revellers until Damo announced; "Here'll do." Swinging the door open to get out, he turned back round to Brian. "Need the cash Monday mate; no excuses." The door was swung closed quickly, causing the yute to shake as Damo hopped out, an inconspicuous part of the human traffic once more.

Excited he had finally scored, Brian lifted his phone to ring his mates. His finger was poised about to dial, when he was distracted by a beautiful girl directly in front of him. She was hailing a cab and had a confident air about her. Brian knew he had seen her before but he just didn't know where from.

He was sitting there with a puzzled expression, desperately trying to figure out when he had been fortunate enough to meet such a gorgeous girl, when he heard someone shout across the street; "Ria!" A bloke with a record bag ran up to her and kissed her and they both bundled into a taxi.

"Jackpot," said Brian under his breath. It was her; Brad's ex-girlfriend, the one who had left him a few months ago. Perhaps he would get back in his good books again now? God he missed his tips. He dialled Brad's number, it was late but he had told him anytime, day or night.

The phone started ringing as Brian pulled out and slowly started to tail the cab. "Hi Brad, it's Brian here, I'm one of your concierges remember?"

"Oh yeah, I remember. What are you calling for Brian?" The voice on the other end sounded tired, tense.

"I have some news. Just seen your ex, that Ria girl come out of a club. She's in a taxi now and I didn't know what to do so I am following her."

"That's great mate. Do me a favour and keep following her. If you find out where she's living mate there will be a big bonus in it for you."

Brian smiled as he heard the excited tone of Brad's voice. "Yes sir," he answered, thrilled to hear the word 'bonus' coming from his lips. The last couple of months had been a struggle without the extra money he usually had from Brad. It was a relief to know it would soon be on its way back to him.

"Just whatever you do don't lose her," the voice warned down the phone.

"Don't worry sir, that won't happen," and with that Brian put his foot down on the gas and sped off in hot pursuit of the white taxi in front, his eyes practically lit up with dollar bill signs.

CHAPTER THIRTY-FIVE

It was a Thursday night; the best night for earning apparently, but plastering on a fake smile was beyond me, even with the help of six glasses of champagne. Ever since I had found out about Andy going missing it had been a struggle. That was the thing about being a stripper, it could be fun if you were in the mood, but if you weren't it was hardly worth it. Approaching men, charming them, trying to exude a light-hearted sexual persona was impossible. My mind was a mess. And so after an evening of half-arsed attempts to hustle some customers I slumped next to Diane, who patted the seat next to hers with her perfectly manicured hands.

"How are you darl?" She squeezed my hand lightly and handed me another glass of champagne.

"I'm okay, thanks," I said, graciously taking her offering, although the last thing I felt like doing was drinking another glass of bubbly. It just wasn't hitting the spot, I felt inescapably sober; a mixture of my growing tolerance to alcohol and the shock of Andy's disappearance.

"So have you heard anything else from the police?" she asked, with a worried expression.

"No nothing. I just can't stop thinking about him though Diane, I have an awful feeling about it."

"I must admit, it is rather strange that he just disappeared like that, but there's nothing you can do now. You've told the police everything you know darl. It's only been a couple of months since he was last seen; there could be a perfectly plausible explanation for it all. Like you said before, maybe he met some people and went off with them; it happens. You young'uns can be pretty impulsive." She shot me a compassionate look, and I realised then that she didn't quite believe her own words.

"It's just so scary though Diane. I was with him for a month and a half, and then the day after I leave him he vanishes. Someone could have attacked him or anything. If I'd have been with him maybe I wouldn't be sitting here now."

"You don't really think he's dead do you?" Her words hung in the air; a terrifying question which I had been trying to avoid.

"I don't know Diane, I hope not. The police seem to think it is suspicious though. They found traces of blood in his van."

She gasped then and I felt my stomach sink. I had been trying to pretend to myself that he was alright, my thoughts had been in battle since the police had come in the week before; wishful thinking against rationality. The more I thought about it though, the more rationality was winning. Why would he not have called me? I could feel the tears beginning to well in my eyes.

"Pearl it's going to be alright I'm sure of it. I am always here for you if you need me." She gave me a hug and I noticed a few sideways glances from the customers as I subtly dabbed at my eyes. Pulling me away again she held me at arm's length and looked at me warmly. "Look it's almost the end of the night now, go and see Natalia, get your money, and go home."

"Are you sure that's alright?"

"Of course it is; besides you're not exactly going to make much money with a face like that are you? Go home and relax."

"Thanks Diane." I smiled at her and made my way through the club; all eyes were on me for all the wrong reasons; I had become the hottest topic of conversation in the place and I hated it.

As I got into the cab I hesitated briefly over whether or not to go and see Eddie but decided against it. I just needed to be alone.

"To the Cross please," I instructed the driver, and as the car pulled off I longed for my family in England and the comfort of their presence. Maybe it was time to go home?

*

I swung open the door to my flat feeling exhausted and ready for bed. It was awash with darkness; only the outdoor street lights were illuminating the sitting room. My eyes darted across it anxiously as they adjusted to the dim lighting, and satisfied all was well I sighed and closed the door behind me. Throwing my bag on the floor, I kicked off my shoes and made my way towards the kitchen for a glass of water. I poured myself a glass and took a sip, when there was a shuffling noise behind me and I felt alarmed as it dawned on me I wasn't the only one there.

"What's wrong surprised to see me?" said a menacing voice. My stomach lurched as I turned to see the silhouette of a man. Brad was stood on the opposite side of the room, an evil glint in his eyes twinkling through the gloom, and he began to move across it towards me closing the distance between us.

"Help!" I attempted to scream, but he dived at me, clamping his hand against my mouth and slamming me against the wall.

"You left without saying goodbye bitch," he said, thrusting me onto the floor. My head knocked against its wooden surface as I fell, and a throbbing pain burst across the back of my skull. He paced towards me, his domineering stature towering above my body as I lay beneath him frozen in terror; helpless.

"Well?" he said. "Haven't you got anything to say for yourself?"

"Sorry," I pleaded, my heart hammering against my chest as I tried to determine how to react.

"Sorry?" he repeated, looking down at me with a sneer. "Sorry? You fucking disgust me."

"What are you doing here?" I asked timidly. He folded his arms and stepped over me, sandwiching my torso between his feet like a vice, and I became more aware of my vulnerability by the second.

"I missed you darlin," he replied coolly, kneeling down so his face was just inches from mine. "What's wrong, aren't you happy to see me?" He smirked as I edged away from him, the smell of alcohol emanating from his breath making me feel sick with fear.

"I missed you too," I lied. Perhaps if I pretended I still loved him he would back off? My statement caused him to laugh unsettlingly. He threw his head back, unable to contain his mirth.

"You missed me?" he exclaimed. "You missed me? Now that's a fucking joke."

I slowly shifted across the floor away from him, too scared to get back up in case he knocked me down again.

"I did," I stammered. "You just really hurt me. I, I…. had to get away."

"Had to get away? You had to get away? I treated you like a fucking princess you ungrateful bitch!"

"I didn't think you were that bothered," I said under my breath.

"Bothered!" he repeated. "Fuck! What does it take to impress you hey? Who do you think you are anyway?" His fists tightened and his voice rose. "You're nothing but a fucking stripper. A stupid little whore. You completely humiliated me."

"Sorry," I said again, glancing nervously at the front door behind him. If only I could get past him somehow. He caught my eye and abruptly locked it, bolting it closed and sealing my only escape route.

"You're not getting away this time bitch." He turned back round to face me again, and as the dappled light from the street outside fell onto his face I caught a glimpse of his expression; a calculated hatred. He certainly wasn't here to win me back; it was obvious now that his intentions were a lot more sinister. I had to get away but I knew that fighting, screaming, or running wouldn't work. I stood up and made my way over to him, my only other hope of escaping this unscathed now resting upon my charms.

"I still love you Brad," I said softly, cautiously ambling over to him. "I really have missed you, you know."

"Bullshit," he said, sneering at me.

"It's true, I've thought about you every day since I left. I hoped we could figure things out eventually, that's why I didn't go back home. I was hoping we could be together again. You've got to believe me, I didn't want to go Brad, I was just scared you would hurt me again."

His reaction shocked me as his enraged demeanour crumbled instantly and he began to weep like a baby.

"I fucking loved you!" he shouted at me, tears welling up in his eyes. "I never really loved anyone before and you just took the fucking piss out of me."

"I'm sorry," I said, on tenterhooks as I tried to navigate his turbulent emotions. "I just didn't think you did anymore. I hoped you might realise if I left and you have." I reached out to touch his arm and he pulled me closer to him, crushing my face against his chest while he wept. I felt paralysed with fear as I felt the bulges of his muscular arms wrapping around me; too frightened to move in case I provoked his rage again. Just as I thought it was becoming safe he jerked me away roughly.

"No it's too late for that now; I know what you've been up to."

"What do you mean?" I asked, horrified.

"The other men, the stripping." He shoved me away, and I used the opportunity to back towards the door slowly.

"There haven't been any other men," I replied, trying to appease the psychotic wreck of a man in front of me.

"You fucking liar," he shouted. Flecks of spit were flying from his mouth, his icy blue eyes glazed over with tears and hatred.

"Honestly," I pleaded again. His face tensed, causing blue veins to bulge from his forehead. I hardly recognised him, he looked so different to how I remembered, evil almost.

"Do you have any idea what trouble you've caused?" he asked in a vindictive tone, his demeanour becoming threateningly volatile again.

"What do you mean?"

"I know you're lying, do you want to know how?" he said, the corners of his mouth beginning to rise into a twisted looking smile.

"I'm not lying," I affirmed. Ignoring me, he continued.

"The reason I know you're lying is because this isn't the first time I found you darlin." He walked towards me his large fists clenched, and I flinched as I remembered how they had rained down upon me so mercilessly before.

"What?" My stomach tensed as I heard his words. "What are you talking about?" I was shouting now despite my fear; demanding an answer.

"I found you a couple of months ago, only a few weeks or so after you left. Funny, your boyfriend was a fucking liar as well." A sickening realisation hit me as he spoke, with such a powerful force that I felt myself stumble. Surely not? He studied my face, sensing that I had connected the dots.

"Yeah that's right, I found your little boyfriend," he added, pausing for a reaction.

"What did you do to him?" I screamed until he was next to me again, grabbing me by the hair, jerking his face towards mine viciously. He spat into my face and laughed, yanking my head dangerously to one side so my neck felt like it was about to snap. Then leaning over my ear he whispered, "I fucking killed him!" uttering the words slowly and deliberately, as if they gave him pleasure.

"No!" I screamed, tears rolling down my face. "No! You bastard!" My anger momentarily made me forget my dangerous situation, but I was quickly reminded as a fist swung into my face, cracking against my temple with such a force, that the room became a blur as I flew across it.

"It's your fucking fault darlin," he said and laughed again. "If you weren't such a little whore he'd still be alive." I heard his feet pacing towards me again, reverberating off the wooden floor as I struggled to maintain my balance.

"But don't worry bitch," he said. "Cause you'll soon be joining the little scumbag!"

I leapt up instinctively at the sound of his threat. Images of being carried off in a body bag, my family in tears as they searched for me flashed through my mind. I would not let him get away with it. I could not let him kill me too. Grabbing the first thing that came to hand, I threw it in his direction. The sound of shattering glass pierced through the air and echoed in slow motion, magnified by my adrenalin. As the shards flew across the room, glittering as they reflected against the street lights, I caught a flash of his vindictive smile penetrating my tunnel vision and I raced for the front door. He got a fistful of my hair from behind and pulled me backwards onto the floor.

"Help." I tried to scream again, but I felt his large hands wrapping around my neck and squeezing, the pressure gradually increasing until I was gasping for air.

"I didn't want this," he said kneeling over me, tears welling in his eyes and splashing on my face as I struggled to break free from his grasp. His body was heavy and strong, like a brick wall weighing down upon me; my attempts to release myself were useless. My neck throbbed in agony as he crushed it mercilessly; it felt like it was about to break. The panic rose inside me as my hand searched for a weapon, my urgency increasing as my need for oxygen grew. I didn't want to die, I didn't want to die like this, being killed by him. My arms flapped about desperately until I felt something cold and hard brushing against my fingertips; the neck of a champagne bottle. I teased it into my reach until it was wedged tightly in my fist, and using all the energy I had left, I swung it as hard as I could at his head. I heard a sickening sound of crunching bone as it connected with his skull, causing him to fall backwards.

Kneeling on all fours I sucked the air from my surroundings, making a hollow whistling sound as my lungs filled back up. I continued to take long drawn breaths violently, whilst checking on my attacker. He was still. But then he made a low groaning noise, crawled onto all fours and looked at me.

"You fuckin bitch," he snarled. Crouched down like a demented tiger about to pounce, he leapt up; a vicious look in his eyes, and I swung the bottle back above my head and down onto the back of his. He fell down face first again, but this time he didn't move.

Motionless on the floor, his big hulk of a body resembled a mountain. Blood poured from his head, spilling across the floor in a crimson puddle. In that instant I knew he was dead, and a new form of panic took over as I reached for my phone.

"Eddie!" I cried. "Eddie. Oh My God. I just killed someone! I just fucking killed someone! Help me." And with that I collapsed onto the floor, next to my assailant's body, convulsing with shock and wishing that my mum could be there to wrap her arms around me and make me feel like a safe little girl again.

CHAPTER THIRTY-SIX

I was paralysed with fear, in disbelief over what had just happened, and in confusion as to what I should do next. Every time I attempted to move from my spot I was overcome by a weakness which diminished my ability to do anything. And so I lay there next to the body of Brad, his wide open mouth gaping at me reminding me of a dead fish, his glassy eyes deadly still, as wide open as his mouth. He had fallen face first onto the floor; his neck twisted in a disgusting position, and as much as I tried I could not avert my eyes from the sickening image. The reality of seeing his lifeless body before me was a stark reminder of the horror of the situation.

I was shaking and it was a while before I noticed that I was still clutching on to the champagne bottle, so tightly that my knuckles were white. My hand was so numb it no longer felt connected to my body. My insides were numb too, devoid of emotion as I lay there as wide mouthed as Brad's corpse, trying to digest the enormity of the situation.

Brad had tracked me down. Brad had killed Andy. Brad had been about to kill me and now he was dead. I had known he was volatile towards the end of our relationship but there had been no signs as to the extent of his insanity. I had just thought he was an egotistical man, with a bad temper and a coke problem. I thought I had been forgotten by him long ago replaced with a long stream of unfortunate women since, queuing to take my place by his side, as defensively clueless as I was. I had been wrong.

Poor Andy. He had taken his life; the life of a young innocent man. He hadn't even met Brad before and he had died because of his involvement with me. I replayed Brad's words in my head. "If you weren't such a little whore he'd still be alive." Perhaps he was right? If I wasn't so bloody stupid, so frivolous and obsessed with fun, maybe I wouldn't be such a strong magnet for dysfunctional men? Maybe Andy would still be here? It should have been me who was killed. Not Andy. I deserved to die, not him. It wasn't fair. I wished that I had gone home when I'd had the chance and not been so foolish. I felt a tear rolling down my face, being pulled by gravity towards the floor as I lay sideways facing Brad's body. Even in death he looked handsome. How could I have been so wrong about him? What the hell was wrong with me?

It felt like I had been there for years, but the clock on the wall told me otherwise. I listened to its ticking, the only noise to be heard over the deadly silence. The puddle by Brad's head was spreading wider now, its colour getting deeper, darker. Still I was unable to move.

I was awoken from my trance like state by a banging on the door.

"Ria! It's me. Are you there? Ria!"

Eddie was hammering on the other side of it hysterically. I slowly picked myself up from my position, and dazed, wandered over to the door, unbolting it. Eddie pushed it open, burst in and grabbed me. "Oh my God," he said. "What the fuck happened?"

Unable to speak I merely turned and pointed to the crumpled body on the floor, the moonlight reflecting off the dark pool of blood surrounding it. Eddie's mouth dropped open in shock at the sight of Brad laying there, the champagne bottle next to him.

"He was trying to kill me," I cried.

"Fuck," Eddie muttered at the scene before his eyes. "Come here." He pulled me into his arms and held me. I felt like I needed to cry, but still no tears came. His arms enveloped me; his warmth slowing down the rapidity of my trembling body.

"We need to call the police," he said eventually.

"What if they take me away?" I replied, petrified at the thought of it. I was unable to face what had just happened. All I wanted was to crawl into bed in a pair of pyjamas, and wrap myself in a duvet until I woke up and everything was back to normal.

"He was trying to kill you! It will be alright." He started pacing up and down nervously, and jumped as the light from a car's headlights shone in, illuminating the room for a split second before carrying on into the night. "No we definitely need to call them," he said.

"I can't," I replied. "I can't do it."

"Yeah well, it'll look better if you do it I think. Just do it Ria. It will be okay I promise. You just tell them what he did. I am here for you."

Without the energy to argue, I reluctantly agreed. "Okay."

The next thing I knew Eddie had dialled zero, zero, zero, and I could hear the sound of the ring coming from my mobile as he handed it to me. I slowly raised it to my ear.

"You have dialled emergency triple zero. Your call is being connected," said a recorded message and shortly after I heard the voice of a woman pick up the call.

"Emergency services, do you require the police, fire or ambulance service?"

"I don't know. Police, and an ambulance maybe, but I think he is dead."

"Who is dead Miss?" said the concerned sounding voice on the other end of the line.

"My ex-boyfriend." My heart was racing so fast that it felt like it would burst out of my chest.

"Okay," said the operator calmly. "I am going to need you to check to see if he is still alive. Can you bend down and see if you can feel a pulse for me."

"No I can't. I can't touch him."

"Look Miss I know it's scary but we need to know if he is alive."

"You don't understand. I killed him. I think I killed him!"

"Ok, now don't panic," the woman replied. "What is your address?"

"It's two hundred and twenty two, Roslyn Street, Flat 4A." I willed myself to display some kind of emotion, to sob uncontrollably; anything to make me look innocent. However I was still numb. Numb and weak.

"He tried to kill me," I told her, in case she thought I was some kind of psycho murderer. "He was strangling me and I hit him on the head."

"Okay Miss, we are dispatching an ambulance and police crew to you now. It should only be a few minutes." I felt Eddie's arms around me and my body trembling next to his.

"Are they coming?" he asked.

"Yeah," I replied flatly, dropping the phone on the floor.

"It's gonna be okay. Don't worry. You just tell them he was attacking you and it will be fine."

"He killed Andy!" I told him, pulling away, the tears finally forming. "He killed Andy!"

"It's okay," he said soothingly. "I'm here now, he can't hurt you again."

Within minutes a myriad of blue flashing lights arrived on the scene, streaming into the dark sitting room, lighting up the walls around me. Then a uniformed officer came, handcuffed me, and began leading me into the back of a windowless van.

"Ria Kimura, I am arresting you on suspicion of murder. You are not obliged to say or do anything unless you wish to do so, but whatever you say or do may be used in evidence. Do you understand?"

I looked up and realised that I recognised the policewoman. It was the same one who had come into Flirt to question me about Andy. Her face was as cold as stone, her voice callous as she told me my rights and she shoved me into the dark, windowless pit in the back of the police vehicle. I placidly followed her direction and watched as the vivid flashing blue on the outside street was replaced by darkness as the van doors slammed behind me with a bang.

I could hear Eddie outside arguing with the officers but was unable to make out what he was saying and then there was a sudden jolt as the officers climbed in front, the engine was fired up, and we began our jerky way to the station, while I sat in the back trying to keep my balance wondering how on earth it had come to this?

CHAPTER THIRTY-SEVEN

It seemed like an eternity to the police station in Kings Cross, when in actual fact it was only round the corner. I felt like a caged animal in the back of the dark police van. After a bumpy ride, the journey came to an end and I waited patiently for the police to unlock the back of the van and let me out. As the door opened the light streamed in, so bright and un-natural I squinted to take in my surroundings.

The first thing I saw was Detective Harlow's sour face. Under her steely glare, I felt like a germ being inspected under a microscope. She and Detective Mikos were stood in front of me and I stared back in bewilderment at the events that had just unfolded.

"Get out," she barked. I cautiously navigated myself through the back of their meat wagon; my unsteadiness worsened by my tightly cuffed hands. I got the distinct impression that Harlow detested me and even if I had just been fighting off Ted Bundy for survival she wouldn't have believed me. She grabbed my arm impatiently and yanked me out so roughly, even Detective Mikos looked surprised. Like a wounded deer caught in the headlights, I followed her direction as I was ushered into a cell.

"I haven't done anything," I cried. "He attacked me. He tried to kill me and he killed Andy."

Neither reacted to my pleas, Mikos swung closed a barred door, leaving me alone in the tiny whitewashed cell in the station. I curled up on its wooden bench and sobbed silently, what little energy I had left expended on my tears. I couldn't believe they hadn't even let me make a statement; surely I was entitled to put forward my side of the story? As far as they saw it though, I was just a cheap stripper with a drinking problem; my victim an upstanding businessman with a respectable reputation that preceded him in the state.

I lay on the hard bench in silence, overcome with exhaustion, grief, and shock. I waited for further signs of any development apprehensively, wishing that my family were there to support me and that they weren't so far away. I needed help.

After what seemed like an eternity, Detective Mikos and Harlow returned, the sound of their footsteps echoing in the polished corridors. They peered in through the metal bars and I sat up from my position.

"We are going to be taking you in for questioning soon. You have a right to seek legal assistance and to make a phone call." Detective Mikos watched for my reaction, looking sympathetically at the bruises on my face. It was the first time I had actually even thought about the damage Brad may have done to me, and I instantly became aware of the heat coming from my throbbing temple and the soreness of my neck.

"Can I have a cigarette?" I asked, in desperate need of something to calm me down.

"I suppose, quickly," Detective Harlow warned. I held out my arms and noticed they were covered in blue bruises, as my hands were re-cuffed.

I was led into the back room and handed a cigarette. I clumsily fumbled with the lighter for a flame and watched as the end grew amber. A deep sense of relief hit me as the smoke permeated my lungs; I inhaled deeply, the nicotine rush made me feel lightheaded and sick.

Frantically I searched my mind for someone who could help me. With all my relatives on the other side of the world there were few available options, and I had a strong suspicion that Eddie had probably been arrested too after I had heard him shouting at my arrest. My mind went blank and then I had an epiphany. Diane. She was the only one I could turn to.

"I want to make a call," I informed the officers as they returned.

"We've got to take some photos and prints first, and then we will be taking you to a proper cell. I've got a feeling you will be here for a while," Harlow answered smugly, a vindictive tone in her voice.

She stood me against a wall and I flinched as some hot white lights flashed into my swollen eyes and my mug shot was taken, probably the ugliest photo I have ever had in my life, the contours of my white swollen face probably now resembling the features of the Elephant Man. Detective Harlow threw me an icy glare, then grabbed me by the wrist and began pressing my fingers against a computer screen, scanning them one by one, finishing off the procedure by swabbing the inside of my mouth for my DNA.

She took me to a room further down the corridor. "We are going to perform a strip search on you now," said a butch looking female officer as I entered it. "Please remove your clothes," she said with an air of nonchalance.

"What?" I protested. "I've just been through hell and back and now you want to examine my body!"

"It's standard procedure."

"Thought you would have been used to it by now," Harlow sneered.

I started to remove my clothing bit by bit, a feeling of shame washing over me as the two women sat opposite in silence, scrutinising my body under the unflattering glare of the linear ceiling lights.

"Right then open your mouth," the officer ordered, shining a flash light into it. "Now raise your arms please."

I obliged, wanting the ordeal to be over with and to have the comforting feel of my clothes against my skin again. I grimaced as the officer instructed me to bend over, shining the flash light in between my legs. Then satisfied that my dignity had been successfully stripped, they passed me a bag of clothes to change back into.

"We'll be needing these for evidence," Detective Harlow stated, as she placed my clothes into a polythene bag and watched as I clumsily redressed.

"I would like that phone call now," I demanded. Surely it was a basic entitlement? I had watched enough movies and crime programmes to know my rights. Harlow reluctantly led me to a phone, standing metres away while my finger tapped against its metal key pad hurriedly.

The pay phone in the corridor rang, and I clutched firmly on to its receiver, willing Diane to answer. It was almost five in the morning, hours since my arrest, and I felt desperate and tired. I was about to give up and ring my mum instead, when I heard a muffled, "hello," on the other end of the line, causing my heart to leap.

"Diane?" I said, the emotion rising in my throat at the sound of her familiar voice.

"Who's this?" she asked, obviously still half asleep and trying to come to her senses.

"It's me Diane, it's Pearl. I'm sorry to disturb you but I am in big trouble. Something happened when I came home from work last night." I heard her gasp; she instantly sounded jolted out of her reverie.

"What happened? Are you okay darl?"

"No Diane," I cried, tears streaming down my face, the seriousness of the situation becoming all the more apparent as I shared it with her. "My ex-boyfriend Brad was waiting for me when I got home last night."

"What did he do? Did he hurt you darl?" she asked, her voice panic stricken at my revelation.

"He tried to kill me," I said, struggling with the words as I choked on my own tears. "He...he...he killed my friend Andy, the one I went travelling with." I was stammering now as I tried to tell her what had happened in between gasps of air, my shoulders shaking as the grief flooded out of me.

"Oh no!" she cried. "Where are you?"

"I am at Kings Cross police station. I... I...I killed him Diane. I was trying to get him off me. I didn't mean to do it."

"Of course you didn't," she agreed. "Listen, don't worry. I am on my way over there now with my lawyer. We will sort this out."

"Thanks Diane," I replied, feeling slightly relieved to have someone to fight my corner. Then hanging up the phone I turned to see Detective Mikos and Harlow standing watching me with their hands on their hips.

They led me back to the cell, throwing me a thin blanket. As awful as it was being in the cold police station, at least here I was safe. Wrapping the cover around me tightly, I shivered beneath it, my body finally relenting as I was submerged into sleep by my exhaustion.

*

Diane hung up the phone and her manicured hand trembled as she replaced the receiver.

"What's up Di?" came her husband's voice from behind her. Standing in his boxers by the doorway to their extravagant living room, he had come to investigate when he had heard his wife's anxious voice on the phone. "Who was that?"

"It was Pearl, she's in trouble at the police station. She has just been arrested for killing her ex-boyfriend." Dave groaned at the news, and put his arm around his wife.

"My God. What the hell happened?"

"He was attacking her Dave," Diane answered defensively. "He was trying to kill her. Luckily she killed him first."

"What does she want you to do about it then?" He was growing sick of his wife burdening the problems of her dancers. Abusive boyfriends, drugs, unplanned pregnancies and now murder! Diane always seemed to be the first person they turned to. Their dramas were infesting their lives.

"She has no one over here to help her. I am going find a lawyer and get down to the station. Where's my diary?" She was noticeably shaking now, her body trembling in her silk dressing gown as she searched their desk, pulling out drawers frantically.

"Diane, it's not our business. You are not responsible for the welfare of the girls. It's not up to you to save them." Dave blocked her path, determined to stop her.

"Yes but she is different Dave. She's not like the others. She told me that he attacked her a while ago and I did nothing. I should have made her report it then."

"Would you listen to yourself woman," Dave said agitatedly. "It's not your fault, it's not your responsibility." He put his hands on her arms now in an attempt to make her still, calm; to make her see sense.

"The girls need me Dave don't you understand? They need me and I am not going to turn my back on them!" She continued with her rifling, getting increasingly aggravated by the second as she hunted for her vitally important possession.

"I need you Diane! I need you. I am your bloody husband." Dave was shouting now passionately, trying to deter her from continuing with her mission.

Diane stared at him in disbelief. Why was he being so selfish, when there was a young frightened girl who really needed her? "You are just being childish," she declared, brushing off his outburst and continuing with her search.

"Seriously Diane. Why do you feel the need to save them all so much? How about us? Does saving your marriage mean nothing to you?"

"Look Dave, this is me. I am the woman you married. I am compassionate and caring and that is why you fell for me in the first place. I care for her, and that's all you need to know. Why can't you just help me?" She was shrieking now, her perfect mane looking almost wild for once as blond strands of hair danced around her face while she hurried around their house, her silk dressing gown billowing behind her like a regal cape.

"No Diane!" Dave shouted back, not backing down. "I won't have it this time. That club has taken over our lives. I've had enough!"

She paused for a moment and turned towards him. "Are you giving me an ultimatum?" she replied coolly.

"Yes, I am," he said, abruptly remembering that Diane wasn't the kind of woman that took kindly to being controlled.

"Well in that case, I suggest you pack your bags, because if I have to choose between a man who wants to control me and being in control of my own life, then I will choose living my life by my rules every time." Diane's chest was heaving as she spat out her words, not even entertaining his demand for a second.

Dave's demeanour sunk back at the realisation he had pushed her too far this time. He loved Diane; all he had ever wanted was for them to make a life with each other. But living with such a strong woman was no good for any man's pride. He had had enough of being second best; of being talked over at their dinner parties while she stole the spotlight with her witty conversation and alluring presence; of always being the plus one partner, the after-thought; of being the secondary provider in the household. He realised then that maybe all he wanted was a quiet life, with a woman who would make him feel secure.

"Fine," he replied dejectedly whilst staring at his slippered feet.

"See, you won't even fight for me," she said when she saw his deflated stance. "See that's the difference between me and you Dave.

I'm a fighter and you," she said pointing at him accusingly. "You are just a coaster." Grabbing her leather Filofax from the kitchen side, she waved it triumphantly, another sign that his presence was an expendable surplus in her life. "See, I found it myself. Thanks for your help."

Dave watched helplessly as she darted back up the stairs, and when she was out of sight, he slunk into the living room. He sank onto the sofa with a sigh, wondering if he had ever been good enough for such a spectacular creature, and deciding that next time he might set his sights a bit lower.

CHAPTER THIRTY-EIGHT

Detective Griffwell studied the swollen face of the girl sleeping in the holding cell. She was curled up like a ball on the bench and he could see she was shaking slightly; she looked like she was being tormented with nightmares while she slept. What an ordeal she must have gone through. How had she come out unscathed? Tony remembered the chilling way that Brad had pursued her, and how his threats had caused him to break out into a cold sweat, even over the phone.

His morals and instinctive need for self-preservation were at war; his emotions torn between fear for himself and guilt over his hand in this sordid affair. It was supposed to be his job to prevent this, and the knowledge that he was partly responsible made his skin crawl. Yet despite it all he felt himself secretly wishing for a brief moment that Brad had succeeded in killing her. Then he wouldn't be facing such torment right now. God if only his mother knew what he had become.

It was about three in the morning when the commotion had begun in the station. The Cross was not exactly an uneventful place, but the murder of a notorious business man committed by a lowly stripper was big news. Tony's colleagues had rushed around, the talk spreading like a wild bush fire, and had reached him before she had even been detained. Being the most senior detective on site at the time he had been obliged to check on the progress of the situation, and from the safety of his office he had requested updates; too frightened to emerge from his sanctuary in case the homicide detectives on the case smelt his fear.

"What's the low down?" he asked Detectives Harlow and Mikos, as they came to his office to report the details.

"Ria Kimura, arrested under suspicion of murder. She made a triple zero call at exactly two forty five am this morning. Informing the operator, and I quote, 'he's dead, I think he is dead.' Then she was asked to check his pulse and refused saying; 'I killed him, I think I killed him'." Mikos confidently spouted off the details to him. He had always been an admirer of his work, always looked up to him. His reputation had taken so many years to build and Griffwell realised in that moment that if he lost it all, the lost respect would be the hardest thing to cope with.

"Right," Griffwell said distractedly, "then what?"

Harlow cut in now, her turn to shine for her superior had come and she was revelling in it, her recent promotion as a detective still fresh and causing her to be annoyingly eager.

"We arrived on the scene to find the victim's body on the floor face down. He had been hit on the head twice with a champagne bottle. Ria Kimura was with her boyfriend Eddie Steele who was either there at the time of murder or appeared shortly after. She claims the victim was attacking her and that he killed the missing English traveller, Andrew Wilson as well."

Griffwell nodded, trying to compose himself and act as naturally as he would in any other investigation. It was a hard task though and he finally understood the fear his detainees must experience when getting caught for a crime.

"Her boyfriend is a DJ in the club Flirt that she works in, and he started going crazy when she was arrested. We have detained him also, for suspicion of accessory to murder." She continued talking, firing off the information robotically, while he struggled to digest it. It was lucky that he would be leading the investigation, the chances were that he could deflect any attention away from himself if need be. It would be alright, he reassured himself.

"Does she appear to have been hurt?" he asked, hoping that his former associate hadn't battered her too badly.

"She has a bruise on her left temple, and defence bruises down her forearms. Other than that, no visible marks," Mikos said.

"I see, well I want you to question her as soon as possible. We need to start building a case against her if we are going to formerly charge her. Sounds like we may be looking at a man slaughter case rather than first degree murder though," he informed his colleague. Harlow opened her mouth to protest and he raised his hand to silence her. "Judging by the evidence so far, he appeared in her flat, died from a couple of blows to the head, and had been attacking her."

"I don't know sir," Harlow protested. "Her last boyfriend disappeared, this one she killed. What's to say she didn't have a hand in Andrew Wilson's disappearance as well? That DJ boyfriend of hers is a shady character as well; he could be involved too. We need to look at all the possibilities."

"With all due respect, I don't need to be reminded by you how to do my job. I didn't get to where I am from just having a pretty face you know." Griffwell snapped impatiently at his colleague; she seemed determined to bring the girl down. She looked wounded by his comment. "Just get her in that interrogation room as soon as possible. Make sure the submission form is sorted and her prints are done."

"Yes sir," she replied flatly. The detectives gently closed the door behind them as they strode back to continue with their investigation.

God the young blood of the force, Griffwell thought bitterly. So enthusiastic, so hungry for action and arrests. She would realise sooner or later that she was fighting a lost cause.

When he felt certain they had gone, Mikos decided to go and inspect the damage for himself. He walked over to the holding cells and stared in at the girl. She looked irritatingly innocent. What was he going to do with her? How should he approach this whole thing? He felt torn, his guilty conscience instinctively making him want to help her get off with it; but if he did that he would have to build a case to prove that Brad was an unstable character capable of murder. If it was discovered that Brad did kill Andrew then that could lead the investigation back onto his own doorstep. The other detectives would want to know how Brad had found them, which could open a whole new can of worms and be detrimental to his own concealment.

However if he collected enough evidence and doubt against her to make people believe she was guilty of killing Brad and involved in the disappearance of Andrew, then maybe he would be safe? Perhaps he could leave this whole thing behind him with his integrity and honour intact? It was going to be very tricky; he knew he would have to play it very carefully indeed. One thing was for sure though; if he ever managed to get through this unscathed then he would retire from the force as soon as possible. He felt like running away from it now with the urgency one might feel from escaping from a burning building. He just had to stick this one out, to see it through to the end. He could see the finish line in sight, complete with cocktail umbrellas, white sandy beaches, and his beautiful wife lying next to him. Just one more case. Just one more.

Hours later I woke up. My body ached and I groaned as I lifted myself up from the hard bench. Taking in my surroundings I was horrified to see that I was alone in an empty cell; it really had happened. I had killed Brad, it hadn't been a nightmare. A whirlwind of despair churned through me making me feel sick and disorientated, and I was startled when I saw two figures peering through the bars; quietly observing me.

"Ria darl, it's me Diane."

"Diane," I cried, rising to my feet and rushing over to her.

"I'm Grant Peterson," said the man next to her, holding out a slender hand to shake mine through the gaps in the door.

I held my hand out to meet his and he shook it forcefully, a confident powerful shake which made my arm feel limp and weak in comparison. "Diane has asked me to represent you," he informed me, whilst peering at me through silver-rimmed spectacles.

"He is the best in the business darl," Diane added. "We are going to get you out of here."

I inspected the man who had been given the thankless task of getting me out of this hell hole. His willowy frame towered above Diane, and he was dressed in a dark grey suit which was doing a good job of not swamping his malnourished looking frame. His physique certainly didn't look very strong or imposing, but his body language said otherwise as he forcefully ordered the police officer standing by him to, "open the cell so I can speak to my client properly."

The officer unbolted the door at his order. "I have been briefed on the case and the evidence so far," he informed me when the cell door was no longer imposing a barrier between us. "We have been granted some time to talk before you are questioned."

"Thank you Diane," I said feeling so relieved to have someone to help.

"Come along," he said, "we don't have long." He marched ahead, his authoritative stalking of the corridors causing any passing police officers to instinctively move out of his way, and Diane and I scurried behind him struggling to keep up. He stopped abruptly when we reached a small office and ushered us in, quickly closing the door behind us and gesturing for us to sit at the desk in the centre of the room, before seating himself next to Diane. It was the same room I had sat in not long ago when I had been questioned on the whereabouts of Andy. Back then I had been hopeful he would come back, but now it was clear that he would never return. The image of his smiling face flashed in my mind causing a stabbing pain in my heart as I sadly acknowledged the awful truth; that his sweet smile would never grace the world again.

"Now Ria, Diane has told me about you and I have been informed by the police of the circumstances of your arrest. Firstly let me begin by ascertaining your personal wellbeing. Have you had any food or drink since your arrest?"

"Erm no," I replied hesitantly, "but I haven't been hungry."

"Right well that's the first thing we need to do. We can't have you being interrogated when you are exhausted and haven't even had so much as a drink of water."

"Here darl," Diane said, putting a paper bag in front of me. "I brought you a sandwich and a coffee, thought you might be needing something." I pursed my lips together and attempted to smile as I took her offering, delicately sipping the cold sweet coffee through the slit in its plastic lid. The sandwich remained untouched folded in a greasy white napkin. Food was the last thing I could stomach.

"Right," he continued with a business like tone. "How long have you slept for?"

"I don't know since about five probably," I replied, unsure of the time.

"Okay well you've had a couple of hours then which they will argue is adequate. Any mistreatment of any sort?"

"No," I replied unsure of what qualified as being mistreatment, before quickly deciding that a few snide comments about me being a stripper from Detective Harlow probably didn't compensate.

"Fine," he stated. "Now I need you to tell me your version of events. What happened when you came home last night?"

"Brad was waiting for me in my flat."

"So he broke into your apartment and was waiting for you to return with the intention of hurting you?"

"Yes," I said, reaffirming my statement.

"Then what happened?"

"He grabbed me over the mouth so I couldn't scream and he said; 'you left without saying good bye bitch'."

"Yes, continue," he urged, whilst clicking on the end of his silver pen and scribbling notes in a black leather binder.

"Then he threw me on the floor. I was so scared. I hadn't seen him for months, I thought he had forgotten all about me but obviously he hadn't. I told him I was sorry, and he said I disgusted him. Then when I asked him what he was doing in my flat he told me he had missed me. I didn't know what to do so I said I'd missed him too, and he burst out crying. I was trying to comfort him, to calm him down. He grabbed hold of me so tight I could hardly breathe."

"Right so he was very emotional, very threatening in his behaviour. Then what?"

"He suddenly turned again. Told me I was a whore; that he knew I had been with other men. I denied it, but he told me. He told me it wasn't the first time he had tracked me down. When I asked him what he meant, he told me that he had found me before and that, and that he killed Andy." I felt a lump rise in my throat, my disturbing admission causing me to relive the terror of the night before. Undisturbed by my statement, Grant simply nodded. I felt Diane's hand grabbing on to mine as my voice began to wobble with emotion.

"When you say Andy, you mean Andrew Wilson, the boy who went missing a couple of months ago?"

"Yes," I replied. "Then he knocked me down on the floor again." I felt tears rolling down my face as it dawned on me what a lucky escape I'd had.

"How did he knock you? Did he hit you?"

"Yes."

"Where did he hit you?"

"Here on my face," I said whilst gesturing to the swollen mound of flesh on my temple.

"With a closed fist?"

"Yes."

"And then what did he do?" Grant Peterson nodded ferociously; causing his thinning grey hair to become dishevelled from the carefully concealed bald patch on the crest of his head. His face possessed a look of intense concentration as he soaked in the information like a sponge.

"He told me he killed him and not to worry because I would soon be joining him. Then he started strangling me." I felt Diane's hand squeeze mine tighter as my painful tale reached its crescendo. "I, I, couldn't breathe. I tried to push him off but he was too strong. He was crushing my neck. I felt a bottle next to me, and then," I paused as I tried to regain the strength to continue, choking back my tears.

"Yes?" he urged, a frown creasing together the lines on his narrow forehead.

"And then I hit him on the head with it. He started to get back up, so I hit him again." I took a deep breath, my windpipe felt tight and sore; the panic rising as I remembered Brad's big muscular hands wrapping round my neck.

"When I looked, I saw he wasn't moving. I didn't know what to do. Then I saw all the blood. That's when I knew," I said struggling to dispel the words though my tears. "That's when I knew I had killed him!"

I glanced over at Diane who looked like she was about to start crying too at my distressing tale. "Oh sweetheart," she said. "It's going to be alright. You're safe now."

I wept, my emotion and fatigue making me feel dizzy.

"Look," Grant said firmly, causing me to take a break from my hysteria for just long enough to catch the gaze from his impenetrable, steely blue eyes and see the determination in them. "What Diane said is right. I am the best in the business and I am going to do everything in my power to get you out of here."

I felt myself relax slightly as I heard the tenure in his voice. "However," he continued, causing my stomach to lurch. "Brad was a very successful man, very well respected and powerful. You on the other hand are just a stripper. Now they are going to try to sully your name as much as they can to make you look like you killed him in cold blood. They are already trying to link you with the disappearance of Andrew Wilson."

I gulped in response, horrified that they could possibly suspect me of intentionally hurting anyone, let alone Andy.

"Now we are going to have a fight on our hands here so I am going to need you to be cooperative. Don't let your emotions get the better of you during their interrogations, don't say anything which they could use to implicate that you are a bad character, and lastly and most importantly of all, don't ignore any of my advice."

I listened silently to his instruction. It was up to me now. I felt some of my fight return like a rush of blood to the head. I couldn't allow myself to go down for defending myself; he would have killed me if I hadn't fought him off. Surely they would see it was a mistake?

"Now we are going to need you to be physically examined by a doctor. If we are pleading self-defence then we are going to need as much evidence as possible to prove that he was attacking you. In fact I am appalled they haven't done so already," he said sounding convincingly shocked. "Now we are going to go in for questioning at any minute. Just remember, do as I say and you should be alright."

I nodded passively; glad to have someone else taking the reins of the beast I was riding. I took another sip of the cold syrupy coffee before me in the hope it would give me some much needed energy to survive my next battle.

CHAPTER THIRTY-NINE

I felt my chest tighten as I anxiously waited for the questioning to begin.

"I am Detective Inspector Griffwell," said a man, before seating himself opposite me. He was quite handsome, tall, with light brown hair, probably in his mid-forties, and possessed a more friendly tone to his voice than his harsh colleagues. I lifted my head wearily as I looked at him, feeling slightly relieved I was not going to be interrogated by Harlow. "I am going to be leading this investigation," he explained.

I grunted in response, trying to preserve what little energy I had left for avoiding imprisonment for the rest of my life.

"Well before we continue," he said whilst pushing back his brown hair from his eyes. "I need to remind you that we have arrested you on the suspicion of the murder of Brad Harrison. You are not obliged to say or do anything unless you wish to do so, but whatever you say or do may be used in evidence. Do you understand?"

"Yes."

"Is there anything I can get you before we proceed?" he asked. I groaned with disappointment as I saw Harlow walk back into the room, displaying the air of a terrier about to catch a rabbit.

"Yes please. Could I have a tea please, milk and two sugars?"

"No problem." He instructed Harlow back out of the room to get it and she scowled in response. A few moments later she was back, and slammed a weak cup of tea in front of me resembling brown dish water. I wondered if she had spat in it while she had been out there. She seated herself next to him quickly, eager to not miss anything no doubt.

"Can we get you anything else?" he asked.

"Yeah. A gun so I can put myself out of my misery."

"Like you put Brad out of his misery you mean?" Harlow hissed at me from across the table. My lawyer shot her a warning look.

"I didn't shoot Brad," I retorted.

"Oh of course, I forgot," she snapped. "How about a champagne bottle instead?"

"I don't think that's necessary," Grant protested.

"Look Ria, you are facing some very serious charges here," said Detective Griffwell. "Very serious indeed. Now Brad Harrison was a very well respected man. So why did you decide to kill him?"

"I didn't decide to. He was trying to kill me, I had no choice. I was just trying to get him off me." Grant looked satisfied at my answer and I felt relieved that I had said the right thing.

"You expect us to believe that he was waiting at your flat with the sole purpose of killing you. Now why would he want to do that?"

"Because I left him."

"You left a multi-millionaire, a man who had whisked you away from your life as a stripper, a man who showered you with gifts and affection. You expect us to believe that?" Harlow said.

"He beat me up. He changed when we came here. I had a night out and I got home and he beat the crap out of me."

"When was that?" Griffwell asked.

"A few months ago," I replied.

"What date exactly?"

"I think it was the fourteenth of January."

"So did you leave him immediately after that then?"

"No I left about a couple of weeks later," I said staring at the table.

"If your boyfriend beat you up, then why would you wait so long before you left him?" Griffwell was staring into my eyes. I shifted uncomfortably under his scrutinizing gaze which was evaluating my every movement. I felt scared to blink out of place and my eyes were stinging as a result.

"Because I was ashamed to show my face. Because I was scared. Because I didn't want anyone to see me that's why." The truth fell out of my mouth easily, but judging by Harlow's expression it was not a plausible enough explanation.

"Or maybe it's because it never happened after all? Maybe you are lying? You know I find it hard to believe a girl of your status would up and leave a man like Brad, even if he did hit you, which I doubt. I think that he dumped you. That you were angry, that you met a young man on your travels and took your rage out on him, and then when you returned to Sydney you finally lured your ex back to your apartment where he rejected you again and you attacked him maliciously, killing him." His voice was stern.

"No. that's not true," I insisted, feeling myself helplessly drowning in their questions.

"So how did you get involved with Brad? You met him at work, isn't that true?"

"Yes," I said, as I recalled the excitement I had felt when I first met him.

"Swept you off your feet, showered you with gifts, treated you like a queen didn't he?" Harlow said and sneered.

"Yes he did."

"Exactly what a girl like you is looking for isn't it? A rich man, that's the ultimate goal for girls like you isn't it?" She spat out the latter part of her sentence, like it was poison on the end of her tongue.

"No actually," I said, growing tired of her constant stereotyping of me. "I worked there while I was at uni, to make money. I was trying to look for a job in fashion when I met Brad. It was a stop gap."

"Right but you just saw an easier alternative when you met Brad?" Griffwell jumped in.

"No actually I loved Brad. I wanted to be with him. He asked me to come with him and I decided I didn't want to lose him."

"So everything was a bed of roses. Then he just beat you up? You expect us to believe that? No one can verify that he was ever violent towards you. You never confided in anyone. No one ever saw so much as a mark on you." Griffwell was cutting me down, hacking at me swiftly like a shear through some reeds and I could feel myself falling. "Brad was an upstanding citizen, not so much as a blemish on his record. Surely if he was a violent man as you would have us believe, then there might be some kind of evidence to back up your claims?"

"Not a zip," Harlow chimed in.

"If what you say is true, then why didn't you tell someone?"

"I did," I said. "I told Diane. I told Eddie. I told Andy."

"Convenient," Griffwell said, pursing his lips unattractively. "If he attacked you as you claim he did, then why not just go home?"

"I wish I had now."

"Seems unlikely an abused woman would want to stick around," he said, accentuating the word abused as if it were as highly unlikely as a snowstorm in the Sahara.

"I wanted to have fun. I didn't want him to get the better of me," I said.

"Well you made sure he didn't in the end didn't you?" Harlow said.

"What I want to know is this Ria," Griffwell said. "Brad was a big guy. He weighed about two hundred pounds. You claim he was strangling you, trying to kill you. All you have is a bit of a bruise on your face and a slight mark on your neck. If a man of his size was trying to kill you, you wouldn't be here now would you?"

"Ria don't answer that," Grant said, practically springing from his chair. "This is all speculation and not based on hard facts." He pointed his index finger at him like it was a loaded gun as he spoke. "You are deliberately putting my client in a corner."

"I am simply pointing out the lack of physical evidence there is to corroborate her story that she killed him in self-defence." Griffwell shot back. He stiffened and turned his attention back towards me.

"Forensics have been into your flat and there was no sign of a break in. Which leads me to believe that you invited him into your home. Isn't that true Ria?"

"No!" I argued. "I hadn't seen him for months. I didn't want to either."

"How did he get in then?"

"I don't know," I said searching my memory for an answer. "Maybe I forgot to lock the door properly." I remembered the large marijuana joint I had smoked just before leaving for work that night. I was about to tell him about it, but abruptly stopped myself. I could have kicked myself under the table. That was it. I had stupidly left my front door unlocked. I felt sick with regret. Another mistake, another way in which my hedonistic lifestyle had led me into trouble. Their questions were like a mirror, reflecting back my thoughtless actions until I felt a sense of shame wash over me.

"So how long did you know Andrew for?" Harlow asked.

"About six weeks."

"He was on his way to Mount Isa to meet his family. Why didn't you want to go with him?" Her eyes shifted over me uncomfortably and I fidgeted to avoid meeting them.

"My money had run out, so I went back to Sydney to work."

"If you had run out of money then why were you staying in a luxury hotel together?" she said bluntly.

"Because I wanted our last few days together to be special."

"I think that you did want to go with him. That he dumped you as well. That you killed him and then got a flight back to Sydney." Her words were calm with a twinge of bitterness hanging off them.

"He dropped me off at the airport for God's sake. Surely there must be a way you can check that? That was the last time I saw him." Their assumptions were causing me to feel frustrated and I felt on edge; my nerves raw.

"Right, well if you are lying then you're right we can verify your claim," Harlow said.

"Do you really think that I am capable of killing someone in cold blood? I really cared about Andy. I was so upset when I heard he had disappeared." I could feel my demeanour weaken further as they bombarded against it, with the brute force of an army wielding a battering ram.

"Yes," Griffwell replied coldly. "We obviously do think you are capable; you wouldn't be here otherwise. So let's get to the bottom of who you really are." He cleared his throat, and edged forward in his chair, closing the distance between us. I shuffled back in my chair, eager to keep my distance.

"So let's see, a girl who is working as a stripper. A heavy drinker who engages in the partaking of drugs regularly."

"Yet more unsubstantiated claims," Grant said.

"Won't be unsubstantiated for much longer, once we have her blood test results back," said Griffwell and I felt my stomach lurch as I realised he was right.

"So, as I was saying. A stripper, meets a millionaire, who sweeps her off her feet. He grows bored of her and dumps her, then she goes off, meets a young man, whom she entangles in her web. He disappears off the face of the earth, and then shortly after she returns to Sydney, where she kills her ex after an altercation in her flat. She conveniently blames the disappearance of her former lover on her now dead ex-boyfriend and defends her violent behaviour by pretending that she was being attacked by him."

I opened my mouth to protest but was stopped by Grant's raised hand. "Don't answer that Ria. This is preposterous." He turned towards Griffwell and pounded the table with his fist. "I object to this battery of my client. You are bullying her."

Griffwell ignored him and continued. "Do you deny that you take drugs?"

"No. I do recreationally. I smoke weed and occasionally do a bit of coke."

"So you admit to being a drug user?"

"Yes," I said reluctantly, knowing the toxicology result would soon prove his accusations were true.

"Must have been hard, losing a man like Brad? Losing his money? Having to go back to work to fund your habit?" His face was hard, unmoving.

"I don't have a habit. I'm not an addict; I can very easily go without!" My palms were sweating, and I realised he was doing a very good job of portraying me to be a druggy stripper.

"What is your relationship with Eddie Steele?" Harlow asked.

"We are friends."

"He seems to think it's a lot more than just a friendship," she said.

"We are close."

"Have you and Eddie ever had sex?"

"Yes," I replied, weakly.

"Another man to add to the list," she said throwing me a look of disgust.

"Have you ever had sex for money?" Griffwell asked me from across the table.

"No!" I exclaimed, horrified at the suggestion.

"Yet you feel quite happy gyrating round naked in front of strangers?" he said, his eyebrow raised.

"There's a difference between dancing and having sex with someone for money." I explained.

"But you used Brad for his money didn't you?" Harlow cut in.

"Ria, don't answer that!" Grant commanded.

"No he used me!" I cried. "I loved him, and he treated me like crap! He was a nasty piece of work, he deserved to fucking die and I'm glad I killed the bastard!"

Harlow and Griffwell exchanged glances at my outburst and I realised that I'd taken it too far. Harlow looked self-satisfied and smug, and Griffwell rose from his seat. "Ria Kimura. I am officially charging you for the murder of Brad Harrison. You are not obliged to say or do anything unless you wish to do so, but whatever you say or do may be used in evidence. Do you understand?"

I felt my heart hammering against my chest, as the whitewalls of the room began to spin around me nauseatingly. "Do you understand?" he repeated.

"Yes," I heard myself reply meekly.

"Interviews over, take her to a proper cell," he said, ushering at Harlow who proceeded to cuff my wrists. My legs wobbled as she began to lead me out of the room.

"No, I didn't mean to do it," I pleaded, as I frantically searched for the face of Griffwell with the false hope that if he saw me now, he would surely be able to see my innocence. However he refused to meet my eyes and promptly turned his attention towards the wall, his face blank and shoulders slumped.

"I didn't mean to do it!" I screamed again. The panic raced through my veins at the realisation I would now be returned to an enclosed, bolted cell for God knows how long. I resigned myself to my fate, sobbing wildly as I was led through the station into the back of the police van again.

"Don't worry," Grant shouted in through the doors before they were closed behind me. "I will get you out of here. I will meet you as soon as I can."

The vehicle jerked to life and began taking me to my next destination. "Please God," I whispered, clutching my hands together

tightly. "Please help me get through this. Please help me to be strong."
I instinctively put my hands to my neck to reach for the angel pendant
Aia had given me and realised it was gone. I felt so alone.

CHAPTER FORTY

The sound of phlegm being repeatedly coughed up from the back of my cellmate's throat and being spat on the floor had alarmed me at first. After days of listening to it though, as frequent as the sound of a tick on a clock, it was becoming unnoticed, like the sound of traffic would after a few months of living by a main road. Still, one would definitely prefer to be woken by the sound of birdsong, just another reminder of the hell I was now living in.

It felt like I had been there for years. Unfortunately for me it had only been five days. Five days of being confined, of having no privacy, of having to pee and crap in front of strangers, and sleep on the bottom bunk, all the while hoping that the Aboriginal girl on the top wasn't going to climb down and slit my throat in the night. She didn't talk. She had never said a word to me. All she did was cough up phlegm, and I spent most of my time hoping that it wouldn't land on me. I don't know how she managed to do it but it was obvious she was on something. Whatever it was, it seemed to be preserving her from attacking me in a narcotic fuelled come down, and so I thanked my lucky stars that she was in plentiful supply and kept my fingers crossed that she wouldn't run out.

I could scarcely imagine what would become of me if I was found guilty of Brad's murder. Even a day inside was tortuous and dragged at the pace of a snail, while I was left alone with only my own thoughts to keep me company. Only the hope of getting out was preserving my sanity. I didn't know what the girl in my cell was in for, and I wondered if she had possessed the same vacuous air in her black eyes when she had arrived, or if years being in and out of prison had driven her to her unhinged state. When I had first been thrown in the cell I had asked myself how the hell I had ended up sharing the same fate as someone like her, but now I wondered if perhaps we had more in common than I'd previously thought? Maybe I would end up like her; I couldn't imagine anything more harrowing.

The impending day of judgement was looming over me, casting a shadow over my future which could inevitably destroy my life with one fail swoop. I felt certain of one thing, and that was I couldn't endure a life sentence, the thought of a year incarcerated was bad enough. I suddenly understood where the expression 'rotting away in jail' came from, because I felt like I was rotting already, from my core outwards.

Bail had been denied, and I had wept openly in the stand at the deliverance of the judge, the prospect of being held in custody until the hearing, a daunting prospect. The date had been set for mid-September. It was only the second of June.

Still one thought comforted me as I sat on the creaky bunk bed, watching my cell mate pacing and spitting simultaneously; I was going to be seeing my mum today. One shred of light to grasp on to, one reason to wake up for. Not long now until visiting time. I wondered what she would say, whether she would be angry with me. I hoped my family would be alright and not completely in pieces at the news.

I was disturbed from my thoughts by the sound of a guard clearing her throat in announcement of her presence.

"You've got a visitor," she said, and unlocked the door.

I got up from my spot and she led the way. I paced behind her eagerly, so fast that the brick walls became a blur as every step got me closer to her. It had only been six months since I had seen her but I felt like I had become a different person.

We arrived at the visiting hall and I scanned the room longingly until I saw her. She was sitting at a table in the visiting room, her eyes fixed upon the doorway anxiously.

"Ria," she cried upon my arrival and I burst into tears at the sight of her familiar, tender face.

"Mum," I cried back and she hugged me, with so much intensity that I felt like I was being drowned by her love.

I released myself from her grasp as I remembered the resolution I had made myself to conceal my emotions from my prison peers. I could feel their steely eyes on me, seeking out my weaknesses like metal detectors.

She instinctively understood the reasoning behind my actions and contained herself also; swallowing back her tears as we both seated ourselves.

She studied me worriedly. "You look sick," she announced.

"I feel sick." The admission seemed to unsettle her further and I felt a stab of guilt as I remembered the upset this situation was causing my whole family.

"I didn't mean to do it Mum," I said, searching her face for any sign of doubt. The notion that she might not believe me was unbearable and more than I could deal with.

"I know you didn't," she said soothingly, dispelling my fears. "You're my daughter, and I love you no matter what, always." Her voice wobbled with emotion and she paused briefly, attempting again to contain the volcano of tears threatening to erupt from her eyes as I dabbed at my own.

After we had both successfully controlled our desire to sob uncontrollably she continued. "I knew there was something not right about that man," she said, her anguish transforming into anger. "I couldn't put my finger on it. I knew you wouldn't listen to me though so I kept my mouth shut. I wish I hadn't now. I should never have let you come here."

"Mum, it's not your fault. I would have come anyway, no matter what you said. I loved him; I thought he was a decent guy."

"Well he had us all fooled," she said, stroking my hand. "Why didn't you tell us that he hurt you?" She sounded hurt that I had excluded her from my pain; that she'd had to learn the story from Diane and not from her own daughter.

"I don't know Mum. I felt like such a disgrace, I couldn't even look at myself after it happened. I just felt like such a failure. I didn't want anyone to know about it." I hung my head in shame. Shame at what had happened, shame at my concealment of the events which had led me to this nightmare. I wished that I'd had the courage to have told her now; maybe confiding in my family would have made me come to my senses and gone home.

"You're not a failure," she reassured me and squeezed my hand tightly. "You are a strong, beautiful girl. It's going to be okay."

"What if I end up being locked up here forever Mum?" I gasped, my lip trembling with fear.

"That's not going to happen." She looked at me determinedly with her warm brown eyes. "Here. I got you something to keep you safe." She placed a figurine of an angel into the palm of my hand. It was made of rose quartz, and I could feel the warmth radiating from it after being clasped in my mother's grip for so long.

"Thanks Mum," I said, clasping it tightly.

"They said I could give it to you. Your dad is watching out for you too, don't ever forget it. And here, I got you some books as well, keep your mind busy." I nodded, still struggling to keep the floodgates from opening. I looked away and wondered what my dad would have made of the whole sorry situation. I caught a glimpse of a stocky girl staring sadistically in my direction out of the corner of my eye, and quickly turned my attention back towards the angel.

"What are you going to do then?" I asked, as I considered the upheaval that her absence must be having on my family. "Are you staying here now?"

"I am here indefinitely. Nanny's holding the forte at home. You need me. Everyone sends their love. We all just want you out of here." I breathed a sigh of relief as I felt the reinforcement of my family taking some of the burden of worry from my painfully hunched shoulders.

"Has it been on the news in England?" I asked as I reflected on the numerous reports there had been in the Sydney papers that Diane had brought in for me.

"Brad Harrison, murdered by stripper," the Sydney Morning Herald's headline had read. *"Respected business man bludgeoned to death with champagne bottle,"* had been on the cover of another. I imagined my old friends and acquaintances back home, gossiping about me over similar sensationalised headlines, anyone who had ever disliked me, relishing the thought of my dramatic incarceration in a

foreign prison, excited by the prospect of my demise.

"Not really," she said.

"Thank God." I exclaimed, in relief.

"Well people don't know him in England so it's not big news." I wondered if she was lying to make me feel better but the outside world felt so distant I decided to forget it.

"So where are you staying?" I asked.

"Diane kindly offered to put me up, so I am there at the moment. We are having regular meetings with your lawyer Mr Peterson to try to see what we can do to help." She looked perplexed as she continued. "The police seem very uncooperative though. We have pleaded with them that you didn't mean to do it. That he killed that Andrew boy, but the detective seems unwilling to even listen to the possibility that Brad's death was an accident."

I felt defeated as I was reminded of the single-minded nature in which my case was being dealt with. Every time I was questioned I felt like the detectives were less interested in the truth, and more in conspiring to place the blame on me and to make me look as guilty as possible. It was frustrating, whenever they interviewed me, I felt like I was being backed into a corner. They were like vultures circling their prey, pecking away at my version of events persistently, their questions shredding my resolve until my inexperience and volatility of emotions eventually caused me to give them the reaction they were hunting for. Anything they could use to highlight an unflattering facet of my character they did. It was exhausting.

"They hate me Mum. They just think I am some crazy druggy stripper who attacked him on purpose."

"Well don't you worry about it. Grant is working very hard to get you out of here. He is a very brilliant man, and very determined. He is regularly getting updates on the investigation and building your case. You just need to stay strong."

"Any new developments?" I asked, anxious for some good news.

"Well," she said, tightening her mouth into a false smile. "He has been finding character witnesses, people who can shed some light on the kind of man Brad was."

"Anything?"

"We are trying to speak to some of his ex-girlfriends, to see if he ever attacked them. So far though, none of them have been prepared to make a statement." I glanced down, unable to conceal my disappointment at her news.

"Is there anyone you can think of who might have seen you after he attacked you? Anyone at all?" She looked at me in desperation, as she tried to conjure up any recollections which could help with my case. I searched my mind, feeling at a loss.

"No one," I said morosely. "I hid away in his apartment afterwards for weeks after it happened. I didn't want anyone to see me. Neither did he." I berated myself once more for my foolishness.

"Yes I'm sure he didn't the bastard," she said, her maternal instincts stirring up her anger again.

"Oh Mum. It's no use is it? I'm going to end up banged up in this shit hole with all these nutters, on the other side of the world from everyone I love."

"No you're not. Don't you dare say that. We're going to get you out of here. You are innocent. That bastard was stalking you; he was trying to kill you. You did what you had to do, what anyone else would have done in the same situation." The conviction in her voice bolstered up my spirits and I searched my mind again for anything which could help my case. Just then I had a thought; an epiphany which emerged from my clouded mind. I couldn't believe that I hadn't remembered it sooner.

"Oh my God!" I cried urgently, causing the guard to jump and look at me suspiciously. "I had a camera. I had a camera, a disposable one!"

"Yes?"

"I took some photos of myself with it, the day after he beat me up. Oh my God I remember now. I woke up and looked at myself in the mirror, and I took some photos of my bruises." I shuddered as an image of myself standing in front of a mirror, surveying the aftermath of his destruction flashed through my mind. However, as painful as the memory was I realised it might well be my saving grace.

"Where is it?"

"I don't know," I said, searching my memory again.

"Think!"

"Urm," I said, fumbling for an answer.

"Well when did you last have it?" she snapped, as annoyed at my

213

carelessness as I was.

After a long pause I replied. "The last time I had it was at the Japanese night at Flirt. It must still be there. Oh my God Mum. This will prove that he was violent. That I was protecting myself."

"We need to find it," she said. "Right, I will go to Flirt with Diane. We will turn the place upside down to look for it. It has to be somewhere. I will ask that Eddie guy to help as well. Maybe you left it there."

"Excuse me, but visiting time is over now, time to go back to your room." A prison warden stood over us interrupting our time together, and I clung to my mother's hand, reluctant to let go. We stood up slowly and I fought the urge to cling to her and weep like a baby.

"Be strong. I love you," she said. "We are getting you out of here."

"I will," I replied.

"I'll come back as soon as I can. Don't worry, it will all work out, I know it will." She gave me a quick hug which was interrupted by the prison officer, and with that I was led out of the visiting room to my cell while my mother stood watching helplessly. Back to the company of my deranged cellmate and the sound of her expectorating, although this time with a renewed sense of faith, and a small crystal angel to keep me safe.

CHAPTER FORTY-ONE

I got out of the shower and wrapped myself in a towel, thoughts of my upcoming case haunting me. It had been a few days since my mother's visit, and I hoped that the next time I saw her she would have some good news. So far though it seemed my chances of being found not guilty were extremely slim. I had previously been unaware of the power and respect Brad and his family possessed, it felt like I was swimming against the tide. It seemed that the world was against me, every paper I read seemed to portray Brad as some kind of charitable hero, and me as a washed up stripper who had vindictively taken his life. Brad's parents were desperate for my prosecution to the point where I wouldn't have been surprised if they were paying off the detectives on the case. It would certainly explain why they were being so closed minded about me.

I had thought that my admission that Brad was responsible for Andy's murder would have made them pursue other lines of enquiry, but if anything they were treating my involvement with Andy as yet another indication of my guilt. Still at least they were no longer directly linking me to his disappearance. It had since been proven that I had last seen Andy at the airport so I was no longer a suspect with regards to his missing person's case. However my insistence that Brad had murdered him was falling on deaf ears; I felt like I was trapped in a nightmare and trying to scream but no noise was escaping from my mouth.

The whole situation felt like a conspiracy, and the reality of ending up in prison was worse than I could bear. I was trying my hardest to blend into the background, but amongst the myriad of characters in Silverwater prison I stood out like a sore thumb. I was concealing my accent, avoiding make up, and only leaving my cell to wash, go to the library, and eat, but when I did emerge from the sanctuary of my cell I could feel the eyes of the other inmates boring into me menacingly while I tried to avoid contact with them. I felt constantly on edge, even sleeping was a challenge as I imagined my crazy Aboriginal cellmate, strangling me while I slept.

I quickly began brushing my teeth in front of a circular mirror, which was steamed up with condensation from the showers. Eager to get dressed and leave my vulnerable surroundings, I looked intently in it for any sign of hostility behind me and my fears were confirmed when I saw the figure of a woman standing behind, staring at me, causing me to visibly jump.

"You're that fucking little stripper bitch aren't you, the one from the paper?" she announced callously, in a thick Australian accent. I could just about make out her appearance through the steam; a tall, thin, white woman, with straggly brown hair. She was probably about thirty but her weathered looks made her look at least ten years older, her face no doubt haggard by hard drugs and an even harder life.

I looked away and continued brushing my teeth, my heart racing with terror as I realised that the moment I had been dreading was about to eventuate.

"Hey bitch. I'm talking to you," she shouted, as she inched closer. My sense of vulnerability was heightened by my nakedness, shielded only by a damp towel. She was fully dressed; already at an advantage. I reluctantly turned to face her, realising that ignoring her would not make her go away.

"No, that's not me," I lied, hoping my acknowledgment of her might lessen the level of aggression emanating from her. She smiled in response, her thin dry lips parting just enough to reveal a set of brown, discoloured teeth.

"It is you, you fucking liar," she insisted, now close enough that I could smell her fowl breath; a rancid aroma that reminded me of a men's urinal. I clutched my towel tightly around me and tried not to display my fear as I quickly stepped away, my bare feet moving cautiously against the moist tiled floor. It was obvious from the malevolent look in her eyes that reason or sense was not something she understood; my only hope was to get away as quickly as I could.

"Don't walk away from me bitch!" she called from behind me. "I'm talking to you." Her voice was rising in volume and contained a venomous anger, which I knew would be dangerous if encountered. I had almost reached the exit for the shower room when I felt my legs slip from under me as my hair was yanked, causing me to land painfully backwards on the hard wet floor and my towel to drop open.

"You fucking liar," she shouted, as I lay exposed, trying to cover myself. An audience was beginning to gather and my fear escalated at the daunting prospect of them all joining the attack.

"Get her Tammy," I heard a voice chime in. "Get the bitch." With that she was down, grabbing my hair and swinging me round by it, her fist crashing into my face repeatedly while I stumbled around sliding against the ground. I felt an explosion of heat as her fist connected with my nose and warm blood began to pour down my face. I could taste it as it streamed down into my throat, almost choking me.

"Get off me," I screamed. "Get off me!"

"You bitch!" she shouted back. "You think you're better than us don't you?"

"No," I screamed, clutching at her hand as she pulled my hair roughly. She hit me again harder, causing me to slide across the floor, back towards the sinks. I saw her feet coming closer as she approached me to continue her assault, and I automatically jumped up and shoved her backwards as hard as I could.

She slid onto the wet floor, her eyes fixed on me all the while, before jumping back onto her feet determinedly. The crazy glint in her eyes was magnified, her need to prove herself in front of her peers now an added motive in continuing her attack. I made a run for the door again but she was on me like a shot, pulling me across the room.

"Get the bitch!" A woman screamed in the background, and the crowd thickened around us. My wet hair was tangled round her fingers, my naked body flailing and then I saw the ceramic sink underneath me as she raised my head above it. There was a deafening crack as my skull connected against it and the white tiled room was replaced with a cloak of blackness.

CHAPTER FORTY-TWO

Vinnie Murphy hadn't been to Flirt for weeks when the sensational story first hit the headlines.

Brad Harrison found dead in stripper's Kings Cross apartment.

He was sitting on his veranda overlooking his decadent pool when he heard the news. His housekeeper had brought him a tray containing his daily collection of papers, alongside his usual breakfast of eggs benedict and orange juice. Vinnie had sighed smugly, taken a luxuriant stretch like a cat, soaking up the sunshine and the lifestyle that he still regularly felt blessed to have had bestowed upon him. "You lucky son of a bitch," he congratulated himself, and was about to tuck into his morning ritual of eggs and print when the front page of the Herald hit him in the face, with the force of a meteorite falling to earth.

He picked up the paper ignoring his breakfast, and began devouring the words hungrily, his eyes widening in shock with each word he read.

Respected business man and entrepreneur Brad Harrison has been discovered dead this morning, after an altercation with his ex-girlfriend. Ria Kimura, a stripper at the notorious gentlemen's club Flirt, in Sydney's central business district, was arrested in the early hours of the morning on suspicion of murder. An investigation has begun to determine the events which led to his death. The business world is in shock today for the tragic loss of a great man. Brad Harrison became successful in his own right after following in the footsteps of his father; Arthur Harrison. He was best known for his chain of juice bars, Juiced Up and a vast property development empire, which spanned the length of Australia. He was also renowned for his generous contribution and donations towards many charities, namely, Youth Action Australia, to which he was an ambassador.

"Jesus Christ," Vinnie declared. He couldn't believe it. His mouth dropped open in shock at the discovery. Brad had once been a friend many years ago; their parents had been close associates. Yes the man had grown up to be an arrogant arse, but murdered, cut down in his prime at the age of thirty five? No one deserved that. More chilling still was the revelation that it had been done by one of the strippers at Flirt. Who could it have been? The pseudonyms of the dancers concealed the real identities of the girls; he really had no clue at all. Still it was a rather exotic sounding name. "Ria Kimura," he repeated to himself. Had to be an Asian girl. Something clicked in his brain as he put two and two together. Pearl! It had to be. She was the only Asian girl at Flirt.

"No way," he said, shaking his head in astonishment. He knew that he didn't really know her, not as much as he would like to have fooled himself into believing. But surely not; Pearl, responsible for Brad's death?

She seemed like such a lovely girl. She was no doubt his favourite, had been for a while and his reasons for liking her apart from being drop-dead gorgeous, was that she seemed innocent, or as innocent as a stripper could be. Pearl was completely focused on having fun in an endearing, childlike way. She had no inhibitions and was totally at ease with herself; no false pretences, completely natural. He found it very hard to believe she was capable of murder.

It had been a couple of months since they had first met and he had been lured by her immediately. He had to admit that his admiration for her had developed into a bit of an infatuation. He had even sneakily stolen her disposable camera at the recent boat party. He felt his cheeks flush with embarrassment as he recalled what he had done. He reassured himself he had been drunk as he began to worry if his actions were beginning to border on the verge of obsession.

Striding back into his bedroom, Vinnie dived for the drawers next to his four poster bed. Pulling out the camera he eyed it curiously, fondly remembering the day he had acquired the plastic lump. It had been a perfect day, the party was in full swing on his sumptuous yacht. The deck had been filled with gorgeous girls tanning themselves and dancing, and yet he had still been unable to tear his eyes from her.

"Didn't know they even made these things anymore," he had said, as he wound up the shutter, taking a shot of her posing by the boat's wheel in a captain's hat.

"I'd rather spend my money on shoes and booze," she'd laughed in response. She had looked even more stunning than usual that day in a cut out white swimsuit and sailor's hat, her dark windswept hair bringing to mind images of a Hollywood screen siren. He had drunkenly decided that he wanted the photo he'd taken as a souvenir. I'll get her a proper camera, he had told himself, to ease the feeling of guilt that had briefly permeated his drunken stupor. He had been so legless he had forgotten all about it.

Now however he realised he was potentially holding in his hands a piece of evidence. Hastily pulling on his suit, Vinnie tucked the camera into his jacket pocket and strode from his large, modern, beachfront property, onto the driveway. Hopping into his red Ferrari he started up the engine; the sound of it roaring to life making his fingers buzz and his hairs stand on end, as he held the steering wheel in his hand and sharply pulled off to begin his commute into work. He would get his assistant to get the photos developed for him; he could scarcely wait to see them.

CHAPTER FORTY-THREE

"Ria, Ria," said a tender voice repeatedly. It had a soothing sound and I felt myself being gently lifted from the darkness. I knew before even opening my eyes who the voice belonged to, and half expected to be in my cosy bed at home in England, my mother waking me from an alcohol induced slumber. When I opened my eyes I was startled to see that I was in fact in a hospital bed.

"Oh my God!" she cried when she saw me looking back at her. "Ria!" I struggled to assess my surroundings through the searing pain across my forehead.

"What happened?" I asked weakly, the pain amplified as I attempted to remember.

"Someone attacked you when you were in the prison." I felt tears filling my eyes as I recalled the precariousness of my situation, and that I was as far away from my little room in Surrey as I could possibly get.

"It's going to be okay," she said, stroking my face. "No one's going to hurt you again."

"What did she do to me?" I asked, concerned by the throbbing in my head.

"Hopefully nothing, just superficial the doctor said. Concussion, you needed some stitches on your head, a few bruises."

I felt slightly relieved that my condition wasn't serious, but then my concern was re-directed perhaps vainly, at the aftermath of my face.

"Has she ruined my face?" I asked; scared as I remembered the repeated blows she had made against it.

"No babe it's fine, don't worry about that now."

"Have you got a mirror?" I needed to assess the damage that had been done.

"No Ria, I really don't think that's a good idea right now."

Her response made me feel even more fearful. "Please Mum, I need to see."

Reluctantly she fished around in her hand bag and pulled out a compact. "Look, don't get freaked out. You're just very swollen at the moment. The doctor has reassured me that it will go down and you will be back to normal before you know it."

I held the mirror, slowly raising it to my face and gasped at what I saw. Both my eyes were black, my nose swollen, and I had a bandage around the top of my head. "I look like I've been in a bloody car crash!" I exclaimed. Then a swell of anger took over as I remembered the vindictive expression of my attacker. "What a bitch!"

"Yes. She never should have been in that prison. The woman's mental, spends her time in between the nut house and the streets apparently. They should never have put her in there." She glanced down at my face again and attempted to smile whilst squeezing my hand. "But don't worry. I've spoken to the lawyer and he is going to make sure that you won't have to go back there. You are going to be put in protected custody from now on. The case is too high profile for you to be mingling with the likes of them. It's too dangerous."

"I knew this would happen," I said, my voice cracking with emotion. "I was just waiting for it."

"Well it's not going to happen again," she said, kissing my head.

"So what are they going to do with me now?"

"Well you're in the hospital wing of the prison at the moment. When you're ready they will take you to a special part of it, where you will have your own cell and be away from everyone else."

"Why has this happened to me?" I cried at my reflection again. I thought of Brad, of the way he had beaten me, of everything I had endured in the last six months.

"I don't know babe. But you are being so strong, I am so proud of you. We are going to get you out of here. It's going to be okay." She sounded like she was reassuring herself as much as me, but it made me feel a bit better all the same. "I am going to have to go and get the nurse now and tell her you're awake, won't be long. Here," she said handing me an envelope. "I have a letter for you, from Eddie. Hopefully it will cheer you up."

I watched helplessly from the hospital bed as she walked out of the room and noticed the prison warden standing by the doorway wearing a solemn expression, a reminder of my clipped wings.

Sighing, I turned my attention to the envelope, at the way Eddie had written my name across it so artfully, like a piece of graffiti. I had not seen him since my arrest and had spent many nights wondering how he was, and what he now thought of me. After everything I had put him through I wouldn't have been surprised if I had never heard from him again, and yet he had written to me, proof he still cared. I teased the envelope open and pulled out the paper inside it, gently unfolding it.

Dear Ria,

I hope you're alright. I have been thinking about you constantly since you were arrested. I wish I could come and see you but as your visits are restricted to only a couple a week I haven't been able to yet.

Diane has filled me in on everything that has been happening, she sounds confident that she will be able to help you, but I still worry. There has been so much stuff in the papers, everyone at work won't shut up about it, it's been doing my head in.

I really miss you, I think about you all the time, every minute of the day. I know you said you didn't want to get involved with anyone and that you just wanted to be friends, but I hope that if you do ever get out that we can be together. I miss spending time with you, your beautiful smile, the way you make me laugh. Everything that has happened has made me realise that I really love you. I wish I could take care of you and this would all end. You don't deserve all this.

Look after yourself in there, and watch your back. Be strong and stay positive. I don't know how, but we are going to get you out of there. Looking forward to the day I can see you and hold you in my arms again.

Yours always,
Eddie.

A warm sensation enveloped me, as I finished the letter and tucked it under my pillow. He loved me and I realised now just how much I loved him back. I just hoped I would be able to see him again.

CHAPTER FORTY-FOUR

Vinnie was sitting at his desk, his mind wandering as he sipped from a large cup of coffee, and stared out at the aspect offered from his office. It was a perfect day, the impressive looking Harbour Bridge framing the spectacular view; an endless expanse of blue, interspersed with boats, meandering across it freely like the silhouettes of birds against the sky.

He was thinking about Brad's murder, the countless reports he had read over the last few days covering it, and his surprise over his once favourite girl's involvement in it all. Although he hadn't been too fond of Brad recently, his family loyalty and connection towards the Harrisons meant that he had heard detailed accounts from his parents as to the ins and outs of the case. Despite it all though, he was still struggling to believe that Pearl could have deliberately killed him. There must have been more to it surely?

He was interrupted from his thoughts by the sound of his assistant knocking on the door. "Come in," he yelled impatiently.

Tentatively she shuffled in, looking every inch the fantasy secretary with her long blond hair, and cleavage threatening to burst from her buttoned shirt. "I picked up those photos you wanted developed," she said and waved a yellow envelope in her hand. He could tell by her unusually subdued demeanour that she'd had a good look at them, and felt aggravated that he'd had his privacy invaded. Still, he probably would have done the same in her position he supposed. He couldn't even remember the last time he had ever seen one of those crappy disposable cameras, so it must have sparked a bit of curiosity in his assistant when he had asked her to get it developed.

"Thanks," he said, taking them sharply from her hand. "Anything else?"

"No, not at the moment."

"Good," he remarked. "Oh before you go Lucy, can you run down the road, get me one of those breakfast baguettes I like. Oh and buy yourself something as well," he added, pulling a twenty dollar note from his wallet.

"Sure, be back soon." She departed from the room with a strange expression on her face. God there had better not be anything pornographic in there, Vinnie thought, hoping that his assistant hadn't seen anything too seedy.

He took another swig from his coffee and started to leaf through the photos eagerly. The first ones were from the recent boat party and he studied them with appreciation. "What a glamour," he remarked under his breath, as he came across the photo he had taken of Pearl posing by the steering wheel. They were followed by some entertaining shots of the Japanese night, a couple with the girls at work on the beach, one with her and the DJ fellow. He felt a stab of jealousy as he came across a few of her frolicking on the beach with a handsome blond boy. Hold on, he thought as he studied his face. It was the English boy. The one who had gone missing! He eagerly flipped over to the next photo and his heart almost stopped with the shock of what was on it. It was Pearl looking far from her radiant self. In fact she had been horrifically beaten, her face swollen to almost twice its size, black and blue, her eyes like slits in their enlarged battered sockets. There were further photos, bruises covering her arms, her torso, her legs even. He checked the dates in the bottom right corner of them.

"Fuck." Round about the same time she was supposedly with Brad. So it was true. He had beaten her. He felt sickened by the thought of it. He knew Brad had been an arrogant prick at times, but capable of doing this to a woman? A young girl like Pearl? It was disgusting. He felt the overwhelming urge to pick up the phone and call the police, but he remembered his disconcerting family ties and decided against it. He would have to send them in anonymously; he really didn't want his name splashed in the papers amidst all of this mess. Not to mention the embarrassment of having to admit he had a crush on Pearl and had nicked her camera. His wife certainly wouldn't be too impressed either. He could just see her now, standing with her hands on her hips judging him hypocritically, as if she didn't know what he got up to. Still she deserved better than to have her nose rubbed in it by him. They had an unspoken agreement; he could do what he wanted as long as she didn't find out. So far it had worked well for both of them; he didn't want to ruin the arrangement now.

He thumbed through the photos, taking out the picture he had taken of Pearl on the boat and placing it into his Filofax. Then he got out an envelope and put the rest of the pictures into it, addressed it to the homicide department in Kings Cross Station, and sealed it closed. Just as he had finished there was another knock at the door.

"Come in," he yelled.

Lucy shuffled in, his breakfast treat in her hand, still possessing a distinctive awkwardness in her mannerism.

"Oh for God's sake Luce. I know you had a good look through the photos, so you can stop pretending now," he said. "No need to worry; your boss isn't a woman basher." Her face relaxed, and as she opened her mouth to apologise, Vinnie raised his hand to silence her. "Gonna need you to take this personally down to the police station for me in the Cross. If they ask you who it's from or what it is, just say you have taken it there anonymously; it is evidence to be used for an important case. Then get the hell out of there before they ask you any questions. Got it?"

She nodded in response.

"Oh and one more thing Lucy; don't look through my personal stuff again okay?"

"Okay," she said apologetically. She took the photos from his hand, and quickly turned on her heel, out of his office. Vinnie watched as she left and sighed. It was a good job she was such a looker or he'd have fired her by now.

*

Harlow was making herself a coffee in the kitchen of The Cross' police station, eager to inject her body with a much needed dose of caffeine, when her partner Detective Mikos burst in knocking her back to consciousness from her hazy daydreams.

"Look what's just been handed in," he announced, waving a yellow envelope in his hand wildly.

"What is it?" she asked, curious to see what could have possibly made her usually relaxed colleague so excited.

"Here, see for yourself," he said, handing it to her with trembling hands.

Harlow frowned and pulled out its contents; a stack of photos, and carefully began leafing through them, studying each one with a puzzled expression on her face. As she neared the photos at the bottom, her mouth dropped open in surprise. "So this means…." she said, gasping in shock.

"Yes. Looks like that Brad guy did beat up Ria after all."

"Has Griffwell seen these?" she asked, wondering what his take would have been on them.

"No not yet. He's not in yet."

"So who brought them in?" Harlow questioned; a perplexed look on her face.

"Apparently a young woman, suited and booted. She just came in, put them on the desk at reception, said she was handing in evidence and darted off again, as quickly as she could."

"Hmmm," Harlow said. "Well we are going to have to include these in the evidence case file, and her lawyer will need to be informed I suppose. Maybe we are going to have to start looking at this case from a different angle?"

"Yeah well, I've believed her from the word go," Mikos said, with an I told you so air to his voice. "It's you and Griffwell who have had it in for her from the start."

"I have not," Harlow said, protecting her integrity. "You don't understand what kind of pressure the department is under to make someone pay for Brad's murder. The Harrisons are very important people, and up until now there was no evidence supporting her claims. And in case you've forgotten, evidence is what we have to go on smart arse."

"Yeah well if you ask me, maybe we need to stop looking into her background and activity and start investigating Brad Harrison's," Mikos answered, pressing the button on the vending machine for a black coffee for himself and watching as the dark liquid filled the white plastic cup.

"You're right," Harlow said and departed down the hallway so hastily that the walls became a white-wash in her peripheral vision.

"Where are you going?" Mikos shouted after her.

"I am going to go through the reports on Brad Harrison's activity for the last few months; thoroughly. Card, cell, you know the drill. See what else we can dig up."

With that she was round the corner out of sight; lost in her thoughts, an endless stream of possibilities racing through her mind.

CHAPTER FORTY-FIVE

It had been a few days since the altercation in the shower and I had reluctantly been returned to Silverwater prison, except this time I was in protected custody. I had expected it to be better with the risk of being attacked by a lunatic minimised, but in fact it was just as bad, if not worse. Before I had had access to the library, more free range, but now the confinement was even more intense, the four walls of my cell closing in on me offering no distraction from my solace. It occurred to me that boredom was perhaps a worse emotion than fear, the absence of my crazy cellmate had been replaced with a mind-numbing silence, which seemed to be harder to listen to than her constant coughing and spitting.

I was looking forward to seeing my lawyer Grant Peterson and hearing about the developments that had been made on my case. I was hopeful, the alternative to hope being despair; I knew that once I had allowed myself on that road, everything would crumble; especially my sanity.

A welcome disruption to my ceiling staring finally arrived in the form of footsteps reverberating down the corridors. Deliberate and efficient, I recognised them at once as belonging to Grant, and I quickly jumped up from my bed in an attempt to make myself slightly presentable for the man on whom I was pinning all my hopes of release.

"Ria," he said as he arrived at my cell. He looked at my face, at the bruising which still made me indistinguishable from the person I had arrived as and winced slightly.

"Looks bad."

"Feels bad."

"Come on." He ushered me out with the urgency one would expect from a man who charges five hundred dollars an hour for his services. "We have a lot to go over."

I followed him as he paced down the corridors, attempting to keep up with his stride without running next to him. As we reached the small interview room, he gave a weary glance to the guard, who quickly disappeared around the other side of the door.

"How are you?" he asked, with an air of professional concern in his tone.

"I'm fine," I said flatly, which was about as much as I could muster under the circumstances.

"Well you certainly don't look it." He was inspecting my swollen face again with a look of distaste. I looked down, wishing I could hide myself from view. Noticing he had touched a nerve he added; "still, at least you're safe now. That is my main concern."

"I don't know how much longer I can take this though Grant," I said, the desperation apparent in my voice. "I feel like I can't cope anymore." I felt a single tear rolling down from my eye, stinging my sore face. I could tell Grant wasn't a sentimental man; he was a man who had no doubt seen it all, more memories than an elephant, but I could tell he was disturbed at my state by the way he crinkled his thin lips in response; a remorseful, compassionate look communicated by his watery blue eyes.

"I have some news which might cheer you up a bit," he said. "Now we have made some progress with your case. It's nothing too major, but it is definitely going to help."

"What is it?" My ears pricked up in anticipation of the news.

"Well we found your photos. The ones you took after Brad assaulted you. I looked at them earlier and they really are quite horrific. Definitely have the power to sway a jury in your favour I'd say."

"Where did you find them?" I asked, curious to know where my camera had been.

"An anonymous person brought them into the police station. There was a note enclosed saying they are an acquaintance from Flirt, had found it amongst their possessions, and had had the camera developed only to find the photos. I assume they didn't want to get entangled in the case but no matter. They are dated thankfully, as is such with those disposable things, and the dates match up perfectly with your account of the incident, so I can safely say they can be used by us as a solid piece of evidence complying with your statement."

"Thank God," I said, relieved it had been found.

"One thing though which the prosecution will no doubt ask: what gave you the urge to take the photos in the first place?"

"I really don't know, it was an impulse I suppose."

"Okay, well I might be able to comprehend that, but others might not be so understanding. Try to be more specific please?" He glanced at me through his steel wired spectacles and tapped his foot impatiently.

"I guess I took them because I wanted to remember what he had done. So that when I had the strength I would leave him, for good."

"Now that's more like it," he said with a satisfied tone. "Also, I have been tracking down his ex-partners, anyone who might have experienced a similar abuse as you."

I nodded, hopeful he had found someone.

"Unfortunately, they all seem to be too scared to make a statement. It seems to be a daunting prospect for them to give evidence against Brad, even though he is dead. More reason to believe he has done it before though if you ask me."

I sighed and felt my heart sink in disappointment.

"However, I have questioned his neighbours, people who work in the building et cetera, and have come across a very vivacious lady willing to put some evidence forward to help you. Her name is Sue Ting. She is a cleaner at Brad's apartment who claims she saw you after the attack."

"Oh yeah. I can't believe I forgot about her."

Grant raised his eyebrow disapprovingly. "Neither can I."

"She came in a couple of weeks after it happened. I was sunbathing on the balcony and didn't realise she was there. I walked into the kitchen and bumped into her."

"And…" Grant prompted.

"She looked away at first, but then she sort of warned me about him.

Said she had seen him hurt other girls. Gave me the kick up the arse I needed to leave him."

"Did you leave straight after that then?" He scrawled down some notes in his diary with illegible handwriting similar to a doctors.

"Yes, I left that night."

"Hmmm. Whatever possessed you to hang around in his apartment for weeks after he had beaten you up?"

I felt embarrassed and foolish as I searched for a satisfactory answer to his question. "I loved him, so it was hard to break away from him. He was very upset and I thought he was sorry. I felt like I had nowhere else to go, but mostly I was too ashamed, I didn't want anyone to see me. I just felt like I wanted to hide away. I felt like he knocked all my strength out of me and it took me a while to get enough back to leave him I suppose."

"All very plausible reasons," he said and wrote down some more notes. "Well that's all for now. But if you remember anything at all that can help, you ring me."

"Thanks I will," I said, and we rose to our feet.

"Oh and Ria," he said, as the prison officer came to take me back to my cell. "Hang in there. I am doing everything I can to get you released."

I watched as he walked away, feeling desolate at the prospect of returning to my isolation. I just hoped to God it was all going to be enough.

CHAPTER FORTY-SIX

Tony Griffwell had been feeling uneasy for weeks. He felt like he was walking across a bed of hot coals, without the luxury of being able to flinch as he crossed it. So far he had succeeded in steering the investigation along the right path; a path which would hopefully lead him out into the clear, to his retirement, and a glorified escape from his conscience. He felt like he deserved it after all the hard work he had put into his career. Sure, he hadn't been as straight as a die in recent years, but he saw his demise into the grey area so often overstepped by many of his predecessors, as a payback for what he had achieved over the course of more than twenty-five years in the force. The diffusion of the line which divided the black and white had faded long ago; for Tony it seemed as inevitable a process for a mature officer as grey hair and an addiction to caffeine.

He had spent many a night convincing himself that he deserved the backhanders he had acquired over the last few years. How could he have known it would lead to this? He reassured himself with the thought that Brad would have found his target eventually, whether it had been through him or another route. Brad was a man who had always gotten what he wanted. A sick bastard. Unfortunately, sick bastards were part and parcel of the job. He had avoided getting entangled with one so far, he was sure he could succeed in doing so for just a bit longer.

When Griffwell arrived at the station it seemed like it would be a relatively uneventful morning. He had parked up along the Kings Cross strip, bought a breakfast bagel and a coffee, and made his way up to his bleak office eagerly, his hunger pangs causing him to move at a speedier pace. He had reached his room, sat in his leather chair, and commenced with the demolishment of his breakfast before turning his attention to the tasks for the day.

The discovery a few days earlier of the photographic evidence proving that Brad had, in fact beaten Ria, had only slightly perplexed him. Perhaps it would mean that she would be found not guilty for his murder, the jury would conclude it was in self defence, and he could retire with a clear conscience? Win win all round. He just needed to stay on the alert and make sure that he took the bull by its horns with the proficiency of a rodeo rider with regards to the direction of the enquiry. Just a minor setback. No need to be alarmed.

He heard a knock on the door and was surprised when the instigator of the noise burst in, without waiting for a response. Harlow was in the doorway looking short of breath; her cropped hair pushed back, a purposeful look in her eyes. Bloody dyke, Griffwell thought to himself sourly, annoyed at the intrusion.

"What can I do for you Harlow?" he asked, swinging his chair round to face the doorway, his arms planted on its rests.

"We're about to have an urgent meeting to discuss the Brad Harrison case. Chief needs you asap."

"Have there been some new developments?" He gulped and tried to hide his angst with a professional detachment.

"I think it's best you follow me," she said, and turned on her heel without even waiting for a reply. Griffwell felt the hairs stand up on the back of his neck as he followed her to the conference room, alarmed at her impertinent manner. As he reached the room he observed that the ovular shaped, walnut table was filled with his colleagues. His heart began to race as he noticed the lack of response or greeting from them all.

He took his seat next to the Chief and searched his face. His bald head seemed to merge as one into his flabby neck, it was a wonder he managed to get a shirt to do up around it at all, His face was expressionless, a talent acquired through many years of service. He surveyed him, his beady eyes roving over him as it would a crime scene photo, and Griffwell knew instantly he was in trouble.

"What's going on?" he asked, struggling to maintain his composure.

"That's what we are hoping to find out," Chief Monroe replied. "A few things have come to light over the course of the investigation. I thought they were anomalies, coincidence at first, but it appears they are not."

"What do you mean?" Griffwell said, slightly overplaying his innocent naivety.

"Did you know Brad Harrison?" Chief Monroe asked, his eyes assessing him.

"No," Griffwell lied.

"If that is true, then why was Brad Harrison calling your cell phone repeatedly, shortly before the disappearance of Andrew Wilson?"

Griffwell could feel himself breaking into a sweat under his tight white collar. "Okay," he said, while he attempted to come up with a plausible explanation worthy of saving his career. "He was an acquaintance of mine that's all. I didn't think it was worth bringing it up because I was worried it would put the integrity of the case in jeopardy."

The Chief's suspicious look was unaltered by his admission. "The day before Andrew's disappearance he rang you ten times. Can you explain that?"

"The truth is he was harassing me," Griffwell said, growing increasingly flustered under the scrutiny of his peers.

"Why?" Monroe demanded.

"He wanted me to help him locate someone. I had no interest in doing so. He had been a grass for me in the past on several cases, so thought I owed him a favour. He began trying to blackmail me but I resisted. Then his calls became threatening. In hindsight maybe it had something to do with his ex-girlfriend Ria, but I didn't know that at the time. In fact I didn't even know the name of the person he wanted me to find, so I didn't think it was relevant."

"Is that so?" Monroe said; a mocking quality to his voice.

"Yes," Griffwell re-affirmed.

"Well that might all be very believable if it wasn't for one minor detail. The discovery of a photo in your desk."

"A photo?" Griffwell asked, perplexed.

"Yes a photo. A photo of Ria Kimura."

"Well that was probably one relevant to this investigation." Griffwell said.

"That may be true except for one thing," Monroe said, a glint in his eye. "It had Brad Harrison's finger prints on it."

Griffwell felt the room spin at the revelation, the chairs of the conference room and the faces of his colleagues merging into one nondescript blur.

"Well Brad had obviously sent it to me previously then... I can't remember," Griffwell stammered, his face becoming a pallid white.

"Convenient isn't it?" Monroe said. "That an experienced detective would forget to mention such a major detail? You didn't think it would be relevant to bring up this information in a murder and missing person's investigation? Do you think I was born on a boat yesterday?"

"No sir, no I don't,"

"Good," Monroe snapped. "Because I wasn't. In fact Tony, yesterday I was rather busy. Having your bank accounts scrutinised. Can you explain how the sum of twenty thousand dollars magically appeared in your account, around the time Brad was allegedly harassing you?" He enunciated, "harassing," so it sounded as absurd as if Tony had accused Brad of molesting him.

Tony could not even bring himself to argue. He felt the energy drain from his body, and he dejectedly resigned himself to his fate. The realisation that the moment he had been dreading was upon him, made him feel sick to the pit of his stomach.

"Tony Griffwell, I have no choice but to dismiss you with immediate effect pending a further investigation. But I think you and I both know what the outcome of that will be don't we? Now get your arse out of my station. You're a bloody disgrace." Monroe pointed to the exit and Griffwell gladly obliged, scurrying through it as quickly as he could, avoiding the eyes of his colleagues.

As he turned the corner of the corridor his angst grew, and he wondered how he would tell his wife the news, and worse still his mother. He just hoped that the story wouldn't be leaked to the press. Tony felt a rage encompassing him mixed with an overwhelming insurgence of guilt over what he had done and what it had potentially caused. Still though he felt he was undeserving of being stripped of his career, his honour, everything he had worked for all his life to achieve; all because of one stupid mistake.

He made his way to the glass exit, forcefully pushed its door open, and simultaneously knocked into someone. As he lifted his head he realised it was Harlow. Her smug expression said it all; she was obviously the whistle blower. He should have known; a man wouldn't have dobbed in another officer. In that moment he redirected all his anger at her instead.

"Bitch," he muttered as he walked away from the gloomy building, in which he had spent over half his life working in. "Good fucking riddance."

He stepped out onto the street and surveyed the scene around him, the notorious strip of Kings Cross in all its glory, bustling with prostitutes, drug addicts and criminals. He wondered why he had ever bothered at all? It was as useless as trying to extinguish a bush fire with a stream of piss.

CHAPTER FORTY-SEVEN

I heard the news no sooner than the rest of Australia and no doubt the rest of the world. I was pacing the cell anxiously after having eaten a bit of the unappetising breakfast that had been brought in for me. I looked down at my legs which seemed to be growing skinnier by the day, now resembling a sparrow's. It seemed that my indulgent lifestyle had ill prepared me for the reality of prison life. Even though it had only been just over a month, I still turned my nose up at the majority of the food; the offerings were as much of a punishment as being locked up.

I swigged back a gulp of some bitter coffee and grimaced at the taste, before lying down to do some reading, one of the very few activities capable of temporarily taking my mind off things. I was interrupted by one of the wardens on the shift. She was one of the few who I actually liked; whose head didn't look like it had been cut off and pickled in a jar of lemon juice overnight.

"Hey." She slid open the partition on my cell door and peered in. "Got something I thought would interest you. Talk of the prison."

"What is it?" I jumped off the bed, eager to find out what she meant.

She responded by sliding a copy of The Daily Telegraph through the slit. "Read it and you'll find out."

I sat back down on my bed and glanced down at the morning's headline.

Detective Leading Harrison Murder Investigation, Sacked Over Corruption.

"What the fuck?" I digested the statement in shock and continued to read the story hungrily.

"Detective Inspector Tony Griffwell was suspended yesterday, after he was allegedly discovered to have been acting corruptly with regards to the Brad Harrison murder investigation that he was leading. According to an internal affairs report conducted by the Daily Telegraph, he had been consorting with Brad Harrison around the time of the disappearance of English traveller Andrew Wilson. The internal investigation showed that the pair exchanged 92 phone calls between the time of the 27th January and the 11th March, the contact commencing shortly after Brad allegedly broke up with his ex, Ria Kimura, who is now in remand after being charged with his murder. She has insisted since her arrest that Brad Harrison murdered Andrew Wilson, and was attempting to end her life also. It seems that the evidence points to the conclusion that Detective Griffwell had been assisting Brad in locating her after their separation. Shortly after Andrew's disappearance Griffwell received a sum of around A\$20,000 from Brad Harrison, which he has no explanation for. The investigation into Griffwell is continuing, alongside the investigation into the murder of Brad Harrison and the disappearance of Andrew Wilson. These new revelations have shed a shocking new light on the case, and will no doubt cast doubt over the guilt of Ria, who is currently in Silverwater prison awaiting trial. It is a completely unexpected twist in the trial that is gripping the nation and the world."

"Oh my God!" My hands trembled and my body began to feel weightless as I finished the article. I could scarcely believe what I had just read, but I remembered the strange way in which Griffwell had dealt with me, the compassionate looks he had thrown my way at times, coupled with the intensely biased, narrow-minded interrogations I had endured. He had given off mixed signals from the start. I had sensed a feeling of remorse in his eyes occasionally, and had just thought that he had a soft spot for young girls in a tough situation, but then just as frequently I had felt like he was on a mission to persecute me, his unrelenting questions steering me into a dark corner. Now I knew why he had been acting so oddly. He had obviously been feeling guilty but been trying to cover his own arse at the same time!

Then a thought entered my mind. He had been the one who had found me in Cairns. If he hadn't been such a corrupt bastard, then Andrew would still be alive. He deserved a lot worse than being suspended, unless of course he was being suspended from a tree by a piece of rope around his neck. The way he had spoken to me, accusing me of being a prostitute, a drug addict, a man hating, money grabbing bitch and the whole time he had known I was innocent! I catapulted myself to the slit in the door.

"Julie!" I called to the prison officer who had delivered the news, straining my face against the bars and twisting my neck in an attempt to locate her.

Immediately I heard her footsteps approaching from down the hall; she had obviously been waiting for my reaction.

"I need to speak to my lawyer as soon as possible."

"Yeah well no need to ring him doll, he called a minute ago to arrange a meeting. He should be turning up soon." She widened her eyes to display her surprise at the revelation.

"I can't fucking believe it!" I exclaimed; my body elevated with adrenalin, my heart rushing. "Can I call my mum?"

"Not right now, but I'm sure your lawyer has rung her to tell her the news. Just sit tight and wait for him to show up. Probably only be a couple of hours."

"Okay," I said resignedly, my pent up frustration making me want to climb the walls of my cell. Instead I sat down at my desk, reading and re-reading the article, whilst nervously tapping my foot on the floor. I watched the clock in the corridor impatiently.

Fifteen minutes passed, nothing, I sat back down, perching on the edge of the plastic chair. I tapped some more and got up again. Another ten minutes passed and the only change was the position of the hand on the clock. Slowly the minutes ticked past, until finally after almost two hours, the time on the clock read nine forty seven, and I heard the noise of Grant, the unmistakable sound of his well-polished shoes echoing rhythmically down the corridor as he walked towards me. I breathed a sigh of relief as Julie reappeared and unlocked my cell, and

Grant emerged through the door looking slightly breathless, the fine strands of his combed over hair, flapping gently like feathers.

"Good news," he said excitedly, his long skinny fingers clutching the handle of his briefcase. He gestured for me to follow him with his other hand. "Come along, we have a lot to discuss."

I was given no time to respond as he darted out as quickly as he had arrived, and I followed his trail eagerly with Julie hot on my heels. We finally reached our usual conference room; a small windowless cell containing a few chairs and a desk, and seated ourselves quickly not bothering with niceties.

"Have you read the morning papers?" he asked.

"Yes. I read the Telegraph."

"Brilliant news! Shocking but brilliant." He smoothed down his greying hair.

"What does this mean for me though? Do you think they will let me off now?"

"What it means is we are getting together enough of a case that we will hopefully prove you were innocent and didn't murder Brad Harrison. It is definitely going to help you immensely." He spoke with an air of excitement which automatically rubbed off onto me.

"Thank God," I replied.

"This alongside the pictures we found and the statement from the cleaner, and I think we stand a very good chance. I am putting together as much evidence as I can for the hearing. Hopefully we can make a jury see sense and we can get you acquitted." Flecks of spit flew from his mouth as he spoke and he pulled out some files from his briefcase, commencing his annoying habit of clicking the top of his gold pen. The man was a tower of pent-up energy; he must have been super hyperactive as a child.

"So there's no way you can appeal against my charges?" I had hoped he would tell me I could be out in a matter of weeks.

"Unfortunately not, we still have to wait for the hearing, but your chances are getting stronger and stronger all the time. Please don't get your hopes up too much though Ria; there's a chance they could still find you guilty."

"Oh great."

"Don't be disheartened. I just don't want you to get carried away yet

Ria. It's a very complicated case. I wouldn't be surprised if Detective Griffwell isn't the only corrupt person involved in it." He scratched his head as if the action would help him to magically identify any co-conspirators.

"What's that supposed to mean?" I asked, my earlier excitement rapidly evaporating.

"It simply means that Brad's family are one of the most powerful in Australia. They have many connections and more money than God. That is what we are fighting here. I think it's quite clear now that you are innocent, but we don't know how many crooks are involved in this. In fact it wouldn't surprise me if they had arranged for that girl to beat you up in here."

"Wow." I said stunned. "I thought you were supposed to have good news for me."

"It is good news Ria. Sorry, but I am just trying to be realistic. This isn't a regular case. But rest assured I feel very confident that we are going to get you out of here sooner or later."

"Please let it be sooner."

"The evidence against you is poor. It has just been brought to light that Brad was actually tracking you down, paying to find you. Our case has progressed immensely by this new revelation, it really has."

He looked at me pityingly then, at my bruised face which still looked awful even though the swelling had finally gone down. I was relieved to see my features were still intact, and all that was left to return was the colour of my skin which was still mottled with marks.

"I am putting together character witnesses to testify towards your better nature. The whole case of the prosecution is built upon the portrayal of you as a drug addicted stripper and Brad as an angelic hero. The press were illustrating him as being a national treasure. Well it is all coming to light now what he really was, and it is pretty clear that you are not the character they are trying to pretend you are either. You are quite clearly a well-educated girl, from a good background, who was unlucky enough to get involved with the wrong person. A jury will be able to see that. Anyone will."

"Thanks Grant," I said wearily. "I hope so. I can't take it in here much longer."

"Just hang in there Ria."

"So how about the Andy case; do you think they might start believing that Brad killed him and start looking for him now?"

"The case has become a media circus, Andrew was a fine young man and all this has put a spotlight on the investigation over his disappearance. The police will be under considerable amounts of pressure now to find out what really happened to him, whereas before they were obviously being prevented from delving too deep by Griffwell. It's all over the news in England, and his parents have even made a public appeal for their questions to be answered."

"Good. I hope they actually do something about it now. Brad deserves to be shamed for his murder, even if he isn't alive to pay for it himself."

"I agree unreservedly. They will be delving into Brad's affairs now and I'm sure there will be no end to what they might find."

"Andy's family deserve to know what happened." I pictured his shiny happy eyes, smiling at me. The image was one that haunted me more than any other and had caused me to endure countless sleepless nights, tossing and turning, trying to prevent myself from imagining what Brad might have put him through. It was horrific knowing his final moments were at the hands of such a monster. I remembered the terror I had felt at the hands of Brad and hoped he had not suffered as much as I suspected he had. God only knew what his parents were going through? They'd had such high hopes for their son from what he had told me, and who could blame them; he'd truly had it all. Looks, brains, compassion, and one of the sweetest dispositions I had ever encountered. Life was unfair.

"I wish he had never met me Grant. He would still be alive." I erupted into tears and Grant tried to console me awkwardly by patting me on the shoulder while I sobbed.

Obviously he hadn't missed his calling in life as a counsellor. Law was perfectly suited to his character; the successful arrangements of facts and evidence, maintaining a certain countenance, which luckily a detachment of emotion usually helped to achieve and didn't hinder.

"Now now. You mustn't blame yourself," he said. "The world is a cruel place, filled with cruel people and you weren't to know."

Somehow his attempt to placate me worked slightly, and I dried my eyes and blew my nose on the tissue he handed me.

"I feel like I am going mad in here," I wept. "I can't take it anymore, I can't."

"Now Ria I am only going to say this once so listen to me properly while I say it." He spoke sternly, commanding my attention and causing me to stop with my blubbering. "If you have that attitude then we may as well give up now. You need to fight this and if you don't and start feeling sorry for yourself instead, then you don't stand a chance. Fighting a case like this is like fighting cancer. You can't surrender to it or it will drag you down. Remember that you are innocent, you are the victim in all this. You don't deserve this. It isn't your fault Andrew died, it is the fault of the man who killed him, who was trying to take your life. If you want someone to blame, blame him, and that stupid son of a bitch detective who was helping him to find you. Pull yourself together. That is my professional advice. If you really want to get out of here then take it."

His words sobered me up like a slap to the face. He may not be good at communicating empathy, but he was obviously an expert on tough love. I nodded and realised he was right. I couldn't crumble now. Not yet.

"Now," he said in a business like tone as he assembled his possessions. "Here is some reading material, a collection of today's papers, I think reading these will give you something to focus on. Also your mother and Diane are visiting later on, something to look forward to."

"Thank you," I said as he got up to leave.

"You can thank me when I get you out of here."

I momentarily caught a glimpse of the familiar flash of conviction in his eyes, before he departed and I was led back to my cell.

"Fighting a case like this is like fighting cancer." His words rang in my ears as the cell door slammed behind me.

CHAPTER FORTY-EIGHT

The day had finally arrived. I had dreaded it and looked forward to it with equal measure, but now it was here I felt a deadening feeling in my body as I was led towards the police van. The culmination of everything I had been through now rested upon the events of the next few days; upon the inclination of the jury, the mood of the judge.

I stepped out of Silverwater prison into the car park, its doorway lifted and I felt the soft breeze against my skin, blowing back my hair and for a fleeting moment had a taste of freedom, of what I had missed for so long. I was clutching the angel my mother had given me tightly in my sweaty palm, holding on to it like I had my hope and sanity for the last few months; in desperation.

As I clamoured into the back of the van, my hands tightly cuffed, I had a flashback to the day I had been arrested for Brad's murder and felt a chill descend through my body. I suppose in a way I was lucky to be in the back of the van, the only other alternative to my situation being my death. I remembered the words my mother had written to me, I had memorised them, been grateful for some encouragement and strength on such a terrifying day. She had asked me to open her letter in the morning and I had reached for it as soon as I'd opened my eyes.

My darling daughter Ria.
The day has finally arrived for you to have your trial, the day we

have all been waiting for. I know you must be very scared but I need you to be strong right now, we all do. Sometimes things happen in our lives that no one can explain: unfair, terrible things, and all we can do is to hold on and be strong. So far you have done a wonderful job, just a bit longer to go and it will all be over.

Whatever happens in court remember who you are, and don't ever forget it because you are a special person. You are kind, and good, and beautiful inside and out. No matter what they say about you in there we all know the truth. Hold your head up high. We love you dearly.

It's all going to be alright, I can feel it in my bones. Remember the angel I gave you, your father and the angels will be watching over you today. You may not feel like it now but your dad has been watching over you throughout all of this, keeping you safe, keeping you from harm, and he will be helping you today.

We are all praying for your safe return home. We miss you so much. Not long now and we will all be reunited. I can't wait to see you out of that place and safe and sound. Keep believing and it will happen before you know it.

I am so proud of you, be brave and we will be waiting for you on the other side. There is a light at the end of the tunnel and you have almost reached it. Have faith. No matter what happens, you will always be my baby. I love you with all my heart.

Mummy.

The letter was folded in the jacket pocket of my Cerruti suit, which Diane had insisted upon buying for the occasion. As soon as I had put it on I instantly felt human again; almost elegant. After months of wearing the depressing prison attire and a bruised face; just changing into something new had given me a sense of empowerment, had made me feel like I had got a piece of my identity back. As daunting as it was, I felt ready to face the world again.

I was quickly reminded of what I was so eager to escape from when we reached our destination and the van lurched, causing me to tumble forwards awkwardly, unable to break my fall with my cuffed hands.

"Shit," I muttered as I attempted to pull myself up, and then, just as abruptly as I had fallen the voices hit me. People swarming around the van, their words indistinguishable from each other as their chatter rose upon our arrival, a wrought throng of energy clamouring to get the best spot; enthusiastically, hungrily. I waited nervously until the door was finally swung open by the prison officer and I was led out into the crowd of faces waiting outside the Supreme Court, their features masked by cameras, microphones, and hands as they jostled each other aside in their attempts to get closer to me. I searched past them, my eyes scanning the outside steps of the court until I finally saw my family huddled near the entrance.

"Ria!" Aia cried as she saw me, and as she tried to get closer I was swept past by the prison officer, the throng of reporters now blocking my much cherished view of my loved ones as I was swiftly led into a waiting room.

Grant was waiting for me in the chambers with a coffee and calming words. "So the day has finally arrived!" he exclaimed. I nodded with a sullen face and accepted his offering of coffee, pouring two sachets of sugar into it.

"Thanks," I said, stirring round the brown liquid with a wooden stick.

"It's going to be alright. We have an extremely strong case. The prosecution lawyer isn't going to know what's hit him. Clark Smith," he said with a bitter expression, as if saying his name was like biting into a rotten egg. "He's a cocky man, puts on a better show than the chorus line for Chicago but it's not going to be enough."

"I hope you're right," I added bleakly.

"Of course I am," he said. "You just need to hold it together in there. When they question you, think carefully before answering. You can do it."

I smiled gratefully at him and wished I could see my family before going in.

"Right well I'd better go," he said. "I need to be in the courtroom to prepare for my opening statement. They will call for you soon. Remember you are the victim in this." He gave me a warm smile before heading off, his tall frame billowing through the corridor, and I watched as he departed hoping that the man was as brilliant as his reputation portrayed him to be.

The prison officer watched me intently while I sipped my coffee. My stomach fluttered as I waited to be summoned, and I wondered how the events of the day would unfold and whether or not it would be in my favour.

Before long a police woman knocked on the door and entered. "It's time," she said. "Follow me."

My heart was beating wildly as I was led towards my fate, and as we stepped into the courtroom, I was overwhelmed by the number of spectators who were in there. Every seat was occupied and dozens of reporters stood towards the back of the room, notepads, dictaphones and cameras poised. I felt all eyes on me as I was shuffled into the dock, Grant and my family seated nearby. My mother, Aia, and Shinzo looked as nervous as I was feeling; the tension was almost palatable as we all waited for the hearing to commence. I wished that I could embrace them all, it had been so long since I had seen my siblings and it felt strange to be in the same room but forcibly separated from them.

The silence was abruptly interrupted. "All rise for the right honourable Judge Coleman."

As the Judge's arrival was announced we stood and I looked at the man who was about to decide my fate with curious eyes. He was short, fat, and bald but I was relieved to see that beneath his spectacles was a kindly plump face. Grant had informed me that he had a reputation for being firm but fair and he had seemed glad he was judging the case, but I couldn't help but wonder if he was in any way linked to the Harrisons who seemed to have their claws in the majority of the powerful people in Sydney. They were seated on the far side of the courtroom behind the prosecution lawyer, their usually resplendent presence overshadowed by a cloud of worry crossing their lined faces. Brad's mother Stephanie was shooting contemptuous glances in my direction and Arthur Harrison appeared to be trying to appease his wife, clutching her hand and resisting the temptation to join in with his own dirty looks. They both seemed to have aged a decade since I had last seen them and I was reminded that regardless of what Brad was, he was their only son and their loss must have been excruciatingly painful. I felt remorseful and looked away quickly, telling myself that if I hadn't have killed Brad it would have been me dead, probably buried in the undergrowth of the outback. I doubt he would have had any consequences to deal with.

The prosecution lawyer stood up then, a stocky man with a dramatic voice and powerful persona. Clark Smith was handsome for his age, well groomed, and classically good looking, the picture of virility with his square set jaw and strong features. The courtroom quietened as he began his address to the jury, the elder women amongst them obviously affected by his prowess. I noticed one lady in the front row smile as he strode to the front of the court, with the confidence one would expect to see displayed from a rock star in concert.

"Ladies and gentlemen," he announced in his booming voice as he paced the floor. "Today we are all gathered to decide whether this young woman," he said pointing to me fiercely, "murdered Brad Harrison. Now I know some of you may find it hard to believe that such a beautifully turned out girl could be responsible for murder, but what I am going to present to you are the facts; the cold hard facts surrounding the case. As we all know in life, things aren't always black and white, the baddies aren't always monstrous looking villains, and the victims are not always demure young women. No," he said, shaking his head and turning back towards me. "Evil can take many forms. What I am going to prove over the course of this case is that this woman; this vision standing before us attacked Brad Harrison with the intent of killing him. Brad Harrison was the victim in all of this, a young man with an amazing future ahead of him, which was cruelly taken away from him because of the actions of this woman. He didn't have so much as a grain of dirt in his history. He was respected, a man of integrity who was an ambassador for youth charities, and helped people generously whenever he could. He gave generously to Miss Kimura during the course of their relationship. He was not a violent man and there is nothing to indicate that he ever was. Now I am sure if we look at the facts then we can safely come to the conclusion that Ria Kimura killed Brad Harrison in cold blood and in her own words and I quote, 'I am glad I killed him'."

He stepped down looking pleased with the impression he had created, and I felt nervous by the way he had captivated the room with his drama. Grant threw me a look of annoyance; he was obviously aggravated by the display put on by the opposing lawyer.

Grant looked eager to jump in and when he was told to give his opening statement, he sprang from his seat as if attached to a coil. When on his feet he gave the jury a calculated look as if to mock what had just been said, and I swallowed hard in anticipation of what he was about to say. He proceeded with my defence, slowly articulating each word with a powerful effect.

"This young woman is a respectable girl," he said gesturing towards me. "The prosecution's case is built solely upon the defamation of her character, and the portrayal of Brad Harrison as a saint. Now what is going to be brought to light during the course of this hearing is that the decedent was not the character he appeared to be. Ladies and gentlemen of the jury, I want you to look past the media hysteria surrounding the case and focus your attention on the real evidence. The evidence surrounding his death clearly points to the innocence of Ria Kimura."

He looked at them with a seriousness; his willowy frame and senior appearance almost regal. After a long pause he continued with his deliverance.

"Fact..." he announced emphasising the word so it echoed through the court room. "Brad Harrison was violent towards Ria Kimura and beat her until she was unrecognisable. There is photographic evidence proving this to be the case. Fact... Ria Kimura left Brad Harrison after his vicious attack, hoping to never hear from him again. Fact... Brad Harrison, and this has been proven, paid senior Detective Inspector Griffwell a sum of twenty thousand dollars to track her down after she left him. Fact... the man she met whilst travelling, suspiciously went missing days after Griffwell located her, leading to the invariable conclusion that Mr Harrison, the so-called victim, may have been responsible for his disappearance. Fact... my client had not had contact with Brad since she had left him, yet months after she escaped from his brutality, he happened to be in her apartment waiting for her when she returned from work. Why was he there? Was he there to harm her? It is the only logical conclusion that can be made. Fact... Ria Kimura rang the police herself after the incident in a state of shock; actions of a premeditated murderer? I think not. Now members of the jury ask yourself in light of the overwhelming evidence about to be unearthed, do you think there is a case strong enough to convict this girl of such a heinous crime? Do you think, beyond reasonable doubt that she attacked Brad with the intent to kill, or to defend herself from a man who had maliciously attacked her before, and had tracked her down with such ferocity that he put it upon himself to pay someone to find her? Brad Harrison wasn't the man people thought he was. He was violent, and he was pursuing Miss Kimura with the intent of harming her. All my client is guilty of is being foolish and too trustworthy. She put her faith in Brad Harrison and now she is paying the consequences for it. It is your job to look at the real evidence, at the real facts, and if you do I am sure you will all come to the conclusion that this young lady is the real victim in all of this. Thank you."

He sat down with an air of grace and I realised how lucky I was to have such a talented lawyer working for me. Thank God for Diane. She was seated next to my mother and they were sharing relieved glances between them at Grant's performance. Hopefully it would be enough to convince the myriad of jurors of my innocence. With two men of such enormous capabilities as opponents, I realised what a journey there was ahead of me before I knew whether I would be freed or facing a life behind bars.

CHAPTER FORTY-NINE

It was day two of the trial and I was stood on the stand, the moment I had been dreading about to eventuate. A sense of panic descended upon me as I noticed the smug look on the prosecution lawyer's face as he prepared to interrogate me; pacing before me in such a self-assured threatening manner, he reminded me of a professional boxer stepping into the ring before a fight. I would not have been surprised if I had heard Clark Smith crunching his knuckles in anticipation of the blows he was about to reign upon me, and I felt a trickle of sweat rolling down in between my breasts as I stood before him, the heat from the courtroom intensified by the countless pairs of eyes boring into me.

I made a silent prayer to God as I swore upon the Bible to tell the truth; something I was certain the handsome man before me was about to twist in any way he could. He adjusted his tie and stared at me in an unsettling manner, and when he was sure he had captivated the attention of every person in the court, he began.

"Ria Kimura, you met Brad Harrison at a notorious strip club in London didn't you, Centrefolds if I'm correct?"

"Yes that's right," I nodded.

"And before long you were engaged in a relationship?"

"Yes we were."

"He must have been pretty smitten with you, a man who could

have had anyone he wanted and he suddenly took an interest in you; a stripper. Must have felt good no?" He accentuated the word stripper, spitting it from his mouth as if it were a vulgar obscenity. I took a breath before answering, knowing the direction he was heading for.

"Well yes, but I didn't realise who he was when we met." I noticed then that my hands were shaking and clasped them together in a bid to hold them still.

"I'm sure a woman whose occupation is based solely upon attracting wealthy men must have put two and two together. You knew he was successful, a man of status, isn't that true?"

"Yes, I suppose I did."

"He was very generous to you I take it. Showered you with expensive gifts, extravagant outings?" He turned towards the jury as he asked me the question, his countenance and tone clearly insinuating me as an unscrupulous money-grabber.

"Yes," I agreed dejectedly.

"Do you enjoy working as a stripper?"

"It's okay, it's a job; a way to make money that's all."

"Still must have been nice for you to have someone who was able to offer you a way out of your existence? A multi-millionaire. Did you become a stripper with the intention of finding yourself a rich man?"

"No, I started working there while I was at university."

"But it was an occupation that you got rather sucked into though wasn't it; the glamour, the money, the drugs?"

"I object," said Grant, leaping to my defence. "He is asking my client leading questions."

"Overruled," The judge responded, waving a fat hand at him dismissively.

I answered quickly before he had the opportunity to ask me his question in an even more damaging way. "Well it was exciting but I wasn't aiming to do it forever. I am not stupid, I have got other ambitions."

"I don't think you are stupid at all Miss Kimura, in fact quite the opposite." He raised an eyebrow at me suggestively as if purporting me to be some kind of criminal mastermind. I reminded myself not to react, which would only serve to further illustrate his depiction of me as an unhinged, vindictive woman.

"So when Brad asked you to come with him to Sydney, it must have been a dream come true for you?" He was pacing the floor in front of me now, subtly throwing furtive glances towards the women of the jury. They were clearly revelling in the fleeting moments of attention from him; their eyes fixed on him as if they were watching a ball at a tennis match, moving from one side of the court to another.

"Well it was exciting."

"Yes I'm sure it was. Suddenly you are catapulted from your life as a stripper, to a glamorous life with your new millionaire boyfriend. Exciting is probably an understatement." He lingered by the stand before continuing with his next question. "So how did Brad treat you at the beginning of your relationship?"

"He couldn't do enough for me," I admitted. "We adored each other." I almost flinched as I heard my statement and simultaneously witnessed a wry smile crossing the face of Clark.

"After arriving in Sydney when did the incident happen, in which you claim he attacked you and you ended the relationship?"

"It was a couple of months after."

"Right so for a couple of months everything was fine?"

"Well not really, he was very possessive of me, I felt trapped."

"What I mean to ask is there were no incidents before when you claim he attacked you?"

"No there weren't."

"So after the alleged attack, how soon after did you leave him?"

"A couple of weeks," I said, glancing nervously at Grant.

"Two weeks," he repeated. "Two weeks! If he attacked you with the ferocity you claim he did, then why did you wait so long until you left him?"

"I was scared. I didn't want anyone to see me." I stared down at the stand and studied the grain of the pine across its wood as a silent tear rolled down my nose.

"Convenient really that no one did see you afterwards wouldn't you say?"

"His cleaner saw me." I felt a twinge of bitter disappointment as I was reminded of her sudden refusal to participate in the trial; after her initial enthusiasm it had been a shock. In that moment I noticed Brad's parents exchange furtive glances and realised that they had probably paid her to keep her mouth shut. An integral part of my case gone. A vital piece of the jigsaw on which my freedom had relied upon, erased so easily with some cash. It was a crushing blow.

"That is just hearsay Ria. Unreliable evidence." Clark paused seeming to enjoy relaying the information to me and observing my frustration before continuing. "So suddenly after months of a happy relationship you claim that Brad Harrison; a man with no history of domestic violence, not a single flaw on his criminal record assaulted you? Did you speak to anyone, tell them what had happened?"

"No," I said softly.

"Sorry, I didn't quite hear you," he said in a sarcastic voice; tugging at his earlobe mockingly.

"No!" I repeated more loudly.

"Why not?"

"I didn't want my family to worry."

"Strange that a woman who moved to the other side of the world to be with a man wouldn't just go home to their family after such an ordeal, don't you agree?"

"Objection." Grant was up now, an infuriated expression on his face.

"Overruled." The judge waved him off again as if swatting at an annoying fly; clearly as sucked in by the drama of Clark's address as the rest of the room. Wide-eyed and silent they observed the scene. I could see the pained expressions on my family's faces as they helplessly watched him attack my credibility, ripping it to tattered shreds.

"I'll rephrase my question. Why after the man you loved ferociously beat you; as you claim he did, did you decide to stay in Australia and not just go home to your family?"

"Because I wanted to have fun before I went home, and I didn't want people to know what he had done to me." I answered him hesitantly, scared of saying something incriminating and giving him more ammunition.

"Fun," he retorted, throwing back his head as if my saying it made him want to laugh. "Fun! It seems like fun is pretty important to you, pretty high on your priority list. Seems to me fun would be the last thing on a normal young woman's mind if they had just been a victim of domestic violence, no?"

"Objection." Grant looked outraged as he made his protestation and this time the judge took notice.

"Sustained," he agreed.

Despite the error of his accusation being pointed out, Clark looked satisfied that he had communicated his point to the jurors, some of whom wore contemplative expressions as if mulling over his idea in their heads. After giving them enough time to reflect on his remark he commenced with my next question.

"Miss Kimura. When you were arrested you underwent a toxicology test didn't you?"

"Yes."

"Ladies and gentlemen of the jury, I would like to bring to your attention the toxicology report taken from Ria Kimura the night she was arrested." He handed a printout quickly to them before placing a copy in front of the judge. "As you can see there were high levels of THC in her blood. For those of you who don't know THC is the chemical abbreviation for the drug more commonly known as marijuana. There were also traces of benzoylmethyl ecgonine or cocaine. How do you explain that Miss Kimura? Are you a drug user?"

"Well," I remarked, carefully considering my answer. "I do smoke marijuana, and occasionally take cocaine." I looked down as I answered; ashamed to have to admit the fact in front of my mum.

"Did you know what the side effects of regular usage of these drugs are?" He directed his question towards the jury.

"No," I answered.

"Well, cocaine is known for producing feelings of agitation, mood swings, and depression. It can also cause aggressive, violent behaviour, and hallucinations. Marijuana has many side effects, abuse is common among schizophrenics. Other more common side effects are anxiety, panic attacks, and paranoia. In other words Miss Kimura; perhaps your drug abuse made you feel that Brad Harrison was trying to attack you? Maybe you suffer from a distorted perception of the world due to your drug usage?"

"Objection, the toxicology reports show low levels of both substances, meaning that neither were taken on a regular basis." Grant stood up again, and the judge acknowledged him, nodding in agreement. He was obviously familiar with toxicology reports and from experience knew what would be considered as high levels or not.

"Sustained," he announced.

Clark looked unfazed and stepped closer to me. "Now the night you killed Brad. How did he happen to get into your apartment?"

"I don't know," I replied. Had I really forgotten to lock my door that night? I berated myself for my stupidity. Who knows though, maybe there had been signs of forced entry and Detective Griffwell had covered it up?

"Well there were no signs of forced entry, so clearly you must have let him in yourself."

"No I didn't. He was waiting for me when I got home."

"And you claim he started attacking you with the intent of killing you?"

"Yes."

"Brad was a big man wasn't he? Six foot and two hundred pounds, he worked out regularly didn't he? How many times a week did he go to the gym usually?"

"About five days a week."

"So you'd agree with me that he was a strong man?"

"Yes he was."

"Approximately how much do you weigh Miss Kimura?"

"About eight stone."

"Eight stone. Correct me if I'm wrong but that's about a hundred and twelve pounds am I right?"

"I think so," I said unsurely.

"So Brad was almost double your size?"

"I suppose he was."

As I answered his question Clark Smith swept round to face the judge. "I would like to draw to the attention of the jury some photographic evidence. It is the photo taken after the defendant was arrested for the murder of Brad Harrison." He swept around distributing the grotesque picture of me before placing one on the stand under my gaze. "Please would you look at this photo of yourself carefully Miss Kimura."

As soon as I glanced down at it the tears began to rise inside me and I relived the horror of that evening; the fear and shock I had felt when I had seen Brad waiting for me in my flat, the disgust and terror that had taken over me when Brad had announced that he had murdered Andy, and the sense of helplessness which had encompassed me as he had revealed his intentions of killing me also and I had felt the force of his body pressing down on top of mine; his hands clamped around my throat as I had struggled to breathe. Looking at the photo; surveying my bruised swollen face, I was reminded of the ordeal he had put me through. A fat tear dropped down onto the photo as I studied it.

Clark's next question awoke me from the flashback and I turned my attention back to maintaining my composure. "Can you describe the injuries on your face for us all?"

"I have a black eye," I said, struggling to get the words out through my sobs. "I have a bruised cheek and bruises around my neck from where he was strangling me."

"From where you claim he was strangling you, but could possibly have been caused by him restraining you from attacking him."

"No it was from when he was strangling me."

"Still they appear to be pretty minor injuries. Why is it Ria, a man of almost double your size, inflicted such little damage when you claim he was attempting to take your life?"

"Because I got him off me in time!" The tears were flowing faster now, and I noticed my family struggling to stop themselves from crying also, Aia wiping her tears away with a tissue.

"Is it?" he snapped. "Because I think it's highly unlikely that a man of his physique would have had any trouble ending your life if he had wanted to." He paused for effect, turning to face the jury before continuing. "Brad had two injuries to his head: one on the top left hand side of his skull. The second was on the back of his skull. The blow ended his life, crushing his skull and causing him to die instantly. The angle at which you hit him must have meant that you were standing over him for the second blow. That he was lying underneath you. Can you explain why you hit him with a force of such magnitude as to kill him, when he was lying on the ground at the time?"

"Because he was about to get back up and hurt me again."

"Or maybe he was never attacking you? Maybe it's all been fabricated to cover up the fact that you were attacking him and you intentionally killed him." He was practically shouting at me now. Grant leapt up from his seat again, a look of disgust on his face.

"He killed Andy!" I cried.

"Nonsense," Clark retorted. "For all we know he could be sitting on a beach somewhere drinking a pina colada."

"I object," Grant shouted.

"Sustained," the judge said.

Clark then turned to the bundle of case files he had brought in and pulled from it a folder containing some photos. "Ladies and gentlemen, I am now going to distribute a picture for you to look at. It's a crime scene photo showing the aftermath of Miss Kimura's attack." He handed out the photos amongst the jury, before placing one before me. "Now I want you to see the damage Miss Kimura did. Notice the severity of her attack. Now please compare the two photos."

The photo was a close up of Brad, his mouth wide open, his head swimming in a pool of blood. It was horrific. I gasped as I looked at it and noticed several members of the jury doing the same.

"Now looking at that photo, of the damage you did, how does it make you feel Miss Kimura?" he asked in a mocking tone.

"Shocked," I replied.

"So it doesn't make you feel glad that you killed him as you stated to the investigating officers during one of your interrogations?"

"No, it doesn't."

He surveyed the room and satisfied with the shocked reactions he turned towards the judge. "No further questions your Honour." And with that Clark Smith went back to the bench triumphantly and sat down.

I attempted to take a sip of water with my trembling hands, and wiped away the fresh tears from my face with a tissue passed to me by a court orderly. I had to get out of there; away from the eyes, away from the judgment being passed on me. I felt like I couldn't breathe from the pressure anymore. I was enormously relieved when Judge Coleman announced that the court was in recess until the following day. I was almost looking forward to returning to my cell.

CHAPTER FIFTY

Diane felt tired. Tired and defeated. Dave had left and her home felt empty, even with Ria's family staying with her. The hearing had been a gut wrenching rollercoaster so far, had cost her a small fortune, and it now seemed like it had all been pointless. Diane felt like there was a black sinister cloud hanging on top of her life like a shadow. She sighed deeply.

She missed Dave badly now. In times of a crisis he was the first person she would usually turn to. She felt lost. Maybe he had been right? Perhaps she did always put the club and the girls before him? Maybe it was time to sell up and move on. After five years of owning Flirt though, it had become a part of her identity. Would she be able to cope without it; without the bustle, the drama, the glamour?

She opened the fridge and poured out some Chenin Blanc into some glasses, they frosted as she filled them. Then she arranged some sushi onto a tray, poured some orange juice for Shinzo, before mustering a smile on her face for her guests and making her way into the sitting room. They were congregated on the large white sofa; pale and distraught, Jane seated in between her two children. She gave her a weak smile as she picked up her glass.

"Thanks Diane," she said.

"You're welcome," Diane said warmly.

"Thank you," Aia added as she took hers. She reminded Diane of a porcelain doll, with her raven hair swept up in an elegant bun and one of Diane's silk dressing gowns on. Even with no make-up and her face etched with worry she was a beauty. Just like her sister except less flamboyant. Aia was more refined and composed, her features more oriental, her figure daintier, less curvaceous. She was a fine example of what Ria would probably have turned out like had she not gone off the rails. Like her good twin.

"You're welcome," said Diane. "It's my favourite evening ritual to sit here in the lounge with all the doors open and to look out across the pool, drinking a glass of wine.

"Not just for the wine though Diane; for everything. God knows what we would have done without you. What Ria would have done." She bit her lip then and a tear rolled down her face. Jane pulled her daughter closer to her as she wept, and Shinzo folded against her too sobbing, taking irregular breaths in between his cries, his young handsome face filled with pain.

Diane felt a stab of regret as she watched the family before her huddled together and she wondered if she would have become a different woman had she had children of her own. Her insistence to help Ria had cost her more than she had bargained for, but seeing what her and her family were going through it only reaffirmed the decision she had made. She couldn't just stand back and watch an innocent girl get put away; not when she knew from experience what Brad Harrison had really been. She had made the mistake of turning a blind eye once before. How could she have made the same mistake twice?

Once Ria's family had sufficiently comforted one another, Jane loosened her grasp on her children and they both sat upright; Aia dabbing at her eyes with a tissue, Shinzo wiping away his tears and snot with the back of his sleeve.

"Do you think they will find her guilty?" Shinzo asked, his innocent brown eyes practically pleading Diane to tell him it would all be okay.

"Of course not," Diane replied, trying to sound as convincing as possible. "Grant is the best lawyer in Sydney and Ria is innocent. It will all work out I'm sure."

It seemed to do the trick and he crawled off the sofa and started eating the food laid out on the glass table.

"Time to go to bed," Jane said when he had devoured a plentiful amount. Shinzo obliged, kissing his mother on the cheek, then Aia; and as he walked past Diane he kissed her cheek too, a kiss which warmed her heart. She really did feel like a part of the family now. If there was one good thing about a crisis, it was the way in which it brought people together.

Once he was safely out of earshot Jane turned to Diane. "Do you really think they will find Ria innocent?"

Diane shook her head. "I don't know. I just don't know. If there is any justice in the world then they will."

The women sat in silence for a while, united in their misery, taking gulps of their ice cold wine.

"Why did you never have children?" Aia asked, startling Diane.

"I suppose I never got round to it," Diane replied eventually.

"Sorry," Aia said. "It's just that you would have made such a wonderful mum." Diane smiled to herself. She already was a mum; to about fifty girls.

The wine only served to further unsettle Diane's nerves, causing her thoughts to slosh around in her head, colliding with each other unsettlingly. She had a bad feeling about tomorrow; the Harrisons were the type of people who always had a contingency plan. When Jane and Aia finally went to bed, Diane was relieved to be alone and she went to her room and lay in her empty bed.

She waited until the big house was still. The combination of the warm night air and the silk sheet was almost too good a sensation against her skin, and she felt compelled to stay where she was, but then she remembered Shinzo's forlorn expression when he had asked her if Ria would be okay. The image was enough to catapult Diane back into action. She had to do it. Just one last ditch attempt.

She crept down the stairs; the marble felt cool against her feet as she tiptoed. The living room was semi-lit; there was an eerie glow to it, which allowed her to just make out the silhouette of the furniture and manoeuvre without stumbling. She pulled the patio doors open and walked into the garden, pulling her phone from her dressing gown pocket. Its light illuminated her face within the darkness, and she hesitated for a moment before pressing dial.

"Hello darl, it's Diane," she said, her voice a half whisper. "Look I know I promised you never to bring this up again, but this is an emergency."

The voice on the other end sounded tired and irritated. "Diane, I already told that lawyer guy. I'm not talking. End of."

"I know sweetheart but this is serious now. I really think Ria is going to be found guilty. You need to do this. Don't worry he can't hurt you now, I promise I am here for you."

"Diane, you don't understand."

"Of course I do, you're frightened and worried; of course you are, who wouldn't be, it must be a terrifying thought to stand up in front of a room full of people and admit what you went through, but it is the right thing to do darl."

"No Diane, that's not it, I'm not scared. I wish I could tell everyone what a stupid son of a bitch Brad was but I can't do it. Not now."

"Why not?" Diane asked.

"I shouldn't be telling you this but that's not why I didn't want to talk."

"Well if you're not scared then what's stopping you, this is a young woman's life at stake here?"

"They bribed me Diane. When it happened, they told me to keep my mouth shut and they would make it worth my while."

Diane heard herself gasp then. "What do you mean?"

"What do you think I mean? How do you think I afforded to buy my house and my new boobs? It wasn't from the money I earned at Flirt."

"But he could have killed you. He could have killed you."

"Yes well I was lucky though wasn't I? I lived and I got enough money to change my life. I'm sorry Diane. I really feel for this girl but I am asking for it if I go on that stand. I just can't do it. I just can't."

Diane heard a clicking sound as the phone was hung up. She felt shocked at the revelation she had just heard. It seemed that money could buy you everything after all. At least she had tried though. She would find out tomorrow whether or not it had been in vain.

CHAPTER FIFTY-ONE

Grant paced the room while I sat down; my head in my hands. It was all going so horribly wrong so far. My only witness of the abuse Brad had inflicted on me; Sue Ting the cleaner, had magically disappeared and the prosecution lawyer was doing a terrifyingly good job of demonising me. I could almost feel my freedom slipping through my fingertips.

I eyed the door feeling the impulse to run through it to my family. I imagined myself fleeing from the courthouse like a villain from a movie, taking the prison officer next to me as a hostage and escaping from the impending sense of doom which had been hanging over me like a thick fog since the beginning of the trial. Instead I made do with touching up my make-up, trying to catch my tears with a folded up tissue, before they rolled from my eyes and made my mascara run down my face in black trails of misery.

"Calm down Ria. There is still plenty of evidence to be presented." Grant sounded like he was reassuring himself as much as me; I could see he was nervous by the way he refused to meet my gaze. We fell silent again, lost in our own thoughts.

We were jolted back into consciousness by a loud knock at the door. Grant, the prison officer, and I all turned our attention towards it as a man stepped in, holding his hand out to greet Grant as he introduced himself.

"Hi, I'm David Price, I work for the Police Integrity Commission. You must be Grant Peterson, Miss Kimura's lawyer."

"Yes I am, pleased to meet you." Grant nodded and shook his outstretched hand briefly, before gesturing for him to take a seat. He sat down and I shifted forward on my own chair in anticipation of what he was about to say.

"As you know we are conducting our own investigation of the case and we have come across some evidence that we thought would be extremely important for the hearing." He spoke in a hushed voice, and I felt my heart leap at the mention of new evidence.

"Really?" Grant asked.

"Yes. We don't know if it was deliberately covered up by Detective Griffwell but it's pretty intrinsic information. We ran some basic checks and we have discovered that Brad Harrison was in fact staying in Cairns on the twelfth of March; in the same hotel Ria was staying in with Andrew."

"Really! So that must mean…" Grant prompted.

"Yes," David nodded. "Brad was in Cairns at the time Andrew Wilson disappeared. It seems that he was tipped off by Detective Griffwell that Miss Kimura was staying there, and he arrived the day they left; staying there for one night."

"And coincidentally Andrew just happened to vanish from the face of the earth at the same time!" Grant exclaimed. "This is outrageous. He obviously murdered the poor boy and nothing is being done about it. Now this young lady is being made to pay the consequences." He pointed in my direction as I sat in awe, dumbfounded by the news.

"We have his flight details, record of his stay in the hotel, and the car he hired." The young man handed them to Grant who stood up and shook his hand vigorously.

"Thank you," he said as the man left, leaving us with a new found sense of hope. We exchanged a look of bewilderment over the startling discovery and Grant arranged the papers across the desk, studying them in awe and shaking his head simultaneously. "This is just what we needed Ria. This is just what we bloody well needed."

At that moment the court orderly announced the recess would soon be over, jerking us back to reality, and I was led back to the court by the PO; eager to discover the impact the new evidence would have upon the trial. I made my way to the dock and noticed Clark Smith leaning over the Harrisons, a smug look crossing his face as I passed their line of vision, and from over his shoulder Stephanie Harrison throwing me a contemptuous glare, her mouth curled into a disgusted snarl. I looked away quickly to my mum who smiled at me warmly, and waited as chatter in the court room rose and dimmed to a hush at the arrival of Judge Coleman.

"The court is now in session," he announced.

Grant took the opportunity to take to his feet. "Your honour there has been new evidence brought to light during the recess. Mr David Price from the Police Integrity Commission delivered it and I ask your permission for it to be revealed to the court."

"Very well, bring it here," Judge Coleman said. Grant handed him the evidence eagerly and he held up the sheets of paper in front of his chubby face and casually scanned the contents of its pages. When he reached the middle of the documents he was quite visibly taken aback; adjusting his spectacles as he looked over the new information in disbelief. "Yes I agree it is relevant to the case. You have my permission to present it to the jury."

Grant triumphantly retrieved the papers and passed the documents to the jury, before a bewildered looking Clark Smith.

"Please pass it amongst yourselves," Grant said, as the jury studied the evidence with uncertainty, handing it to one another with blank expressions. "Now what you see before you is new evidence recently overturned by the Police Integrity Commission in the course of their internal investigation," he explained to them. "Now as you know this case has been under scrutiny from them because of the corruption known to have taken place during the investigation; namely by Detective Inspector Griffwell who was heading the inquiry. It was discovered he had been paid the sum of twenty thousand dollars by Brad Harrison to locate Miss Kimura after she left him. There has also been the suspicious disappearance of Andrew Wilson who Miss Kimura met shortly after leaving the Mr Harrison."

"I object," said Clark, looking agitated. "There is no evidence to suggest that Miss Kimura left the decedent."

"Overruled," the Judge said.

"My client got on a flight away from him, and Mr Harrison paid a police officer twenty thousand dollars to locate her. I think we can safely assume she left him," Grant threw back at him. "My client," he said turning his attention back towards the jury, "has always maintained that Brad Harrison was responsible for Andrew Wilson's disappearance, claiming he confessed to his murder the night of her arrest. Her claims were never sufficiently investigated due to the corrupt nature of the case. Well in front of you ladies and gentlemen of the jury is evidence, supporting her claim that Brad Harrison did murder Andrew Wilson."

There was a collective gasp from the courtroom and Clark's face grew ashen. For the first time since I had met him he appeared to have had the wind knocked from his usually unflappable sails.

"Andrew Wilson was last seen on the twelfth of March. He had been staying in the Ocean Plaza Hotel in Cairns with Miss Kimura for two nights. They checked out that day and Andrew Wilson drove Miss Kimura to the airport where she got a flight to Sydney. He then continued on to drive to Mount Isa to meet his family. Well two hours after they checked out, Mr Harrison checked into the very same hotel."

A wave of chatter broke out amongst the press and spectators, but was quickly hushed by Judge Coleman banging his gavel ferociously.

"Continue Mr Peterson," he urged.

"Shortly after arriving at the Ocean Plaza Hotel Brad hired a car, and wasn't seen again in the hotel until the next afternoon. Soon after he flew back to Sydney. Now this evidence clearly supports the fact that Mr Harrison tracked Miss Kimura down to the hotel in Cairns, with the help of Detective Griffwell and undoubtedly he found someone else; Andrew Wilson. Now what he did to him when he found him is uncertain, but Andrew has not been seen or heard from since, his campervan found abandoned in the outback, his personal items left inside it.

Now this new evidence, basic evidence which should have been uncovered straight away, is only serving to shed more light onto the corrupt nature of this investigation. I think it is preposterous that my client, this young lady over here is still sitting in that dock. If Brad Harrison had not been a man of such fame and fortune, this case would have been thrown out of court a long time ago. He was a man who was violent, who was desperate to find her and he was attacking her the night she killed him in self-defence. Thank you your honour."

Grant sat down, throwing me a comforting look. I saw my mum taking a deep breath as if trying to calm her nerves, clutching Aia's hand tightly. The new information was a small victory which had managed to restore the balance of the hearing, and I felt glad to have something working in my favour.

"I object," Clark protested. "Just because the decedent was staying at the same hotel as Andrew Wilson at the time of his disappearance, it does not prove he was in any way involved with his disappearance."

"Overruled," Judge Coleman said dismissively.

The hearing continued and Grant and Clark proceeded passionately with their presentations of the remaining evidence to the jury. I felt powerless, unable to contribute anything to the battle which would decide my fate. I watched the faces of the jurors intently, clutched my angel stone, and prayed that they would be able to see the truth through the mist and the vast complications of the case. The thought of being led back into Silverwater prison, to an existence of solitude and confinement was more than I could bear.

Clark made a point of expressing the magnitude of the case to the jurors, his style of presenting captivating, gut wrenchingly good, and emotive. Grant had a style all of his own; a precise deliverance of his words, a respectable tone, and consistently factual based arguments which anyone would find difficult to discredit. As the day unfolded I saw confusion in the audience of the court room, as the lawyers relayed their interpretations of the information surrounding the case, with flair. My life was hanging in the balance between these two men.

When Judge Coleman announced it was time for them to deliver their closing arguments I held my breath with apprehension and clasped my sweaty hands together on my lap as I silently prayed to God to let me escape this nightmare. It would soon be over and I would finally know what would become of me.

CHAPTER FIFTY-TWO

It was Clark's turn first and he stepped down towards the jury, his head high, his dauntingly handsome face casting a severe look upon the spectators. He knew the art of perfect timing and wielded it like a weapon. Finally, after what seemed like an eternity, he began.

"We are here today because a young man, a beloved son, an inspiring person, and a national treasure was cut down in his prime, by this young lady," he said pointing at me with an accusatory finger. "Now I believe he was a good man, a man of integrity. He met this young lady and fell in love. He offered her the world, shared his fortune and his heart with her. He was heartbroken when she left him. He did try to find her, not because he wanted to hurt her, because he had a responsibility to look after her, he needed to know she was safe, and of course because he loved her; despite her many flaws. Unfortunately love isn't a choice for many and in this case it was a disease. A disease which ended up killing Brad Harrison.

"Now Brad Harrison had no history of violence in the thirty-five years he was on the planet, not one iota of misconduct recorded in his lifetime. He was of a sound mind, successful in his own right, an inspirational character. Now it is because of this that I believe that Miss Kimura's claim that his murder was an act of self-defence, preposterous. A lie fabricated to protect herself, to explain the unforgivable behaviour which ended his life.

"Miss Kimura was with Brad Harrison for approximately six months. In that time there is no evidence he had ever so much as raised a hand to her. No witnesses were confided in; no friends, no family. No doctors or nurses ever saw so much as a mark on her.

"We have established the character of Miss Kimura, through facts. She is a drug addict, an alcoholic. A stripper. She was intoxicated the night she killed Brad. There were also no signs of forced entry into her flat, which indicates that he was invited in by her.

"I believe that Ria Kimura attacked Mr Harrison with a champagne bottle, in a drug and alcohol fuelled rage, beating him over the head with it. She showed no remorse for her actions. No, the first thing she did after she killed him was to ring her new lover.

"The definition of self-defence is the protection of one's person or property against some injury attempted by another. Ria Kimura did not use reasonable force against Brad Harrison. If she had, he would still be alive. She hit him over the head with a champagne bottle and when he was lying on the floor underneath her she struck him with it again; with such force that she crushed his skull and brain, causing him to die instantly.

"It was almost an hour before she called the emergency services, while Brad lay on the floor in front of her, his blood spreading across the floor of her apartment. This in my mind are not the actions of a victim, but of a cold-blooded woman with no feelings of remorse for ending the life of such a fine man. She watched him, was next to his lifeless body for almost an hour. Now during that hour she became scared. Feared for her future.

"She came up with a story to save herself. She conveniently blamed the disappearance of Andrew Wilson on her dead victim. She lied and said Brad Harrison had been attacking her, when all she had to show for it were a few minor bruises; bruises that would have been more likely to be sustained from Brad Harrison defending himself, not from him attacking her. Now I believe that if a man of Brad's size had really been trying to kill her, she would not be here today. But Brad wasn't attacking her. She did not kill him in self-defence. She murdered him. A woman scorned. I find it very hard to believe that she left Brad, I believe he ended it with her and when she ran off, he looked for her purely to make sure she was safe. She invited him over on that fateful night and when she saw no signs of him ever taking her back, she attacked him viciously, ending his life.

"Now when making your decision, I want you to consider that there is no reliable evidence supporting her claim of self-defence. I want you to completely disregard Andrew Wilson's disappearance when making your decision. There is no conclusive evidence to say he is not still alive and well. Thousands of travellers "disappear" in Australia and live here illegally every year.

"When making your decision, please consider the loss of the people who the decedent touched in his lifetime. His parents, his friends, and loved ones; the thousands of young people across Australia who he mentored and supported through his charity work. The thousands of people who he employed through his many businesses, and their families who now have their futures hanging by a thread. All because of the actions of this woman. She has not just ended the life of Brad Harrison but she has affected the lives of so many others.

"Do not let her looks fool you because underneath it all is a cold woman, a murderer, who viciously bludgeoned her victim to death. Her tears are an act, she is an act, an act who is usually parading herself around naked in front of men to fund her drugs and extravagant lifestyle. Brad was just a means to an end and when she saw he would no longer be meeting with her demands, she ended his life. When interrogated by police, Miss Kimura claimed she was happy she had murdered him and I quote her exact words. 'He used me! I loved him, and he treated me like crap! He deserved to fucking die and I'm glad I killed the bastard!'

"I ask that you find her guilty of murder in the first degree. She shouldn't be allowed to walk free. I hope you make the right choice."

I swallowed hard at hearing the prosecution's closing statement. It was convincing. So convincing I felt a chill descend through my spine. Aia looked white, the colour washed from her face. The jury looked touched, I noticed a few of them nodding their heads subtly in agreement as he spoke. Could this be it? Could this be the end for me? The concept of a life in prison was terrifying. I would rather die than face it. I hoped Grant was about to deliver and live up to his glowing reputation, or I was screwed.

Grant took a sip of his water, straightened his tie and stood; all the eyes of the room were resting upon his willowy frame. There was an impenetrable silence as he surveyed the jurors, a serious expression on his face. It was an expression which conveyed that he meant business. It seemed like it was ages until he spoke, the court room anticipating his words. What could he finally say that could sway the jurors' minds in my favour now? I felt like my fate had already been sealed. He cleared his throat and began.

"It is a gross misconduct that this case is even in court. This whole case is a gross misconduct, based upon character defamation and the glorification of a man who was obviously not what he seemed to be. It is wrought with corruption, riddled with it like a disease; so deep, it is impossible to determine what is factual and what isn't. But at the bottom of it, underneath all the layers of corruption and fabrication, there is a young woman's life at stake here.

"There is not enough evidence in my opinion to convict Miss Kimura with murder. To sentence a girl to life imprisonment for defending herself against a man who had tracked her down unrelentingly and showed up in her apartment, uninvited, unannounced, waiting for her in the small hours of the morning. My client did what anyone else would have done when faced with a person twice their size, pinning them down and strangling the life from their body. She fought back. She grabbed the first thing to hand and she hit him with it as hard as she could to protect herself. It wasn't out of anger. It was out of fear.

"I want you as members of the jury to look past your prejudices. My clients is a young woman, is it criminal that she came here to have fun? Is it really so shocking that she has taken recreational drugs, does that mean she is capable of cold-blooded murder? Because she has worked as a stripper does that mean she is a bad person? We are not here to judge her lifestyle. Now I am pleading with you all to ignore the performance of the prosecution. This isn't a theatre, it is a court of law. Please look at this young lady and see her for who she really is; a scared, young girl. Beaten by her ex-partner, ruthlessly pursued by him, and almost murdered by him. Andrew Wilson was probably murdered by this same man, a man who was so desperate to find her that he paid a detective twenty thousand dollars to track her down. She is a girl who has been in custody for the last four months because she defended herself, a girl who is desperate to be with her family, who have suffered almost as much as her from this ordeal, helplessly on the other side of the world.

"Throughout this trial we have seen evidence supporting her self-defence plea. Evidence Miss Kimura left Brad because he violently beat her, leaving his apartment quickly in his absence as if she were fleeing. We have seen horrific photographic evidence of her after his attack. We have been given evidence from the Police Integrity Commission which strongly links Brad Harrison to the disappearance of Andrew Wilson whom my client insists was murdered by Mr Harrison.

"Ria Kimura is a young lady with no criminal history, and no motive for murder. It was self-defence. She had a split second to decide whether to protect herself or let a man squeeze the life from her body. She chose to protect herself. I don't think she needs to be made to suffer any more than she already has. I don't think it is plausible to say she is guilty. She is innocent. Now please let the poor girl go home to her family and continue with a life that has almost been destroyed by a man, who quite clearly came after her with the intent to do her harm.

"Please make your judgements based on the facts and evidence, and not on your prejudices of a young girl who has been villainized wrongfully and your false ideals of a vicious man's façade as a good person. He was attacking her, she grabbed the first thing to hand and hit him on the head with it. It really is that simple. Ria Kimura is innocent, and if there is any reasonable doubt in your minds at all, you will find her so."

The court went into recess while the jury decided the verdict. My family cried as I was taken from the court, handcuffed, and led back towards a cell. Diane seemed to be trying to comfort them, as they all stood, shocked from the ordeal.

"We love you Ria," Aia cried, as my mum held her tightly and I felt myself crumble into breathless sobs as I was taken away from them all again, while the people of the jury made the decision which would change my life.

I lay awake most of the night, my stomach churning in agony, my muscles aching with tension, my eyes sore from my tears. The more I thought about it the more fearful I became. Brad had been a powerful man, his parents wielded more power than I could imagine. Perhaps they had bribed the jury already, perhaps it was a foregone conclusion and all this hope and apprehension was an unnecessary charade? Who knew what tomorrow might bring? It could be the beginning of my life, or the start of the end.

CHAPTER FIFTY-THREE

My body swayed as I struggled to maintain my composure, my heart pounding loudly in my ears as I stood awaiting my verdict. On the other side of the room; a lady stood at the front of the court. Her blond hair was swept back severely, her body attired in a navy blue suit, her face not giving away even a trace of evidence as to what she was about to disclose. We all waited. It must have been only seconds until her announcement was made, but it seemed an eternity until she parted her lips and gave the declaration which would change my life forever.

"Your Honour," she said, pausing mercilessly before bestowing the vital information upon us. "We find the defendant not guilty of first degree murder on the grounds of self-defence."

I heard the elated cries from my family shrieking at the news, the sobs from Brad's mother, my own involuntary shriek, and the deafening chatter amongst the throng of reporters and bystanders. Judge Coleman hammered ferociously as he attempted to make his comments heard. "The defendant has been acquitted and I order her to be released with immediate effect."

The room began to spin, the voices and my emotions causing me to feel dizzy as the hysteria rose within me. I was free. I was free! I ran into the arms of my family, my mum, Aia, and Shinzo embraced me while Diane and Grant punched the air victoriously at the news. Eddie ran over and hugged me tightly. "Thank God!" he cried.

"I can't believe it." I wept as I felt the joy of being immersed by my loved ones again. They whisked me away, my mother kissing me repeatedly on the head as we descended the steps from the courthouse.

"How does it feel to be acquitted?" a reporter asked, thrusting a microphone at me.

Grinning and crying simultaneously, tears of joy and relief, I replied in the only way I could think of. "It feels fucking fantastic!" I heard laughter erupt at my response, before I was bundled into a waiting car by my family.

"I knew you could do it," my mother said holding me tightly, and I cried harder then, releasing the tension that had built within me over the last few months until her jacket was sodden with my tears. She stroked my hair softly. "It's all okay now sweetheart. We will all be home soon. It's going to be alright now."

"I missed you all so much," I exclaimed, so relieved to be in the company of my loved ones again after being away from them for so long.

"We missed you too," Aia said, wiping at her face and hugging me again. "So glad you're okay now Sis. We love you so much, we were so scared. I'm glad you're okay, I don't know what I'd do without you."

We clung to each other in the back of the cab, Shinzo, Aia, my mother, and I; swaying as the taxi navigated through the streets of Sydney. We didn't let go until we arrived at Diane's house. Eddie jumped out and opened the door for us all and Diane promptly led us into her beautiful kitchen, opening a bottle of champagne and filling our glasses.

"To Ria's freedom," she announced, and we clinked them all together in unison with our shaking hands.

It felt like a dream come true and as I surveyed the people I loved around me tenderly I felt like the luckiest girl alive. My ordeal had taught me the real importance of life and it had nothing to do with fast cars, yachts, and expensive things and everything to do with having the people I loved around me and my own freedom. We took our celebration into the garden and I delighted at the feeling of the warm sun against my skin and the sound of laughter and happiness around me. It seemed unreal in comparison to the life I had been living for the past few months. I had finally got through the dark tunnel to the light at the end of it, and it was blinding me with its magnificence.

CHAPTER FIFTY-FOUR

The heat in the air was so thick that the officers were having trouble breathing; the perspiration under their uniforms causing their shirts to stick to their skin as they searched. The police cadaver dog seemed to be struggling further still, panting underneath its fur coat, its long pink tongue hanging out from in between sharpened teeth as it tracked the dusty ground. It was the height of the Australian summer, the parched terrain cracking under the midday sun, the red hue of the scorched soil aptly portraying the sweltering torridity as they marched across it.

It had been three long hours since they had arrived on the scene. The endless expanse of area they had to navigate was overwhelming as they trampled listlessly under the direction of the dog, which so far just seemed to be just getting lost and tired.

"We're not bloody getting anywhere here," complained Officer Kent as he dragged his feet behind the trail of the dog handler. Wiping the sweat from his brow, he stopped to take a swig from his bottle of water.

"Come on, you big girl," mocked his colleague. "We've just gotta get this over with. Another hour and we can go back to the Chief knowing we've given it a good go." Detective Johnson of Queensland police was trying to hide his complacency towards the task at hand, whilst secretly cursing his ancestors for not having invented the siesta in a country with one of the harshest climates in the world. Perhaps if they hadn't been ruled by bloody poms then they would be laying in a darkened room right now with a cold beer. Mmm beer; he could almost taste the amber nectar already, braising against his lips. He couldn't wait for this day to end.

"It's a waste of bloody time though mate. This body we're looking for could be bloody anywhere. It's been eight months. Eight bloody months! It's probably bloody dust by now out here! That dog's not gonna find shit!" Kent remarked.

The female handler turned round sharply when she overheard the comment from behind her. "Actually, dogs can sniff out a corpse at all stages of its decomposition," she said matter-of-factly, before abruptly turning back around and walking briskly behind her canine; its nose sniffing the air around them as they continued with their mission.

"You were told mate!" Johnson laughed once her back was turned and she was a safe distance ahead.

"Do you think it will be able to sniff this out?" There was a loud grumbling noise as Kent screwed up his face comically, expelling some wind.

"You're sick mate!" laughed Johnson, walking further away from his immature colleague. They trudged further onwards sighing and wiping at their sweaty faces with the backs of their hands. "Just think mate, just a bit longer and before you know it, we'll be down at the hotel having a nice cold beer."

The promise of a cold bevvy managed to temporarily motivate them and they returned to silence again, their focus turned back towards preventing themselves from collapsing as their sweat dripped off them in a heavy stream; their bodies threatening to evaporate in the heat. Johnson could feel his feet begin to blister as they slid around in his shoes, rubbing uncomfortably against the hard leather, and he silently berated himself for volunteering for the search.

Then, as if from nowhere, the dog began to bark wildly; a deep husky noise which caused the two officers to stop dead in their tracks.

"Lucy. Has it found something then?" Kent asked the handler.

"What do you think?" she snapped sarcastically, as she tried to keep up with the German Shepherd which was enthusiastically stalking the scent trail it had uncovered, its tail wagging from side to side enthusiastically, its nose to the ground.

They rushed behind it until they reached a crevice in the soil, just next to a dried-up creek. The dog stopped, and began barking and circling manically. Lucy crouched by the discovery and prodded the soil before looking up at the flushed, sweating faces of the men standing behind her. "Looks like you're gonna get that beer sooner than you thought boys. I think we've found what we've been looking for."

They crouched down next to her, studying the heap of cracked soil by their feet and Detective Johnson felt a sudden wave of dizziness hit him, so overwhelming he felt himself losing his balance and had to lean forward on his hand to prevent himself from keeling over. The heat from the sun was really getting to him now. The salty sweat was making his eyes sting and he reached into his pocket for a hanky to wipe it away. He had just finished mopping his brow when something caught his eye. A couple of metres behind the pile of earth which was concealing the body, something was glistening and shining in the undergrowth. Curious, he edged towards it. As he bent over to pick it up his heart pounded against his chest. Held in between his thumb and fore finger was the most exquisite ring he had ever seen. It glinted in the sunlight, the clarity of the large diamond practically blinding him with its brilliance. He stole a fleeting glance at his colleagues, still crouching by the body; they hadn't noticed him or his discovery. He exhaled a silent sigh, then as subtly as he could he slipped it into his trouser pocket. When it was safely out of sight he smiled to himself, resisting the urge to punch his fist in the air and scream in excitement. Volunteering to go walkabouts in the outback hadn't been such a crazy idea after all. He had literally struck gold. Looks like the beers would be on him tonight.

EPILOGUE

A few months had passed since my acquittal, and each day I had savoured and cherished my freedom and the time with my loved ones. I felt like I'd had a near death experience and I intended on making the most of every moment, of the simple pleasures that life had to offer. Good company, good food, laughter, and love.

The first couple of months after my release I had spent my time nestled securely in the family home, as close to my mum and family as I could get, dealing with the feelings of guilt over Andy, and the shock of what I had been through. I had known that I would have to get on with it eventually though and start over, and after two months of hibernating I decided to sort my life out.

My days were now filled with making a business plan and designing clothes to launch my new fashion business. Diane, as always, had helped enormously with her business expertise. My mother and she had become great friends and she had become like a part of the family. I had recently moved into a new apartment in the heart of London, amongst the buzz and pulse of the fashion world. It was beautiful, the kind of place I had always dreamed of calling home. My own little space; my haven. An apartment located in Shoreditch, East London; it was modern, spacious, and sublime. The day I had moved in I had screamed with delight with my mum, we had jumped up and down clutching each other's hands, unable to contain our excitement. It was certainly a big step up from Silverwater prison. I had been bestowed with good fortune since the trial and had been given generous amounts for sharing my story with the world. I had been happy to get my version of events out at last, after months of being villainized by the press and successfully battling against the corruption and unfairness of the nightmare I had been living in. I intended on using my new found money on fulfilling my ambitions. No more stripping ever again.

Today was my birthday, a time for celebration. I was putting the finishing touches to my birthday dinner with the help of my mum while Shinzo lounged on the sofa listening to music. It was Sunday, so we were having a traditional roast dinner with all the trimmings, one of the many things I had missed when I had been in Australia.

As I laid out the cutlery and my mum clattered around in the kitchen looking for condiments, I wondered where Aia, Howard, and my nan were but more importantly when Diane and Eddie would arrive. I glanced at my watch anxiously; any minute now.

Today would be the first time that I had seen Eddie since I had left Sydney. I wondered if it would be the same, if there would still be an attraction between us? We had kept in touch since I had moved home but I had maintained a distance between us, wanting to devote my time and energy to my family; too fearful to get involved with anyone new. I had wanted to see how my feelings would develop and they seemed to be developing stronger every day. But had his?

I felt like I had transformed into a different person since I had worked at Flirt. Pearl was well and truly dead. She had been replaced with someone better; less selfish, less daring, less intoxicated. Would he even like the new me? Perhaps it was the just the drama of Pearl that he had fallen for?

My thoughts were interrupted by the sound of the buzzer echoing loudly in the hallway and I rushed towards it, knocking over some cutlery as I did so.

"You gonna let your old nan in? It's bloody freezing out here."

I relaxed when I saw my nan's face peering at the video phone. "Hi Nanny, come in," I called excitedly.

"Happy birthday," she announced as I answered the door, and she was followed by Aia and Howard.

"What time's your fella coming then? I want to inspect him, give him the once over." My nan delighted in making any new boyfriends nervous, it was a bit of a game for her and I laughed.

"Any minute, he's coming with Diane."

"Don't scare the poor boy off," Mum said, rolling her eyes at her.

"Here Sis, happy birthday," Aia said, giving me a card and an enormous bunch of flowers which my nan proceeded to display on the table I had laid.

"Where's the vase?" she yelled as she went through my cupboards.

"Happy birthday." Howard gave me a kiss on the cheek and followed Aia to the table containing the nibbles.

"Make us a cuppa then, I'm gasping," my nan ordered. I happily obliged, making a round of tea for my family. They sat around the living room, filling the space and I smiled to myself at the sight of them congregated together, chatting happily and bickering. I passed the teas around and gave my nan her cup.

"What has the cow gone dry?" she exclaimed, remarking on the lack of milk I had put in and causing us all to erupt into laughter. Then the buzzer went again; Diane and Eddie had arrived.

I ran to the door, checking my reflection quickly on my way, before swinging it open to be greeted by their smiling faces.

Diane gave me a kiss and went into greet my family, giving Eddie and I a moment alone. Before I had even had a chance to tell him how much I had missed him, he enveloped me in a tight hug, a hug I could have quite happily surrendered myself to all night long. And just like that, all my fears were dispelled at once. It just felt right, like I belonged in his arms and he belonged in mine.

After a few moments he pulled me away and held me at arm's length from him, looking into my eyes with a tenderness that I had forgotten existed.

"So good to see you Ria," he said.

I felt butterflies and murmured back. "It's good to see you too." I tried to wipe the ridiculous grin off my face as I began to lead him through to the sitting room. "Oh and my nan can't wait to meet you; watch out though she's a bit scary."

He laughed and followed me eagerly. "I love your new place," he remarked and I felt a flush of pride.

After some enthusiastic hellos and some embarrassing stories of my childhood were exchanged my mum announced; "it's ready," and we all sat down around the dining table. The sun was shining, and I had all my favourite people in the world around me. It couldn't get any better than this.

My mum raised her voice and stood up. "I just wanted to say a few words to mark the occasion," she said as she surveyed us all. "Firstly I would like to thank Diane, for making all this possible. We will be forever grateful. You saved my daughter. Also thank you to Eddie for joining us; it is a pleasure to have you here and to see you again. But most of all," she said, her eyes welling up with emotion. "I just wanted to say how proud I am of you Ria, for getting through it all and staying strong. Sometimes it takes the bad times to make us realise what we have. So here's to family, the most important thing in the world."

"To family," we all said in unison before tucking into the feast laid out before us.

"Hold on," I said standing up. "I wanted to say a quick word too if that's okay."

"Come on we're bloody starving," said Howard, as Aia gave him an elbow in his side.

"Just wanted to say that it means more to me than anything that we can all be here together today. It's hard to believe that only a few months ago I was in prison. I just want to thank you all for being there for me through thick and thin."

"Well it's all over now love, you've got the world at your feet now," my mum said reassuringly.

"It's certainly one extreme to the other with me isn't it?"

"Yeah well you deserve it after all you've been through," Diane said. "So how's the business plan coming along?"

"Yeah really well, got a meeting tomorrow with a lady from the Hungarian factory. She has made up some samples for me and hopefully, if they are good, then we can start putting my designs into production."

"I am so proud of you Sis," said Aia.

"Thanks," I smiled back at her. "Just so glad to be able to put it all behind me and get on with my life. Today feels like a bit of a turning point. Like I can finally release what's happened and move on."

"At least that poor boy can be put to rest now as well. Awful what that man did to him," my nan said, shaking her head.

"I know, I'm glad they found him. It must be such a relief for Andy's parents but awful as well. They invited me to attend a memorial service for him next week."

"Ah that's nice of them." My mum smiled at me and passed the potatoes to Shinzo.

"Yeah, it will be really sad though. I am surprised they even wanted me there. I feel like it's all my fault." Eddie squeezed my hand under the table.

"How were you to know what a nutter Brad was? You can't blame yourself love," my nan reassured me.

"Yeah I suppose."

"Well anyway let's not dwell on that. We are all together, it's your birthday and you're free. Let's enjoy it today," my mum said quickly, eager for the mood not to deteriorate.

We managed to spend the rest of the day talking without making reference to any of it again. It was a brilliant day and when it was over my family filtered out merrily; Aia unusually tipsy and telling me she loved me repeatedly as she left with Howard. Then Eddie and I were finally alone.

"Your family are great," he said as I sat back down next to him on the white sofa.

"Thanks, they really like you."

"Good. I'm glad. Wouldn't fare well for me if they didn't." He kissed my hand softly.

"Why's that?" I asked as he laced his fingers through mine.

"Why's that?" he repeated. "Do you really need me to spell it out?"

"I guess not, but as it's my birthday…"

"Okay then Ria I will spell it out. I love you. I have loved you for a long time and I can't stand not being near you anymore."

"I love you too," I said, knowing as soon as I heard the words from my mouth that I really did. It wasn't the dangerous kind of infatuation love that I had once felt for Brad. It was something more real. More meaningful.

He kissed me then, the first kiss we had shared for almost nine months. It was intense; passionate but natural. It's funny how distance can amplify feelings sometimes. Since I had returned to England it had been there, an aching longing haunting me, a feeling that something was missing. And now he was here and the yearning was being satisfied. It felt good and suddenly it was clear and simple. I needed him and he needed me.

We began tearing at each other's clothes and I groaned in delight at the sensation of his warm skin against mine. The sex was a release of all the tension in one go, the first time I had even been close to a man since mine and Eddie's first night together all that time ago. It felt as if he knew my body intricately as he made love to me and I didn't want it to ever end.

I woke up, comfortably enveloped in his arms hours later. It was still really early; just beginning to get light. The sacred time when even central London was peaceful, resting as if in anticipation of the commotion which would soon erupt onto its streets. I eased myself up from my bed, gently lifting Eddie's arm so as not to wake him. Stumbling into the kitchen I poured myself a glass of water and sat down. I felt so happy, that I felt like pinching myself.

I put my feet up onto the chair next to me and looked at all the cards around me, the messages from my friends and family. I really was lucky. In between a couple of envelopes I noticed one which I hadn't seen before and picked it up. It was unopened; I must have missed it earlier. I eagerly tore off the envelope, excited to read my final birthday wish of the day and find out who it was from.

On the front of it was a simple, "Happy Birthday," design. It was the type of card that someone would buy from a newsagents' in bulk because it was a good offer and keep in anticipation of a birthday of an acquaintance; then send, grateful to have some space cleared in their bureau. I looked at it curiously and read the words.

'Happy Birthday,' was printed on the inside of it. I squinted to read the scrawled writing on the bottom and gasped in horror, letting go of it instantly. The card fluttered to the floor like a moth as I relayed the words I had read over and over in my head. There were just three words. Three words that chilled me to my very core and made me feel sick with dread…

You will pay.

Acknowledgements

Thank you to all my family and friends who supported me through this journey. To my sister Leah, who first read my manuscript and gave me the encouragement to see it through. To my mum who has always taught me to follow my dreams and has nurtured my imagination since I was a child. To my beautiful little boy Enzo who has changed my life for the better and given my life more meaning than words could ever express. Finally, in memory of Stephanie De La Warr, a brilliant lady who inspired me to write my own story.

You have now been officially
Corrupted!

If you enjoyed reading this book then please spread the word to
friends through word of mouth and social media sites.

 EmmyYoshida

 /corruptedbook

Writing Corrupted

What Inspired You To Write The Book?

I have always wanted to write a book and enjoyed writing. I began Corrupted after taking a creative writing course. It began as a memoir based on my time in Australia working as an exotic dancer, but I decided that I wanted to use my imagination more and devise a plot, and characters.

How Long Did It Take For You To Write?

I finished the first draft in about five months and spent about six months editing it. Most of my writing was done during the night when my son was in bed, and it became an obsession for me. All I thought about and talked about for a whole year was my book, and I am looking forward to becoming as equally immersed in my next book which I have just started.

Did You Plan The Plot Before You Started Writing The Book?

I had an idea of what it would be about and the beginning of the book but the plot unfolded naturally. Usually I had a few scenes in my mind that I wanted to work on and would write them accordingly depending on my mood and what I felt like working on that evening. I pieced together the scenes as I went along until finally I had a completed novel.

Are The Characters Based On People You Know?

I wouldn't want to divulge too much information about how true to life the characters are but I'm sure that some people who used to know me might recognise some of them. Most of the characters however are a combination of different people I have met and I have taken a mixture of their characteristics and added a splash of imagination to create them.

How Similar Are You To The Main Character Ria Kimura?

The character Ria Kimura is similar to what I used to be like. Impulsive, wild but also very naïve. She is an act now think later kind of girl, like many young women are. Her main priority is having fun, but it is a distraction for her as she is carrying a lot of pain in her heart from the death of her father.

Which Parts Of Corrupted Did You Enjoy Writing The Most?

I loved letting my imagination run riot and got completely immersed in the more dramatic scenes. I enjoyed writing the chapter when Ria gets beaten up in prison, when she kills Brad Harrison and when Andy is killed in the campervan. Also I enjoyed creating the court room scenes although they were the more challenging and took more editing to get right. I liked building the drama in those chapters and making it seem like Ria would end up being put away!

Do You Have Any Writing Rituals?

Usually I put my son Enzo to sleep, and spend an hour relaxing. Then I will go to my room, get a big glass of milk and my laptop and sit in bed with my computer on my lap, and work for about five or six hours at a time or until I can feel my head nodding!

What Do You Like To Read?

I enjoy reading all sorts; it depends on my mood and what I am going through. My favourite book as a girl was Anne Of Green Gables, I read all of the series and my mum would get me the next one as a special treat and I'd devour it in a day or two. Nowadays I enjoy suspense novels, crime, thrillers, anything gripping. I am a big fan of Martina Cole and Jackie Collins. I also really like reading Anchee Min books and enjoyed Memoirs Of A Geisha; I find that period of history fascinating. I like books that have strong female characters and are full of surprises.

What Was The Most Challenging Part Of Writing Corrupted?

For me the editing was the hardest part, making sure the story fitted together properly, that it was consistent, that there weren't any holes in the plot. It was challenging having to wake up in the morning and go to work or look after my son when I had been up half the night too, but I enjoyed writing Corrupted so much that the hours flew past before I realised the time!

How Did You Decide On The Ending?

I wanted Ria to have a happy ending, I would have been annoyed if I had read the book and she had ended up in prison. I wanted to write the process of the court case as I felt it would have been cheating to have just skipped straight over it. Ria being acquitted was a major part of the story for me, and I wanted to build the tension and suspense and make readers worry over whether she would be released or not. However I don't like endings to be too soppy so I left it with a bit of a question mark at the end as well.

Will You Be Writing A Sequel?

The book I am writing at the moment is based on completely different characters but I think there is the possibility of a second book based on Ria Kimura in the future. Ria evolved so much as a character in Corrupted, but there is definitely still a lot of scope for development. Who knows what might happen to her next time, it will probably come to me one night when I least expect it and I will be up until the crack of dawn trying to get it all down!

Book Club Questions

What Do You Think Were Ria Kimura's Main Motivations In Becoming A Stripper?

Why Do You Think Ria Was So Eager To Move To Australia With Brad Harrison?

When Do You Think Brad Harrison First Exhibited Signs Of Being Possessive And Violent?

Why Do You Think Ria Chose To Stay In Australia Instead Of Going Home?

What Do You Think Are Ria's Biggest Flaws And How Did They Lead Her Into Misfortune?

Why Didn't Ria Leave Brad Straight Away After He Assaulted Her?

Do You Think Ria Kimura Is A Strong Or Weak Character?

Is Tony Griffwell Responsible For Andrew Wilson's Death? How Much Do You Think Tony Griffwell Interfered With Evidence After Brad's Death?

Do You Think That Brad's Parents Arranged For Ria To Be Beaten In Prison? In What Ways Do You Think They Might Have Attempted To Influence The Course Of Justice?

Why Was Diane Mackenzie So Eager To Help Ria? How Much Did She Already Know About Brad Harrison's True Character?

Are There Any Underlying Lessons To Be Learnt From The Story?

Who Do You Think Sent Ria The Birthday Card At The End Of The Book?

Corrupted is Emmy Yoshida's debut novel.
A combination of memoir and fiction many of the scenes in
the book are based on her own life experiences as an exotic dancer
in London and Sydney.

Find out more at www.corruptedbook.com

 EmmyYoshida

 /corruptedbook